FISTBUMP

LOVER COME BACK

SCOTT HILDRETH

DEDICATION

To the lover that came back.

Thank you for returning, for giving me a chance, and for believing in me as much as I believe in you.

You are my one, my only, and my always.

extends clenched fist

AUTHOR'S NOTE

The events depicted in this book are true. The scenes are described to the best of my ability after recalling facts with my wife, family members, and friends. The narrative is a product of my experiences as well as my thoughts and opinions regarding them. The dialogue has been reproduced with the highest degree of accuracy I am able to scribe. During the drafting of this manuscript, it was reviewed by those in the know. Sentences were added, removed, or modified to maintain this accuracy. I'm certain someone will ask if I don't bring it up, so I'm bringing it up. Yes, the fist bumps described in this book happened. All of them. In one chapter, the number seventeen will be mentioned. Yes, that happened as well.

This book may read as fiction, but rest assured, it is not.

I hope you're able to find a way to enjoy this story as much as I enjoyed living it.

Scott

ACKNOWLEDGMENTS

To all the people who etched a memory in the sidewalk of my life, thank you. You made this writing possible. To Carol Hall and Jennifer Campbell, you are more than Beta readers and support to my writing, you are true friends. To the many readers who wait in line at the book signings to simply get a photo or have a book signed, thank you. Your dedication and support do not go unnoticed. Without you, I wouldn't exist. To my followers, friends, and foes on social media, thank you. The playful banter we're able to share between (and during) writing keeps me sane and keeps life interesting. To my family, thank you for putting up with me during the living of this tale. To my wife, thank you for the unconditional love and support. To my six children, thank you for making my life worth living. Whether you realize it or not, I love you with all I am able to give. Lastly, to the late judge Wesley Brown, thank you for believing me, and believing in me.

LOVER COME BACK PLAYLIST

Listen to the playlist HERE

Lover Come Back - City and Colour
Hold it Kid - The Weeks
Cry to Me - Marc Broussard
New Slang - The Shins
Broadripple is Burning - Margot & the Nuclear So & So's
She Loves You - The Gaslight Anthem
Jolene - Ray LaMontange
First Day of My Life - Bright Eyes
Tennessee Whiskey - Chris Stapleton
Half Crazy - The Barr Brothers
Sinister Kid - The Black Keys
Midnight Rider - The Allman Brothers
Someday Baby - R.L. Burnside
Sideways - Citizen Cope
Down in the Valley - Otis Redding
Hold On - Alabama Shakes

Lonely Boy - The Black Keys
Breakdown More - Eric Hutchinson

COPYRIGHT

LOVER COME BACK 1st Edition Copyright © 2018 by Scott Hildreth

All rights reserved. In accordance with the U.S. Copyright Act of 1976, the scanning, uploading, and electronic sharing of any part of this book without the permission of the author or publisher constitute unlawful piracy and theft of the author's intellectual property. If you would like to use the material from the book (other than for review purposes), prior written permission must be obtained by contacting the author at designconceptswichita@gmail.com.
Thank you for your support of the author's rights

Cover design by Jessica www.jessicahildrethdesigns.com

Beta readers: Carol Hall and Jennifer Campbell

Follow me on Facebook at: www.facebook.com/sd.hildreth

Like me on Facebook at: www.facebook.com/ScottDHildreth

Follow me on Twitter at: @ScottDHildreth

PROLOGUE

I dreamed of being a surfer. Of spending every daylight hour becoming one with the ocean. In the evenings, I would make custom surfboards in the back of a beachfront shop. I'd sell the hand-crafted boards in the hope of sharing my love with anyone courageous enough to attempt to tame the waves at San Diego's infamous Black's Beach.

My dreams, however, were squashed by the Hells Angels Motorcycle Club.

Despite my fascination with the Pacific Ocean – and my hope of becoming a surfer – my parents were moving us from San Diego to the Midwest. The decision, according to them, was in our family's best interest. The biker gangs infiltrating Southern California were bringing drugs into the communities. With the drugs came violence.

Although my sister, brother, and I begged to stay, our pleas fell on deaf ears. My father wanted better for us than he felt Southern California was able to offer. According to him, we were moving away from the Hells Angels, Vagos, Mongols, Chosen Few, Diablos, and all the criminal activity that flourished in the wake of their obnoxiously loud motorcycles.

"It's about time to go," my mother said. "Get your things picked up."

It was to be our last trip to the beach before we left on our voyage to El Dorado, Kansas. The small Midwestern town of five thousand residents was my father's birthplace. When he was eighteen years old, he married my mother, moved to Southern California, and then joined the US Marine Corps.

Immediately thereafter, his mother and father moved to the Golden State. My mother's parents and adult siblings followed. Our family was close-knit, and I liked that about us. We ate dinner with my grandparents on Sundays, took vacations as a group, and attended family reunions every summer – often traveling across the United States to do so.

We may have been leaving San Diego – and the beach – but we weren't leaving alone. The entire family – grandparents included – were coming with us. It didn't make the move any more palatable, though. There was nothing anyone could do or say to convince me that moving away from something as fascinating and rewarding as the ocean was a good decision.

The three of us picked up our beach toys and reluctantly followed my mother. With each step, I pressed my toes firmly into the wet sand, leaving an impression that I hoped would last a lifetime.

I knew eventually the tide would simply wash my footprints away, erasing proof of my existence entirely. If I didn't see it, however, I felt that I could convince myself it never happened. I would remain one with the beach, linked through my footprints, until the day I returned.

One day, without exception, I would do just that.

Return.

With hesitant steps, I walked up the beach, savoring each grain of sand as it pushed its way between my toes.

And, I never looked back.

CHAPTER ONE

I was forty-two years old, and lived in Wichita, Kansas. I had never returned to the beach. I wondered if my life might have taken a different turn had I chosen to do so.

I sat at my attorney's side. We were waiting anxiously on a frail man who possessed a sharp wit, tremendous attention to detail, and a vast understanding of federal law. He could send me to prison for as much as twenty years, or he could send me for as little as five, but he had to send me. Federal law prohibited him from sentencing me to anything lesser.

At the beginning of my legal case, his age caused me concern. President John F. Kennedy appointed him to his status of Senior Federal Judge. He must have been destined to practice law, because he somehow managed to grace the earth with his presence for ninety-eight years, sixty-five of which had been spent as a federal judge.

Having presided over countless federal criminal trials, I suspected he'd seen all there was to see. Yet. During my trial, he took pause. In the end, I was pleased to have him as my judge. He proved to be open-minded and truly impartial.

As we sat in wait, I hoped he maintained these qualities during my sentencing.

My legal case had dragged out in court for four years. It cost me a quarter of a million dollars, several friendships, a marriage, and all but deteriorated my relationships with my three children.

"Will the defendant please rise," the bailiff bellowed.

His voice echoed off the ornate wooden walls of the federal courthouse. Upon realizing my freedom could be snatched from me in a matter of minutes, my right knee began to bounce.

"Stand proud," my attorney whispered. "Remain stoic. Win or lose, don't give these sons-of-bitches the satisfaction of seeing any emotion."

"Yes, Sir," I responded.

We stood in unison.

I was a firearms collector. It wasn't my profession. It was simply a hobby. I used it to occupy my idle time. A crutch, if you will, to help me along my path to clean living. I'd quit drinking twenty years prior. I then applied my addictive behaviors to collecting firearms. Nonetheless, I set up a business, paid my taxes, and made certain every transaction was in accordance with the law. The ATF, however, had testimony obtained from an informant that told them otherwise.

According to him, I had two million dollars in cash, and a cache of machine guns in my safe. Nothing, however, could be further from the truth.

In hope of finding the cash and machine guns, an undercover ATF agent posed as a biker and befriended me. I confided in him. I invited him into my home. We shared stories. He met my wife and children. All the while, unbeknownst to me, he was investigating me.

During the course of that three-year investigation, he had found no wrongdoing on my part. The upper echelon of the ATF was still attached to the belief that I was a criminal. They brought in another undercover agent. This time, they had a woman pose as the widow of a law enforcement officer.

She called me, asking that I give a bid on her deceased husband's firearm collection. She explained that there were complications obtaining the funds from his retirement. She needed to sell the guns to purchase a headstone for his funeral. After visiting pawn shops and having multiple wannabe collectors offer her pennies on the dollar, I was her only hope.

In a last-ditch-effort to obtain a search warrant for my home, the ATF – through her – offered to sell me a collection of firearms that included a machine gun. I couldn't own the weapon, and I knew it. I explained the federal law governing the transportation of the weapon at length while being filmed by a hidden ATF surveillance camera.

I could, however, act as an agent for a machine gun dealer who had been my partner at several gun shows in the Midwest. A week later, after obtaining the prerequisite paperwork to transfer the weapon, I agreed to pick them up.

Upon placing the weapons in the back of my SUV, a helicopter lowered itself onto the street just ahead of me. Federal agents armed with machine guns leaped from the earth's every orifice.

Mimicking the scenes from a Hollywood action movie, I was zip-tied, tossed into the back of a black SUV, and rushed through the city in a convoy of similar black SUVs. Upon reaching the ATF's headquarters, I was handcuffed to a stainless-steel table.

As I watched the agents from various federal entities remove their bullet-proof vests and secure their weapons, I noticed my fellow biker walk past. He wasn't wearing boots, jeans, and a wife-beater. He was wearing SWAT-type gear, a badge, and had a pistol affixed to his tactical belt.

While I was bound to the cold piece of steel, they obtained a search warrant. They searched my home. Upon finding nothing, they got another warrant to search my safe deposit box. After finding nothing once again, they obtained a warrant for my bank records. Then, they searched my retirement account, my investment accounts, and my business records.

Nothing, nothing, and more nothing.

I had no illegal weapons. There were no piles of cash. In fact, their searches, in their entirety, revealed no wrong doing whatsoever. The only crime that had been committed was the one they'd orchestrated.

Frustrated, they released me without any criminal charges. I was quite certain they felt foolish. I surely would have if I'd spent three years attempting to arrest a machine gun kingpin, only to find out that he was a law-abiding citizen.

A year later they charged me with possessing the machine gun. I explained to my attorney about the machine gun dealer, the licensing he possessed, and of the paperwork he'd provided. We both agreed the case would never make it to trial.

The government then offered me a sentence of probation if I plead guilty to the crime. Through my attorney, I declined, choosing to go to trial. No jury in their right mind would convict me of a crime I had no intention of committing.

That was my belief, at least.

The day before the trial was scheduled to begin, they dropped the charges entirely.

The next day, they indicted me on two counts of machine gun possession. According to their Washington D.C. specialist, the firearms they'd sold me included two machine guns. I, according to him, had improperly identified one of them.

How convenient, I thought.

Facing two charges, I was once again offered probation. *You might beat one charge, but you'll never beat them both*, they taunted. *Remain a free man, simply plead guilty.*

I declined their offer, opting to take both charges to trial.

The trial was plagued with lost audio recordings, video recordings without audio reproduction, and witnesses – including federal agents – who were willing to perjure themselves on the witness stand.

Halfway through the first day of trial, the judge stopped the proceedings. He advised the jury that there was evidence to suggest that I was entrapped to commit the crime. He asked that they consider that the government may have coerced me to possess the machine gun. He further advised them to find innocence or guilt only after giving the entrapment doctrine consideration.

On the witness stand, I lost my composure. I screamed, I cussed, and I demanded the truth be told. Despite the judge's orders not to, I challenged the prosecuting attorney to produce the lost recordings.

During breaks from testimony, US Marshalls struggled to keep my attorney and I separated from the ATF agents. Arguments broke out. People pushed each other. Verbal mud was slung through clenched teeth from both sides.

After all the testimony, my attorney and I stood on the steps of the courthouse and smoked a cigarette. I'd given up drinking alcohol and cigarettes twenty years prior, but the stress of the trial had me smoking again. At least they didn't drive me to drinking, I told myself.

The US Attorney walked past, giving his regards as he reached the steps.

"Looks like you've got this one in the bag, Mc Master," he said.

My attorney gave a sharp nod. "The opera's not over until the fat lady sings."

Neither of us knew it, but she was about to sing. In the form of yet another lying witness.

When we returned to the courtroom, the US Attorney's office called a witness that wasn't on the witness list. My former partner. The machine gun dealer.

He claimed he didn't provide me with the transfer paperwork. My attorney produced the ink-signed form which had been confiscated from my vehicle at the time of arrest. The dealer then opted to exercise his right under the Fifth Amendment not to testify any further for fear he would incriminate himself.

I found out years later that they forced him to testify, threatening prosecution if he chose not to.

On that note, the trial ended. The judge provided the jury with instructions to allow entrapment as a legal defense. They deliberated for three days. Moments before the judge was prepared to declare a mistrial, the jury announced a verdict had been reached.

"Have you reached a verdict?" the judge asked.

"We have, your honor," the foreperson replied.

The judge cleared his throat. "How do you find the defendant?"

"On count one, we find the defendant not guilty," the foreperson announced.

I felt faint. I was halfway there. The sweet taste of victory caused me to salivate.

"On count two," he continued. "We find the defendant guilty."

My heart faltered.

According to my attorney, it was common for a jury faced with multiple charges and little damning evidence to find guilt on one count, and innocence on the other.

After the guilty verdict was reached, the judge released me. I went home as if nothing happened. He ordered a ninety-day long investigation into my character. After the investigation, a sentencing date was set.

It was now time for me to learn what my future held. The judge rifled through a stack of paperwork, appeared to read something, and then looked up.

"Mister Hildreth," he said, his quaking voice giving indication to the century-long life he'd lived. "I've reviewed the evidence, the transcripts from the trial, and the notes from the ATF agent's investigation. I do not believe you had any intention to possess the machine gun in question, nor do I believe you had any intentions to possess machine guns prior to the offense in question. There is no place in the law, however, for me to second-guess the jury. That jury, need I remind you, found you guilty."

He picked up a sheet of paper from his desk, scanned it with his eyes, and then handed it to the bailiff, who in turn handed it to the stenographer.

"Despite my belief of your innocence," he continued. "You chose trial by jury. You now stand before me a guilty man. My sentencing today will be indicative of my belief of your lack of intention to possess the firearm in question. Furthermore, I have spoken to the prosecution's office, and they have agreed not to appeal my decision or my sentencing. I hereby sentence you to three years of probation."

My attorney's knees buckled.

Mine did the same.

I'd studied law for three years, spending almost twelve hours a day with my nose stuffed in one of over three-dozen legal books. I knew enough about federal law to know the judge didn't have the latitude to do what he'd just done. The federal sentencing guidelines prohibited it.

He'd done it, nonetheless.

If the appellate court didn't find out about the lenient sentence, nothing would be done to modify it into a prison sentence. I could serve my probation, stay out of prison, and live my remaining days on earth a free man.

The laws of double jeopardy would prevent me from ever being resentenced after the probation time was served. The only way the appellate court would find out about the judge's sentencing was if I chose to appeal the case.

In the absence of an appeal, I would remain free, forever. To accept the punishment of probation, however, I must accept the guilt. Taking ownership for a crime I didn't commit – or intend to commit – wasn't something I could do.

The world I lived in was black and white. There was right, and there was wrong. There was no in between. Gray didn't exist. In this circumstance, I was right. The jack-booted thugs in the ATF had proven their willingness to botch an investigation in places like Ruby Ridge and Waco, Texas. They were now proving it in Wichita, Kansas.

I had news for them. The man who stood before them was courageous enough to take his case to the US Supreme Court steps.

I leaned to the side and whispered in my attorney's ear. "May I speak?"

"You want to address the judge?" he asked.

"Yes, Sir," I responded. "I do."

My attorney, a former Marine officer, Vietnam War combat veteran, retired Golden Gloves boxer, and Notre Dame graduate, was a hard ass on his best day.

He gave me a stern look. "Proceed with caution and respect," he whispered. "No outbursts."

I faced the judge. "Your honor, I appreciate your belief of my innocence, and equally appreciate your expression of such in your sentencing of me today. It saddens me to inform you, however, that I must appeal this case to the appellate court. I would like to go on the record as saying that this decision will be appealed. Consider this timely notice."

My attorney gripped my bicep. "Your honor, my client will be advised of the risks taken if an appeal is filed. Be advised if we so choose to appeal, a notice will be given in writing--"

"Your honor," I interrupted. "In accordance with the Federal Rules of Criminal Procedure, consider that timely notice of appeal has been given on this date."

"Mister Hildreth," the judge said. "It is your right to appeal the finding of the jury, and your further right to appeal this sentencing. If you choose to do so, and the end result is a loss, I will have no other recourse but to send you to prison. Do you understand that?"

"Yes, your honor, I do."

"As we speak, however, you are a free man."

"I understand, your honor."

"If you so choose to appeal," he said. "Good luck, and may God be with you."

I accepted the sentencing. Against the advice of my attorney, I went on to appeal the guilty conviction, risking going to prison in doing so. Based on the grounds that I was coerced by ATF agents to commit a crime I wasn't predisposed to commit, a brief was filed with the appellate court. Two-and-a-half years later, six months before completing my sentence of probation, I lost the appeal.

I went on to appeal the case to the US Supreme Court.

They didn't hear my case. It wasn't surprising, as they only hear one percent of the cases they're presented.

It was the same as a loss.

When I went back in front of the judge, he had already celebrated his one-hundredth birthday. He imposed an unprecedented sentence of just less than three years in prison, rewriting federal law in respect to machine gun possession when he did so. Furthermore, he allowed me to remain at large and later surrender to US Marshalls to begin serving my prison sentence.

Three months later, I surrendered proudly, knowing I fought until the bitter end without giving up, or giving in.

The date was September eleventh.

CHAPTER TWO

I was being escorted by a man who had a swastika tattooed on the back of his shaved head. I followed him toward a prison cell at the end of the cellblock. The door was flanked by two men whose faces, arms, and legs were covered with tattoos. Upon entering the crowded space, the foul odor of hatred enveloped me like a sickness.

Each of the inmates who lined the cell's walls were covered from head to toe in various tattoos, all of which appeared to be the product of a prison-fashioned tattoo gun. Swastikas, *Schutzstaffel* lightning bolts, and the numbers fourteen and eighty-eight seemed to be the common theme amongst the men who were greeting me with clenched jaws and side-eyed stares.

My presence wasn't a matter of choice. I was brought there at the request of the shot caller for the prison's Skin Head gang.

Wearing nothing more than a pair of cut-off sweats and black lace-up boots, a man stood at the far end of the twelve-foot-long cell. In case anyone was uncertain of his loyalties, he had the words *Skin* and *Head* tattooed across his forehead. A swastika centered above the bridge of his nose separated the two words.

His bulging biceps and washboard abs gave indication as to how he'd spent his prison sentence. In prison, men took on one of three body structures. Skin and bones, from not eating entirely. Obese, from eating everything in sight, or they were covered in muscles from head to toe from spending all their idle time exercising.

After sizing me up, his sinister blue eyes met mine.

I held his gaze, knowing if I looked away that it would be perceived as a sign of weakness.

He stroked his six-inch long goatee with the web of his hand. "Ever done time before?" he asked, his voice raspy and dry.

"I have."

He walked half the short distance that separated us, which was just enough to give me a demonstration of his exaggerated prison swagger.

He looked me up and down. "Where'd you do time?"

"I did state time in Kansas twenty years ago. Drugs."

"Ever done Federal time?"

"Not until now."

He crossed his arms over his chest. "You've been here three days, and you about popped off a riot in the chow hall. You've got a lot to learn about doing time *here*."

In the seventy-two hours that I'd been incarcerated, someone had taken it upon himself to call me a snitch. The instant the words passed his lips, I unleashed a flurry of punches, stopping only when he was lying in a pile at my feet.

In prison, having the label of a snitch was comparable to being a child molester or a rapist. I was victim of an undercover ATF sting operation for firearms violations. I had never spoken a word to an ATF investigator short of a *fuck you* in passing.

I was the polar opposite of a snitch.

"He got his ass beat because he was a disrespectful prick," I said dryly. "I don't see the problem."

He lifted his chin slightly. "Might have been different in a state joint, but in here you can't go busting every black in the head that pisses you off. If you do, it'll pop off a riot. A riot puts all of us on lockdown. When we're on lockdown, I'm out of business. When I'm out of business, I get ugly."

I didn't bother telling him that there was nothing he could do to rid himself of the ugly that oozed from his every pore.

I stood within arm's reach of him, considering my response in silence. I was raised to believe that all men were created equal. Neither religion, race, nor creed were grounds for segregation. Witnessing a man's actions was the only way of knowing who he truly was. In my forty-three years on earth, I'd learned that there was good and bad in all religions and races.

I'd fought the man in question because he was disrespectful toward me. Skin color had nothing to do with it. His actions alone earned him the ass whipping.

"It wasn't a black-white thing," I explained. "He was disrespectful. I didn't know I needed to get permission to stand up for myself."

His eyes thinned. "There's a hierarchy here. Following it is critical to this joint's success. If a white treats you with disrespect, bust him up. If a black or Mexican does it, come tell me. I'll have a sit-down with their shot caller. Depending on the circumstances, you might get permission to take care of him. That permission comes from me, and me only."

The prison had a set of unwritten rules that, if followed, allowed it to function in a manner that minimized arguments and fights amongst the inmates. The men were separated into cliques, with each group sharing the belief that they were superior. In the absence of threat or argument, they were left to believe their opinions of themselves were true and correct.

Raining on the man's parade who stood before me wasn't going to do either of us any good. So, without necessarily agreeing, I agreed.

"Fair enough," I said.

He looked me up and down. "It's tough finding a man willing to fight for what he believes in. We can always make a place for another stand up white boy."

"I've got three years to do," I said. "I'll just stay out of everyone's way and do my time alone."

"Fair enough," he said mockingly.

I turned toward the door and peered into the cell block. Four televisions were mounted high on the ceiling with the screens angled toward the men who were gathered beneath them.

One was surrounded by whites, one by blacks, and one by Hispanics. The last was being watched by various other races who were in the minority. The segregation of the men wasn't by choice. A television was assigned to each race by the prison's warden.

He was of the opinion it solved problems.

I was of the opinion it was the first step in creating them.

With a mesh laundry bag draped over my shoulder, I gazed through the glass door and into the prison's courtyard. No differently than the other eighteen hundred prisoners housed inside the brick walls of the institution, I'd spent every waking hour locked inside. I hadn't seen sunlight or stood beneath the open sky for almost three years. I was anxious to gulp the fresh air and feel the warm summer sun on my face.

The door's bolt shot open with a metallic *clank*. I glanced over my shoulder. Four sets of doors separated me from the cell block to my rear. I turned toward the one door that separated me from freedom and took a few hesitant steps.

Nothing happened.

I took a few more.

Still nothing. Apparently, they were truly going to let me walk out of there.

I inhaled a deep breath and walked through the door with

authority, pushing it open as if I'd earned my place on the free side of the three-inch thick steel-reinforced glass.

The sweet smell of freshly-cut grass hit me like a clenched fist. Immediately behind it, the scent of various flowers tickled my nostrils. I closed my eyes and grinned.

It was over. I was free.

"Hildreth," a familiar voice said from beside me.

I opened my eyes and turned toward the voice. Dressed in full uniform, one of the prison's guards stood at the edge of the steps.

Cambridge was an intimidating figure. Physically fit to a point that it disguised his age of fifty-five, he loomed over most of the inmates, standing six-foot-eight in boots. He wore his gray hair in a buzz cut, despite being out of the military for twenty years.

I'd worked under his watch for my entire prison stint. We were far from friends, but we'd become as friendly toward one another as an inmate and corrections officer could.

"Cambridge?" I asked. "What's going on? You're not taking me back in there, are you?"

He pushed his hands into his pockets, looked me over, and then shook his head lightly. "I've worked here for eighteen years. In those eighteen years, I've never encountered anyone like you. Hell, I've never met anyone like you, *anywhere*."

A look of confusion washed over me. "You waited out here to tell me that?"

"I waited out here to ask you to do me a favor," he explained.

Despite my newfound freedom, it seemed odd having a prison guard ask a favor of me. I set my bag on the ground at my side. "You want a favor from *me*?"

"Promise me you won't do anything stupid," he said. "Don't kill that guy that testified against you, and don't kill that ATF agent, either. Just get back to living life. A man like you can make a difference on this earth, but not if he's in here."

Early in my incarceration, I'd expressed anger toward the two men he'd mentioned. Eventually, however, I forgave them for what they'd done. I found it troubling that he'd learned of conversations I had in private, but quickly remembered that nothing was truly private in prison.

"I'm not going to kill anyone," I assured him. "At least not either of those two idiots."

"What are you going to do?" he asked. "For work?"

"I don't know." I shrugged dismissively. "Maybe I'll write a book."

"A book?" His mouth twisted into a half-assed smirk. "What kind of book?"

"Something heartwarming," I responded jokingly. "Infused with my opinions and beliefs, of course. Maybe a little sex."

"If anyone could do it and succeed at it, it'd be you." He extended his hand. "Take care of yourself, Hildreth."

I didn't simply shake a man's hand when it was offered. I'd offended many by not shaking their hands, and looked at doing so as an endorsement, of sorts. An agreement that the man attached to the hand I was shaking was morally equal to me. It was a habit that I developed from twenty-five years of being a biker.

I accepted his outstretched hand, shook it, and grinned. "Do the same, Cambridge."

CHAPTER THREE

I pushed the garage door up to shoulder-height and peered inside the unlit space. What was left of a lifetime of accomplishments was shoehorned into a ten-foot-wide by twenty-foot-long storage facility.

After I surrendered to US Marshalls, my home – and a good part of what I owned – was sold by the men in my Motorcycle Club. Ironically, even though my father despised the men who forced him to move away from what he considered to be paradise, I'd become one of them.

A biker.

The proceeds from what was sold was used to pay attorney's fees, fines, and provide me with a monthly *income* while in prison.

My remaining belongings were set aside and placed in storage. I wasn't completely certain of what was left, because I hadn't spoken to anyone in the MC for two and a half years. Short of my father and children, I'd chosen to separate myself from all friends and family while I was incarcerated. No phone calls, no visits, and no opened letters.

It allowed me to serve my sentence alone. Dragging anyone else into wide range of emotions that were associated with incarceration wasn't something I cared to do.

Just inside the garage door, my chopper sat, covered in dust. Upon seeing it, a lump rose in my throat. I faced Teddy and swallowed heavily.

"You guys kept it?" I asked.

"Chico took out a loan against it so he could give your kids Christmas presents and buy 'em clothes. He paid it off a couple of months ago."

Beyond the motorcycle, my BMW M3 was parked. On either side of it, cardboard boxes were stacked to the ceiling.

"Kept the car, too?"

He chuckled. "Nobody wanted that ugly fucker."

Often described as *baby shit yellow*, the Phoenix Yellow BMW was a love or hate color. I was colorblind, and I loved it. It seemed, however, that I was the only one.

"Want to take it out for a hundred and fifty mile an hour run?" he asked.

I traced my finger over the gas tank of the chopper, wiping the years of accumulated dust away from the purple flames that were painted over the underlying black paint.

"Not so much," I said. "I need to ride."

I doubted the motorcycle would start. After sitting for years, at minimum it would need a new battery and to have the carburetor rebuilt. Nonetheless, I was eager to start the process.

I lit a cigarette, admired the bike for a moment, and then looked at Teddy. "Wanna take me to get a battery for it?"

He stroked his beard and grinned. "Doesn't need one."

"What do you mean?"

"Chico put one in it a couple of months ago, when you were supposed to get out. Had the carb rebuilt, too."

I was released from prison three months later than expected, because I wouldn't sign a form that allowed me to accept a reduction in sentence for good behavior. In signing it, I had to admit guilt, and that was something I would never do.

"How'd he know when I was supposed to get out?"

"He called up there once a month to make sure you weren't catching any new charges or doing anything stupid." He wiped the dust from the motorcycle's seat, and then looked at me. "I know it wasn't easy for you to be in there, but it wasn't easy for any of us, either. We missed ya, Brother."

"Missed you fuckers, too." I slapped my hand against his shoulder. "Where's the key?"

He gestured toward the left side of the motorcycle and chuckled. "Hanging on the fucking coil wire."

I laughed to myself.

I despised carrying anything in my pockets, keys included. As a result, I'd kept the key to the motorcycle attached to the coil wire for the ten years that I'd owned it. An invitation for theft, it was a miracle that the bike had never been stolen.

The club joked that the only reason no one had taken it over the years was because everyone in the Midwest knew it was mine.

I poked the key into the switch, turned on the ignition, and pressed the *start* button. After the high-compression engine turned over a few times, it started.

The exhaust echoed off the storage facility's walls, filling the alleyway between the buildings with proof of its brutal power. I stretched my leg over the fender, sat down in the seat, and grinned.

Most men, upon being released from prison, had one thing on their mind.

Sex.

I'd never had meaningless sex with anyone in my life and wasn't about to start. For me, the relationship came first. Being in a relationship with a woman was the farthest thing from my mind, and I doubted it would change any time soon.

My luck with finding a woman who had the ability to be loyal to me was nil. I was convinced I was going to spend the rest of my life married to the men in the MC, and to my motorcycle.

Oddly, I was okay with the concept.

I had one thing on my mind, and one thing only. I gestured toward Teddy's truck. "Follow me back to your place so you can get your bike?"

He glanced at his watch. "The fellas are having a barbeque to celebrate your release. Everyone's meeting at the clubhouse at six."

"Gives us about eight hours," I said. "I need to ride. And, I want a cheeseburger. A *real* cheeseburger."

Teddy wasn't much different than me. In the ten years that I'd known him, he hadn't been in a single relationship. His lack of trust, however, didn't stop with women. He simply didn't trust mankind.

His free time was spent building motorcycles and riding them.

"Ride out to the airport in Benton and get a burger?" he asked. "Watch the planes do touch and goes?"

Stearman Field was a small biker-friendly airport an hour away. It often sponsored our MC's poker run, and allowed us to park on the runway, away from the cars that often packed the parking lot. Many of the planes that flew to and from the airport were the bi-winged Boeing-Stearman, and the facility was named after them.

Because I didn't drink, I preferred to patronize establishments whose focus was something other than drinking. The rest of the MC didn't always agree with my suggestions for places to eat, but Teddy often did, as he didn't drink, either.

"Sounds good to me," I said.

I maneuvered the motorcycle out of the storage building and alongside Teddy's truck. He pulled the door closed, locked it, and turned to face me.

"I'll follow you," he said.

I rode between the buildings slowly, getting a feel for the extended forks of the chopper. After a moment, muscle memory set in, and riding it became second nature.

When we reached the highway's on-ramp, I glanced over my

shoulder, checking for oncoming traffic. A long line of approaching cars acted as an invitation for me to accelerate rapidly to get out in front of them.

Instead, I waited for them to pass. I had a lifetime ahead of me, and I planned on enjoying every minute of it as if it were my last.

CHAPTER FOUR

For the two years that followed, I worked as a project manager for a construction company. Twelve hours a day was my typical work schedule. After leaving the office at six pm, I would ride my motorcycle until two am. After four hours sleep, I'd eagerly go back to work. In my eyes, I was living life to the fullest.

While on the motorcycle, and only while on the motorcycle, I felt free. The time I spent on the open road was cleansing to my soul. The memories of prison, of the trial – and of the people who I believed had wronged me – all evaporated as the wind rushed past me.

My body's fuel was coffee. Lots of coffee. On my way home each night, I would stop at a local donut shop that was open twenty-four hours a day. I wasn't big on sweets, but it was one place I could unwind and get a cup of coffee late at night. Stopping there had become part of my daily routine.

I'd grown to like *The Donut Whole* more than my former hangouts. If I frequented the predictable places, I was surrounded by people who wanted to hear stories of prison, how I'd fought the ATF, and how I'd miraculously returned to the motorcycle club unscathed.

I wanted to forget my past. Doing so required separating myself from the people in my past. The remote donut shop had become my refuge. Short of my MC brethren, no one knew about it, and I planned on keeping it that way.

On a Monday evening after work, I sat at the worn wooden table I'd claimed as my own and sipped my coffee. Dressed in a pair of tattered jeans, a wife beater, and boots, I didn't quite fit in with the hipsters and high school kids who sat cross-legged on the floor and ate multi-grain bagels, but I never really fit in anywhere.

I liked it that way.

The little brass bell jingled as the door opened, warning of another patron entering the establishment. I'd developed habits in prison that I feared would always remain with me, one of which was positioning myself with my back to the wall.

Another was being aware of everyone who was in my presence.

With my back to the wall, and my cup of coffee gripped loosely in my hand, I shifted my eyes toward the door. To thwart the approach of any random strangers, my face wore a stern scowl.

A young woman with curly blond hair stepped through the door and glanced around the seating area. Her hair was golden in color and fashioned in a series of curls that bounced with each step she took. Describing her as simply being beautiful would have been an understatement.

She was elegant. She stood as proof of God's ability to create things of sheer beauty.

In awe, I watched eagerly as she peered into the open seating area. After satisfying herself it was okay to enter, she walked sheepishly toward the corridor that led to the other end of the building.

I possessed an uncanny ability to read people. Watching a person's eye movements, how they walked, and their manner of interacting with strangers revealed a tremendous amount about their personality – and their past.

Watching her divulged all too much about who she was and what she'd been exposed to. She made eye contact with no one, looking away from those who took so much as a precursory glance in her direction.

She carefully surveyed each passageway before entering, as if assessing the area for threats. Her arms didn't dangle loosely at her sides, they were cinched tight against her body. Her hands were stuffed deeply into the pockets of her light jacket, which was an unnecessary accessory considering the ninety-degree spring temperature.

In my opinion, she was the victim of some form of abuse.

I sipped my coffee and watched intently as she disappeared into the back room. After a few moments she reappeared, holding a porcelain plate in one hand and a cup of coffee in the other.

She scanned the room for a place to sit. Upon realizing there wasn't an open table, her gaze fell to the floor.

I cleared my throat, gathering her attention in the process. When she made eye contact, I gestured toward the opposite side of the table. "You can sit here."

She lowered her head, walked toward me, and then looked up. "Pardon me?"

I slid my cup to the side, motioned toward the seat across from me, and grinned. "I'm leaving in a few minutes. You can have this table."

Clutching her coffee in one hand and the plate in the other, she met my gaze. The depth of her brown eyes was bottomless.

"Are you sure?" she asked.

I was lost in admiration. After regaining my composure, I tore my eyes away from hers. "Quite," I said. "This place is always packed this time of day. You'll have a hard time finding somewhere to sit until about midnight."

She pulled out the bench, set down her things, and then lowered herself into the seat. "Do you come here a lot?"

"A few times a day, and then again late at night, on my way back to the house. I'm not normally here this time of day, though."

She picked at her donut with her thumb and forefinger, eventually tearing a bird-sized bite from the side of the circular pastry. "Do you work nights?"

"I work days," I responded. "I ride at night."

She poked the morsel into her mouth. After swallowing it, she gestured toward the parking lot. "Is that your motorcycle? The big one parked on the sidewalk?"

"It is."

She began picking at the donut again, alternating glances between it and me. "It's pretty."

I rested my forearms on the edge of the table and looked right at her. "You're pretty."

Her tanned skin quickly blushed. She raked the curls away from her face with the tips of her fingers and grinned a slight smile. "Thank you, but I don't feel pretty."

"Why not?"

"I just had a baby," she said, seeming embarrassed by what she revealed. "I need to lose weight."

She was just north of five feet tall and might have weighed one hundred and fifty pounds – if she had a brick in each of her jacket pockets. Her hair and DD boobs weighed twenty pounds. The jacket, another five. I loved her hair, and wasn't about to suggest a breast reduction, so I mentioned the jacket.

"You could start by tossing that jacket. That'll free up five pounds," I said with a laugh. "If you lose much more than that, you'll blow away."

She smiled, revealing whiter teeth than I'd ever seen. "I needed to hear that."

"Well, it's true," I said matter-of-factly. "You look fabulous."

Still wearing the smile, she flipped her blond locks over her shoulder. "I'm Jessica."

I extended my arm over the table and offered her my hand. "Scott. Pleasure to meet you."

She shook my hand. Her smile faded. "Do you have to leave?"

"I don't *have* to do anything."

"Can you stay for a while?" she asked, her voice filled with hope. "It's nice to have someone to talk to."

The last thing I needed was for her husband or boyfriend to wander in and see us sitting together. I had no ill intentions, but I was quite sure a confrontation of any kind wouldn't end well. With me, they never seemed to.

I reached for my coffee cup. "I doubt that'd go over well with your husband."

"I'm not married."

"Husband, boyfriend, they're both the same as far as I'm concerned."

"I don't have one of either. I'm single."

I released the cup and leaned away from the table. "What about the father of your child? The baby you mentioned?"

She went back to picking at the edge of the donut. "He's not in the picture. It's a long story."

"Unless that long story ends with him being dead, he's still in the picture."

After I spoke, I regretted it. The war in Iraq was coming to a close, but it was far from over. A strong possibility existed that the father of her child was a war veteran who had lost his life defending our country's freedoms. I felt like an inconsiderate jerk.

"I wish he was dead," she said. "Life would be a lot easier if he was."

Relief washed over me. "Want to talk about it?"

She let out a sigh and pushed the donut aside. "He was an abusive jerk. We've been apart for a few years. After I left him the last time – the final time – I found out I was pregnant. I had the baby alone, and I've been alone ever since. He still comes around every now and again to threaten me, but that's about it."

Without consciously doing so, I sat up straight. "He threatens you?"

She stared beyond me, blankly. After a long pause, she shook her head lightly. She then met my gaze with watery eyes.

"On our first date, he put a gun in my mouth." Her eyes welled with tears, but she continued, nonetheless. "He told me if I ever left him, he'd kill me. I could go on and on about him stabbing me, beating me, and tell you about the cops constantly coming over and doing nothing, but I won't. I'll start crying if I do."

She was already crying, she simply didn't realize it.

My blood began to boil.

She forced a heavy exhale and looked me in the eyes. "Now, I'm twenty-four, have two kids by him, and wonder every night if it's going to be the night he shows up to kill us."

My hands began to shake. My jaw tightened. Abusing women was one thing I couldn't tolerate. I drew a long breath, said a silent prayer, and then reached for her hand.

"I'm going to need you to tell me what his name is and where he lives. Maybe show me a picture of him."

Her face washed with worry. "I don't know what good that'll do."

"It'll be the first step in solving your problem."

She pushed herself away from the table and looked at me as if I was a lunatic. "You don't understand. He's mean."

I flashed a crooked smile. "I know someone meaner."

She wiped her tears and coughed a laugh. "You're funny."

"I'm not trying to be."

"If he comes around again, I'll let you know." She reached for her purse and pulled out a tissue. "How's that?"

I wasn't going to press the issue. She was uncomfortable with the thought of anything happening to him, that much was clear. I doubted it was a result of her having feelings for him. More than likely it was from fear of repercussion.

If we kept in touch, in time, she'd eventually tell me.

"You've got a deal," I said. "Before I go any further, I need to ask you three questions."

She wiped the trails of mascara from her cheeks. "Okay."

"Ready?"

"Yeah. I guess."

"Can you use chop sticks for their intended purpose?"

She squinted. "What?"

"Can you use chop sticks for their intended purpose? Can you eat with them?"

She shook her head. "No."

"Have you ever eaten a grapefruit?" I asked. "If the answer's yes, did you like it?"

"I have." She smiled. "I love grapefruit."

"Last question," I said. "If the opportunity presented itself, would you consider dating a black man?"

She cringed, apparently afraid to answer the question.

"There's not a wrong answer," I assured her.

"I have dated a black man," she whispered. "A black cowboy."

I laughed. "Really? A cowboy?"

"He was nice. Had a hat, and everything. He even had a ranch. We didn't hit it off, though. It didn't last long. What's with the weird questions?"

"Your answers tell me a lot about your personality," I said.

The questions gave a hint as to whether she was determined, open to trying things, and if she was open-minded. Without asking those specific questions, and then being given a canned response, I could obtain answers that were truthful without her knowing what I was truly seeking.

"What do they tell you?"

"They tell me you're a pretty remarkable woman."

Her eyes glistened. Then, the corners of her mouth curled up slightly. "Thank you."

"I need to tell you something," I said.

She shrugged one shoulder. "Okay."

"I'm a convicted felon," I said. "I've been out of prison for just under two years now. In being honest, I thought I'd tell you."

"Can I ask why?" She dabbed her eyes with the corner of the tissue. "Will you tell me what you did?"

"Sure," I said. "Possession of a machinegun."

She scrunched her nose. "Why did you have a machinegun?"

"It's a long story," I said. "I'm hungry. Care to discuss it over dinner?"

She dropped the tissue into her purse and grinned the best she was able. "I'd love to."

CHAPTER FIVE

All I had to do to enjoy my time with Jessica was exist. I could be my natural self. She accepted me entirely and cared nothing about my past. She didn't get frustrated with the present and never mentioned her expectations of the future.

She truly lived in the now. She asked for nothing, was satisfied with simply being in my presence, and was grateful for every moment we were able to spend together. If she were a man, I would have asked her to prospect for the club.

Instead, I offered a little more of myself on each day, hoping she would continue to hold me in high regard despite my colorful past.

I picked up a piece of pita and swiped it through the hummus. "I can't believe you like this stuff. No one likes it."

"I love it," she said.

I bit the bread in two, and then nibbled on what was left. "It's a staple in my diet."

"Mine, too."

My friends in the motorcycle club didn't care much for Mediterranean food. Sharing my favorite foods with someone who enjoyed them as much as me was exciting. Wichita had a heterogeneous array of people, many of which were restaurateurs. In the thirty-five years that I'd lived there, I'd become quite a foodie.

"Have you ever eaten pho?" I asked excitedly.

She draped the tip of her pita in the chickpea purée. "What?"

"Vietnamese noodle soup," I said. "It's called pho."

Her eyes widened with excitement. "I love that stuff."

"I eat it every Saturday afternoon. There's a place on Central, down by my house. You'll have to try it with me sometime."

"It seems like you've got a schedule for everything," she said. "You have biker meetings on Thursday nights, you eat that curry soup out east on Friday afternoon, pho on Saturdays, and you eat sushi on Sunday evenings. Oh, and you exercise on Tuesdays, Thursdays and Sundays, at midnight."

"I go see my parents every Sunday afternoon, too." I chuckled. "You forgot that."

"Every Sunday?"

"Every Sunday."

"That's awesome," she said. "My parents live in St. Louis. I see them a couple of times a year."

Spending time with my parents was something I looked forward to, especially since being released from prison. I was aware their days on earth were coming to a close, and I valued our Sunday afternoons together.

"I spend three or four hours every Sunday with mine," I explained. "It's kind of a tradition."

She wiped her hands on her napkin and relaxed against the back of the booth. "It seems like you know everything about me, but I know very little about you."

"I'm an open book. If you want to know something, all you've got to do is ask."

She finished eating the piece of pita bread she held, and then wiped her hands on her napkin. "You said you got divorced before you went to prison. Did you do it because you were going to prison?"

The question surprised me. "No," I responded. "That had nothing to do with it."

She reached for another piece of pita. "Is there a chance that you two will get back together?"

I choked on my response, coughing the words out onto the table between us. "Not a chance in hell."

"What's so funny?"

I blew out a long breath. I hadn't discussed it with anyone since it happened. The men in the MC feared mentioning it would cause me to react in a manner that would earn me a trip right back to prison. The time I'd spent incarcerated was therapeutic for me, and I'd managed to find a way to forgive her for what she'd done. It didn't make talking about it any easier.

I drew a breath of courage and then spoke in one rambling sentence. "While I was preparing for trial, my wife had sex with my best friend."

Her hand shot to her mouth. "Oh my gosh," she gasped. "I'm sorry."

"Better that it happened before I went to prison. It would have been tougher to accept if it happened while I was in there." I coughed out a laugh and continued. "I guess, in some respects it did happen while I was in there."

I realized I was saying more about matters than I wanted to. I reached for my glass of water.

"So, did it happen while you were locked up, or afterward? I'm confused."

"Before I went in. The fellas kept seeing her with him at the coffee shop. They said it didn't look like they were just friends. I figured he was comforting her, and let it go. Hell, I knew it was hard for her to accept that I chose to fight my case and risk prison when I could have simply accepted their offer of probation. Six months later, I felt like the fellas were probably right. So, I asked her. She confessed to having an affair with him."

"Holy crap." She shook her head. "That's awful."

"It is what it is. I forgave her. I said if she cut her ties with him that we could get through it. She apologized, agreed, and I figured it was over. A month or so down the road, I caught them together on a Friday night. She was supposed to be working late. She wasn't. They were out on a date."

Her eyes slowly widened. "What did you do?"

I was ashamed of how I reacted to the situation and regretted what I had done. I'd lived my life shielding others from the ridiculous decisions I often made. Confiding my mistakes revealed my weaknesses, and I preferred not to be perceived as being weak.

With Jessica, however, I felt complete transparency was in my best interest.

I let out a long sigh. "That night, after their date, they went to his house. That's where I found them. I went to a friend's house, got a gun, and then parked across the street from his house. I sent them each a text and explained if I saw either of them come out, I'd kill them."

"You're not serious!"

"I'm afraid I am."

She covered her mouth with her hands. "You didn't..."

"No, I didn't. I sat there and smoked an entire carton of cigarettes. I don't know how much time passed. The sun came up, and then went down again, I know that. I smelled like a wet goat. At some point I realized that her falling in love with him wasn't something I had control over. It was human emotion. So, I sent them a text, apologized, and left."

She blinked a few times. "Wow. That's...it's...that's kind of extreme. Is that how you handle everything? With violence?"

"Not really."

"What do you mean, *not really*?"

"I'm not a violent person. I consider myself kind and loving. When someone crosses me, I often feel the need to teach them a lesson, though."

"What was your lesson going to be? On that night?"

I shrugged. "I don't know. I think my frustration with the court case came to a head. I'd been battling with them for three years at that point and things didn't look good. I'm ashamed for what I did. For what it's worth, I apologized to him the next day and wished him the best in his endeavors with her."

Her eyes bulged. "Seriously?"

"Seriously."

"Are they still together?"

"They got married while I was in prison."

"Oh, wow."

I rarely offered my personal experiences to others. If someone wanted to know something, they had to carefully extract the information from me. In an effort to maintain complete transparency with Jessica, I decided to continue, offering her a little more.

"I dated a couple of women after that. I was trying to cling to some form of normalcy during my legal battle, I guess. The last relationship I ended up in continued until the day I surrendered to US Marshalls. She said she'd wait for me until I got out of prison. I had my doubts, but it was nice to think about."

I took a drink of water and mentally prepared to drop the next bomb.

"I'm guessing she didn't wait," Jessica said.

I shook my head. "I found out two months into my sentence that she was pregnant. When the fellas found out when the expected delivery date was, they figured the baby was mine. The date of conception would have been about a month before I got locked up. With me being in prison, communicating wasn't easy. Letters were written back and forth. Then, in one letter, she told me what happened. She had sex with one of my other friends a month before I surrendered. That's when I cut off all communication with the outside."

With her mouth hanging open, she stared back at me. After a moment, she swallowed heavily. "That really happened?"

"It sure did."

"I'm so sorry."

I shrugged. "I'm not. I believe everything happens for a reason. All that crap got me *here*. I like where I am now."

"Do you have trust issues?" she asked.

I did, but I was surprised that she asked. "Why do you ask?"

She pointed at herself. "Because I have them. So, I'm sure you do, too."

"I suppose I do."

"You can trust me," she said. "I'll never lie to you, or cheat on you."

"That's good to know."

She seemed offended by my response. She pushed the plate of hummus aside and leaned against the edge of the table. Her gaze met mine. "I'm serious."

"I believe you," I said, even though I didn't.

I didn't trust anyone at that point. Men, or women. After what I'd been through, my faith in mankind, entirely, had diminished to nothing.

I'd hoped that telling her about my past would cleanse me of what ill feelings I still harbored. My rising blood pressure proved I wasn't prepared to be in a relationship with anyone at that point.

As long as I didn't allow myself to fall in love with Jessica, she wouldn't be able to hurt me. Throughout my life, friends had come and gone, each leaving me with fond memories of the time we shared together.

She would be no different.

I needed to maintain a friendship with her, and nothing more. Doing so would protect me from the inevitable.

At that moment, I made the decision.

Jessica would be a friend, and nothing more.

CHAPTER SIX

I'd seen Jessica several times a week in the month that followed. She revealed a little more of herself each time we met, exposing her innocence and vulnerability as she blossomed before my watchful eyes.

Her clothing, makeup, and hairstyles stood as proof of her growing self-confidence. She was no longer sheepish. In fact, she was becoming bold. Knowing that she felt she could trust me was rewarding. Seeing the changes made each meeting between us a pleasure beyond compare.

She walked around the front of the car and stepped to my right side.

"Are you ready?" I asked, my tone laced with a hint of sarcasm.

She gripped my arm lightly and gave me a look. "Yes."

I glanced over my right shoulder. A playful glare followed. "Is that where you're supposed to be standing?"

Her face washed with confusion. "What do you mean?"

"Left side, Jess." I forced a dramatic sigh. "How many times have I told you? Always walk on my left side."

She released my arm. "I forget."

"Well, I'm reminding you. Again. Left side. Now, and always."

"Why do I have to always walk over there?" She stepped around me. "It seems silly."

"Because I say so."

She slipped her arm beneath mine and gripped the inside of my elbow lightly. "I want to know why."

I turned toward the theater and took a few steps. "There's a reason for everything I do."

She tugged against my arm, stopping me from going any further. "If there's a reason, you can tell me what it is."

I faced her. "My right side is my dominant side. If we're ever threatened, I need my right side to be free, so I can protect you."

Her eyes glistened. The corners of her mouth curled upward, forming a smile. "I like you."

"You're pretty good stuff, too. C'mon, we're going to be late."

She coughed out a laugh. "Pretty good stuff, huh?"

"Yep. You're pretty good stuff."

"I think you're pretty good stuff, too."

After entering the theater and looking over the twelve possibilities of movies, I chose an action-adventure movie. "How does *End of Watch* sound?"

Her brows knitted together. "What's it about?"

"Cops chasing gang members. It's got Jake what's-his-name in it. I like him. He's a good actor."

She glanced at the movie poster. "Jake Gyllenhaal?"

I gave a nod, hopeful that she liked him enough to agree to see the movie. "That's him."

"My stomach knots up when I watch movies like that."

Despite my run-in with the ATF, I respected law enforcement officers, and admired them for the sacrifices they made on a day-to-day basis. Watching believable depictions of their lives was something I found fascinating.

"Movies like what?" I asked. "Cops attempting the endless and impossible pursuit of ridding this world of evil?"

"Suspenseful movies," she said. "They make me sick."

"Seriously?"

She scanned the twelve miniature-sized movie posters. Her eyes became fixed on one in the center. "*Pitch Perfect* sounds better."

I arched an eyebrow. "*Pitch Perfect?*"

She looked at me. "Uh huh."

"College girls in a dance-off?"

"Singers. They're singers. The Bellas."

"The Bellas are better than Jake Gyllenhaal?"

"I'm a girl. Girls like to dream. Movies are an escape. They're like a dream."

"You could dream about Jake Gyllenhaal."

"I'd rather not."

The movie theater was across the street from my house. I often walked there three times a week to see a movie, mostly alone. The few times I took someone with me, it was Teddy.

I'd been looking forward to seeing *End of Watch*. Making Jess uncomfortable in any way, however, wasn't something I was prepared to do. Teddy and I could easily find time to watch it one night after our ride.

I stepped to the counter. "Two for Pitch Perfect."

The sixteen-year-old boy standing behind the ticket machine looked at Jess, and then at me. His eyes scanned up and down my arms, pausing to make note of my full sleeve of tattoos. Dressed in my normal attire of a wife beater, jeans and boots, I looked the part of the biker I truly was.

He met my gaze. His eyes were filled with disbelief. "Did you say Pitch Perfect?"

"That's right," I said. "Pitch Perfect."

He printed the tickets, handed them to me, and fought to conceal the smirk that was etched on his face. "Enjoy the show."

Amidst hordes of giggling high school girls who were updating their Facebook status while their respective faux hawk donning boyfriends talked amongst themselves, we found our seats. While waiting for the lights to dim, I stole a few glances at Jess. She ate her popcorn one carefully chosen kernel at a time.

She was everything I wasn't. She was soft spoken and reserved. I was loud and outgoing. She ate her Vietnamese soup with a fork and spoon, carefully twisting the noodles onto her fork before taking a bite. I used chop sticks and slurped it from the bowl. She drove cautiously – two miles an hour under the speed limit. I drove as fast as possible and accelerated from the traffic lights at a neck-breaking pace.

I couldn't help but wonder how well we'd do together – as a couple. If she would grow tired of me, or if I'd become frustrated with her. I further wondered if we'd simply complement one another.

If she could somehow be the yin to my yang.

The lights dimmed.

She rested her head on my shoulder.

Surprisingly, I liked the movie. In fact, I enjoyed it immensely. Movies, as Jess had indicated earlier, were an escape. If I could watch one that held my interest for ninety minutes, it was worth the price of admission.

If it could cause me to smile or laugh, I left satisfied.

I sat in the theater with her long after the movie ended, staring at the blank screen.

"You want to know something?" I asked.

"Sure."

"When I was in prison, there were two things that I yearned for. Just two. I'd lay in my rack at night and daydream of the day I could return to the free world and fulfill my desires. You'll never guess what they were, so I'm going to tell you."

"Let me guess."

I looked at her. "Okay."

"Get a cup of coffee."

I shook my head. "Strangely, that wasn't one of them."

"Eat pho?"

"That wasn't one either."

"Okay. I give up," she said.

"You'd think it would be seeing my kids, eating my favorite foods, or holding a woman in my arms. Maybe talking to my parents or riding the motorcycle. Something like that. But it wasn't. The two things were coming here to see a movie and petting my cat."

"Oh my gosh," she gasped. "You've got a cat?"

"My youngest son has it now. But, I did. Why?"

"Cats creep me out. They're scary."

"Cats are the best. There's nothing more satisfying than having one hop into your lap, lay down, and curl up into a ball."

She winced in disgust. "That grosses me out."

"If we ended up together one day, and I wanted a cat, what would you say?"

"I don't know." Her nose wrinkled, and she looked away. "I guess I'd have to deal with it when the time came."

I stood. "Are you ready?"

"For what?" she asked. "To go get a cat?"

I chuckled. "No. For a cup of coffee."

She let out a sigh. "I'd love to."

There were differences between Jess and me, that much I was sure of. The effect those differences would have if we were ever in a relationship would have to be seen.

I felt, however, that I wasn't willing to find out, regardless of what the outcome might be.

CHAPTER SEVEN

Teddy, Chico, and I rolled to a stop in front of the bar, thirty feet away from the covered patio. The outdoor seating area was filled with beer-drinking patrons who were anxiously watching the pre-season football game on one of the many flat-screen televisions.

We parked our motorcycles along the sidewalk that connected the bar's front door to the patio. Before I had a chance to get off my bike, the crowd erupted in cheers and drunken applause. There were four men seated at a high-top table, however, that seemed far more concerned with the three of us than the football game.

I glanced at the four over-sized idiots and then looked at Teddy. "Let me guess," I said flatly. "The four frat brothers."

Teddy was in his mid-thirties and looked more like an outdoorsman than a biker. He cut his unkempt hair once a year, and rarely trimmed his unruly beard. Instead of black boots and wife-beaters, flannel shirts and Doc Martens were his attire of choice.

He swept his kick stand down, glanced toward the patio, and then gave me a confused look. "The what?"

I gestured with my eyes toward the four men who were now

fidgeting in their seats. "The four dip-shits with the Greek letters on their shirts."

He glanced in their direction and stroked his beard. After a long study, he nodded. "Yep. That's them."

I climbed off my bike. With my back to the men, I looked at him and arched an eyebrow. "Which one was it?"

"Hard sayin'." He craned his neck and peered over my shoulder. "I just saw the finger, not who it was attached to."

Our MC took part in a poker run earlier in the day. Afterward, fifty or so of us went to a local bar. Then, around five o'clock, the club voted to go to a different bar.

Chico was sweet on one of the bar's waitresses, so we stayed behind until her shift ended. With her on the back of Chico's bike – and us trailing an hour behind the rest of the club – we left in typical biker fashion.

Fast and loud.

We shot out of the bar's parking lot full-throttle, racing toward the downtown district to meet the rest of the club. Upon coming to a stop at the first traffic light, Teddy informed me that someone had flipped us the bird and shouted something as we rode away from the bar.

I treated everyone with respect. I expected the same in return. So, upon hearing of the disrespectful gesture, I demanded that we turn around and go back to the bar. Teaching the men in question a lesson was something I felt compelled to do.

Chico's arms were loosely draped over the top of his ape hanger handlebars. The bubbly blond waitress had her hands in his lap and her boobs pressed against his back.

The Black Keys' *Sinister Kid* blared from his custom Road King's speakers.

"Fuck 'em," Chico said. "I say we stab 'em up. Disrespectful pricks."

Chico was half-Hispanic, muscular, and covered in tattoos. With short black hair and a neatly-trimmed goatee, he could easily pass for one of SoCal's Chicano bikers, but he was born and raised in the Midwest.

His answer to everything was stabbing someone. An awkward look in the coffee shop, a spilled drink, or someone giving his motorcycle a second glance were all grounds for being stabbed.

I glared at him. "Nobody's getting stabbed up." I shifted my eyes to Teddy and gestured toward the rock garden at the edge of the sidewalk. "Hand me one of those rocks without any of those fuckers seeing you. A big flat one."

Teddy's eyes widened. "What's the plan?"

"You two are going to sit here," I said. "And, I'm going to teach them a lesson on respect."

With his hands hidden from their sight, Teddy handed me a four-inch round one-inch thick rock.

"How's that?" he asked.

The rock was heavy in my hand. It would give me the edge I needed to face the four college football players. With my back to the men, I slipped the massive stone into the pocket of my jeans.

"It's perfect," I said with a nod.

Teddy looked at my rock-filled pocket and shook his head. "You sure you want to do this?"

He was the club's pacifist. In his opinion, God would sort out everything in the end. Nothing warranted violence. I disagreed with his theory wholeheartedly. If anyone knew it, he did.

"They need to be taught a lesson," I said dryly. "You know I'll never be able to live with myself if I don't do this."

He let out a sigh. "You're going up there alone?"

If three kutte-wearing tattooed bikers sauntered up to the men's table, it would be intimidating. Intimidation was a form of bullying. I was many things, but a bully wasn't one of them.

I needed to act alone.

I nodded. "Yep."

I glanced at Chico. The ditzy blonde's delicate nineteen-year-old hands were resting in his lap while her head bobbed to the music.

I shook my head at the sight. "If things go to hell in a handbasket, you two can join in. Only if they go to shit, though." I gestured toward the waitress. "Leave her ass here if you come up there."

Chico pulled out his phone. "I'm recording this shit."

I shot him a glare. "No, you're not."

"Why not?"

"Because. It's intimidating," I explained. "You know how I am about that shit."

"You're six-foot-two, covered in prison tats, and have a permanent scowl on your face." He chuckled. "It doesn't matter if you go over there alone or if we go with you. It's going to intimidate them, either way."

"I need to convince them that I'm right and that they were wrong. If you're recording it, it's going to make them nervous, and they might agree with me even if they don't agree with me. I need to make sure their apology is sincere. Put the phone up," I said.

He shoved the phone into the pocket of his kutte. "Whatever, you weird fucker."

I inhaled a deep breath and turned toward the patio. "Wish me luck."

Prepared to beat any – or all – of them into seeing things from my perspective, I strode toward the four men with purpose in my walk. It was the same bravado gait I'd used many times in prison to warn the other inmates that I wasn't an easy mark.

With each step, I kept my eyes focused on the men. I wondered how receptive they'd be to my request. I fully realized teaching people life lessons wasn't my place on earth, nor was it God's will, but I'd spent a lifetime doing it, nonetheless.

I stretched my legs over the waist-high wooden fence that separated the patio from the parking lot and walked up to the edge of the men's table.

While the four of them stared at me wide-eyed, I pulled out a spare stool and sat down at the end of their table. Two of the men were seated on my left, and two were on my right.

I made eye contact with each of them, and then gave a nod. "How you fellas doing?"

Three of them stared at me in sheer disbelief. The fourth, the biggest of the group, took a long drink of his beer and then pushed the mug to the side. "Trying to watch the game," he said. "What's up?"

I locked eyes with him and leaned forward, resting my forearms on the edge of the table. "Well, one of the fellas I was riding with gave me some troubling news."

He glanced toward Teddy and Chico, looked at me, and chuckled. "What's that got to do with us?"

He was obviously the leader of the group and wanted to play the part in front of his friends. I had minimal patience for smart-asses, less for liars, and none for people who treated others with disrespect.

He had crossed all three boundaries.

I sized up his three friends and then looked him up and down. At six-foot-two and just shy of two hundred pounds, I wasn't small by any means. He easily had fifty pounds on me, as did each of his friends.

But, he was the one with the mouth. Therefore, he was the one I needed to talk to.

Hidden from his view by the table, I slipped my hand into the right pocket of my jeans and gripped the rock.

"It's got everything to do with you," I explained in a dry tone. "You see, one of you flipped us off when we were leaving a few minutes ago. I'm sure you're aware that the gesture is a universal sign for *fuck you*. I don't know about the four of you, but when someone tells me to fuck off, I see it as a sign of disrespect. I'm weird about people treating others disrespectfully, so here's how I'm going to handle this."

I paused and looked at each of the men. "Whichever one of you did it has one chance to apologize. Just one. If no one admits to it, I'm going to start beating on *you*." I gestured toward Big Boy with a nod. "And, I'll beat you like you've never been beaten before."

His Adam's apple rose, and then fell.

"I'm pretty sure your buddies will get me off you at some point. But, I can guarantee you *this*." I stood, clenched my jaw, and gripped the rock firmly in my hand. "Tomorrow, at some point, you'll look in the mirror at your missing teeth and the cuts I left on your face, and you'll say to yourself, *damn, I wish I would have apologized to that guy yesterday.*"

Each of the men stared back at me with open mouths and wide eyes.

"I'm going to count to three," I explained. "By the time I get there, someone better be apologizing."

I raised my left index finger in the air. "One..."

"I did it," Big Boy blurted.

I shook my head. "Why?"

He shrugged. "Your motorcycles were really loud, and we were trying to watch the game."

I gestured toward the sign in the parking lot behind him and chuckled. It was one of a dozen that read, MOTORCYCLE PARKING ONLY, and reserved the front twelve parking spots for bikers.

"In case you didn't know it, you're in a biker bar. It's neither here nor there, though. Disrespect is disrespect. If you treat the wrong man with disrespect, you'll get your ass kicked – or killed. You're lucky it's me talking to you, and not that ugly Mexican over there." I raised my eyebrows. "Now, I'm going to need you to apologize."

Big Boy let out a sigh. "I'm sorry."

"Fair enough." I glanced at each of the men. "Look at it as a lesson learned. Give respect, and you'll get it in return. Remember that, it just might get you out of a jam sometime."

I reached into my left pocket, pulled out my money clip, and tossed a twenty-dollar bill on the table. "Next round is on me, fellas."

"I appreciate it," the man on my left said.

"I appreciate the fact your buddy had enough common sense to apologize." I pulled the rock from my pocket and slapped it down on top of the bill with a *thud*. "Have a nice evening, fellas."

CHAPTER EIGHT

I'd worked for more than twenty years in the construction management industry. With my focus being large commercial buildings, I designed, bid, and managed construction projects from concept to completion. Over the years, I'd established quite a reputation for developing cost-reduction options without sacrificing a building's quality or performance.

The day I was released from prison, I had multiple job offers waiting. I accepted the most challenging one. Then, two years later, I walked away from the commercial construction industry entirely.

I felt I needed a change in my life, I simply didn't know what that change was. After a few months of blindly searching for the answer, I agreed to accept a job doing the same thing – on a smaller scale – with Teddy.

He was a General Contractor by trade and owned his own business. He preferred projects that fell in the half-a-million-dollar range or less. I had spent two decades thumbing my nose at such jobs, preferring the complexity and reward that came with work priced in the tens of millions.

I quickly found that working on smaller projects produced less headaches. Less headaches allowed me to live with much less tension in my life. It appeared – at least on the surface – that I'd found the answer to my problem.

Working with Teddy and his indecisive nature, however, ground on my every nerve.

"What if we move that island to the center of the room and put the display case on the south wall?" he asked.

"What if we leave the son-of-a-bitch where it is and save two grand?" I growled.

He gazed blankly at the proposed location. "It will flow better in here if we move it."

"It'll flow fine if we leave it. Kids buying frozen yogurt won't give two shits where that island is."

He stroked his beard with the web of his hand. "I think I'd like it better if we moved it."

"Did the owner complain about where it is?"

Without facing me, he shook his head lightly. "No."

"Then were leaving it."

"I was just thinking--"

"Look, dumbass. Every dollar we spend on this job is a dollar out of our pockets. Fifty cents out of mine, and fifty cents out of yours. It'll cost two grand to move it, re-wire everything, and fix the floor. He isn't going to sell any more yogurt if it's over there. I'm not willing to pay a grand to satisfy your anal-retentive nature."

He looked at me. "I'm not anal-retentive."

"Maybe that's a bad choice of words, but you're weird, and you know it."

He looked me up and down. "Not as weird as you."

"There's nothing weird about me, Brother," I said dryly.

He chuckled a dry laugh. "You weigh yourself ten times a day. You exercise at two in the morning. You sleep two or three hours a night. You're so full of pride that it gets you in trouble. You--"

I'd heard enough. I shot him a glare and interrupted him mid-sentence. "Hold on a fucking minute. So full of pride it gets me in trouble? I might have a boatload of self-esteem, but I don't think I'm an excessively prideful person. I take exception to that comment."

"They go hand-in-hand."

I gave him a look. "What does?"

"Pride and self-esteem."

"Excessive pride makes a man conceited. Are you saying I'm arrogant?"

"No. You're not arrogant."

"I'm confident. There's a difference," I explained. "My Pop and I talked about this. I don't know if I told you or not, but at trial, the judge said I possessed a certain arrogance, and he suggested I find a way to lose it. When my Pop read the manuscript of the trial, he tossed it across the living room and started yelling when he reached that part. He said the judge needed to recognize the difference between arrogance and confidence."

His eyes thinned. "What's the difference?"

"Confidence is inwardly knowing your abilities. Arrogance is outwardly expressing your belief of the same."

He stroked his beard for a moment and then gave a nod. "I'd agree with your Pops."

"Checking my weight isn't weird," I added. "It's maintenance."

He barked out a laugh. "You weigh yourself in the morning. Then, again, before you eat breakfast. Then, after breakfast. And, before we go for a ride. As soon as we get back to the house. Before you exercise. After you exercise. Then, again, before you go to bed. I'd call that weird."

"Fuck you," I snapped back.

"I forgot something. If that chick from the donut shop is so hot, why aren't you throwing her some dick? That's weird, too."

"Same reason you're not screwing that little chick at the coffee shop who's ga-ga over you. I don't trust women. Now that you've mentioned it, she's coming here for lunch."

"Who?"

"Jess."

His eyes went wide. "She's coming here?"

"Yep."

He glanced left, and then right. "Today?"

"That's what I said."

He didn't have to tell me that her expected arrival made him feel uneasy. Teddy couldn't accept outsiders into his life without going through a painstaking process of questioning their intentions. In fact, he trusted only two of the men in the MC enough to allow them into his home. Despite his claim of not being weird, he was the strangest man I'd ever met.

"You'll be fine," I said.

He glanced around the room. "We'll need to get these tools put up. And, all those light fixtures will need to be hidden."

"She's not going to steal the tools," I said with a laugh. "And, the light fixtures are fine right where they are."

"They were a hundred bucks a piece. She could hock 'em for fifty. We need to--"

"They're fine right where they are. You can trust this chick."

"How do you know?"

"Because I know."

"If any of this stuff comes up missing..."

"If it comes up missing it won't have anything to do with her, I can assure you of that."

Teddy had been remodeling his house for the past year. The interior of the home was stripped down to the bare studs and subfloor. Without sheetrock on the walls, one could peer from one end all the way to the other, seeing through each room, including the bathrooms.

As a result of the home's condition, he often slept in my spare room, sometimes for three or four days before returning to his dilapidated house.

Six months prior, when he returned home after a two or three-day hiatus, he found out he'd been robbed. There wasn't much stolen, because there wasn't much to take. Everything of value, however, was gone.

The police told him they doubted they'd catch the guy. No fingerprints were left, there was no security footage, and the neighbors saw no one come or go. It was the work of a true professional, according to the police.

A few weeks later, by happenstance, they caught the guy. He was attempting to sell something he'd stolen from Teddy on eBay. The problem was that there was only one of these particular items on earth. The detective on the case had been checking eBay for the stolen item, hoping the criminal might use it as an avenue for ridding himself of the merchandise.

After the criminal's arrest, Teddy learned who he was.

He was an unpatched member of our Motorcycle club. A hang-around. A friend. Someone who was with us day and night. He rode where we rode, ate where we ate, and attended club functions – less the meetings reserved for patched members only.

The arrest didn't cause Teddy to develop his lack of trust toward mankind, it simply confirmed the suspicions he already harbored. It was a huge step in the wrong direction for someone that was slowly beginning to learn how to trust.

Teddy gasped. "Holy shit."

I realized I'd lost my train of thought and looked up. "What?"

He gestured toward the storefront windows. "Is *that* her?"

Dressed in a pair of loose-fitting pants, heels, and a flowing top with a plunging neckline, Jess was walking toward the front door. Her hair was up, in a braided bun. A few delicate curls dangled along each side of her face.

I grinned at the sight of her. "That'd be her."

"She's uhhm." He swallowed hard. "She's a pretty fucker."

I walked toward the door. "Don't say anything stupid."

He cleared his throat. "I'll do my best."

I pushed the door open. "Have any problems finding the place?"

"Nope. It was right where you said it would be." She hugged me, and then peered over my shoulder. "You must be Teddy."

Without hesitation, she strode toward him. The uneasy look he was wearing earlier promptly returned. In addition to not trusting people, Teddy was extremely nervous in the presence of women. So much so that he often did or said things that were extremely embarrassing.

She extended her hand. Teddy wiped his palm on the thigh of his jeans, and then looked at it before offering it to her. After wiping it a second time, he shook her hand.

"Is that your real hair color?" he asked.

"No." She brushed one of the curls away from her face with a wave of her hand. "I'm a brunette. I'm a hairstylist, so the color is always changing."

Teddy had a thing for blondes, and I knew the moment he met Jess that he'd like her for that reason alone.

"I like that color," he said. "It looks good."

She smiled. "Thank you."

"Should we all go to lunch?" I asked.

"I like the way you've got it fixed, too," Teddy said. "Wedding hair always looks good. Especially when it's blond."

Jess gave him a look. "Wedding hair?"

"Isn't that what it's called? When it's up like that?"

"It's a chignon," Jess said. "It's a fancy name for a bun."

"Well, I like it."

"Should we all go to lunch?" I asked, raising the tone of my voice slightly.

Teddy took a step back. After looking her over from head to toe, he gave a nod of approval. "I like those pants."

Her pants were white and covered in various geometric shapes. They fit her butt like a second skin yet hung loosely around her legs. She wore the style quite often, claiming they hid the size of her thighs, which she described as *thick*.

"Fun pants," Jess said. "That's what I call them."

His brows knitted together. "Why's that?"

She shrugged. "Because they're fun."

"Quit being weird, Teddy," I said in a snide tone. I raised my brows. "Should we all go get lunch?"

Teddy scowled at me. "I'm not being weird. I was being nice."

"You're being weird."

"Hitting guys in the head with rocks is weird," he said. "This is normal."

Jess spun around. "You hit a guy in the head with a rock?"

I glared at Teddy, and then shifted my gaze to Jess. "No."

She looked at Teddy.

"He didn't hit the guy with it, but he had it ready," he said. "Just in case he didn't apologize."

She faced me. "Apologize for what?"

"Being a shithead," I said.

She cocked her hip. "Seriously? You had a rock, and everything?"

I shrugged. "The guy flipped us off."

Her glare sharpened. "So, you were going to hit him with a rock?"

Considering her composure, I figured I needed to downplay the use of the rock. Discussing it made the event sound much worse than it was. At the time it seemed like a practical choice.

Now, it seemed ridiculous.

"If it would have just been him," I said. "I wouldn't have had the rock. I would have just beat his ass. But, he had three friends with him. I needed an equalizer."

Her brows raised. "You were going to fight four guys? With a rock?"

I turned my palms up and shrugged.

She looked at Teddy.

He nodded.

She turned to face me. "Four? With a rock. You would have gone right back to prison."

"I couldn't let him get away with flipping me off," I snapped back. "Right is right, and wrong is wrong. He was wrong."

"But you didn't hit him with it?"

"Didn't need to. He apologized."

"Why'd he flip you off?" she asked.

"Does it matter?"

"I was just curious."

"We were sitting outside at a bar under the covered patio. When we left, he said our motorcycles were too loud. They interrupted his football game."

She scrunched her nose. "So, he flipped you guys off? That's kinda dumb."

"Precisely," I said.

"Threatening him with a rock is dumber, though."

"I didn't threaten him with a rock," I said. "I just threatened to beat the shit out of him. I had the rock in my pocket just in case."

"That's better, I guess." She shook her head dismissively, and then looked at me. "I wonder about you sometimes."

"You're not the only one," Teddy said.

I glanced at them both. The choices I made weren't the same decisions others would make, but to me they made perfect sense. The last thing I needed was to have someone second-guessing my manner of handling my life's problems.

I turned toward the door. "I'm going to lunch. If you two do-gooders want to go with me, that's fine. If not, you can sit here and talk about how you would have hugged your way out of the situation."

"Don't get mad," Jess said.

I turned toward the door. "I'm not mad."

"Seems mad, doesn't he?" Teddy asked.

"Kind of," Jess agreed.

I wasn't mad. Disappointed would be a more accurate statement. I liked Jess. I simply didn't need someone telling me what was right or wrong with my way of doing things, or with my life.

I'd never let anyone tell me what to do, and I certainly wasn't going to start with her.

CHAPTER NINE

Another month passed. Jess and I had become inseparable. She was filling an undeniable void in my life that I'd had for years but wasn't willing to admit. I was only making half as much money as I was accustomed to, but I was twice as happy as I'd ever been. I attributed that happiness to the time Jess and I shared together.

I pulled into her driveway and parked. She lived in a duplex, occupying one side of the building while a co-worker and friend resided on the other. Before I took my first step, Jess' co-worker opened her front door and poked her head through the opening. Her hair was brown, except for two thick strands, which were golden blond.

"You must be Scott," she said.

"I am," I responded. "You must be Sasha."

"I am." She gestured toward me with her hand. "I like the sleeve."

I waved and took a step toward the porch. "Thank you."

"What are you guys up to?" she asked.

I paused. "Just going for a cup of coffee."

She stepped onto the porch and shielded her eyes from the sun. "Seems like you guys drink a lot of coffee."

I grinned and took a few more steps. "We do."

"I like your car."

I let out a mental sigh. "Thank you."

"What was prison like?"

I sighed, this time for real. "It's pretty uneventful. Boring, really."

It was far from boring, but I wasn't willing to share prison stories with someone I didn't know.

"Really? I've got a friend who has a brother that went to prison. He's got a million stories to tell."

"If he's got more than two or three, they're lies," I said with a laugh.

"Do you think so?"

"I'm sure of it," I said flatly.

I made it to the porch before she hit me with the next question. "So, you're in a motorcycle club?"

"I am."

"Like Sons of Anarchy?"

"Exactly," I said, hoping to satisfy her curiosity.

"Why do you pick her up in your car all the time? Why don't you ride your motorcycle?"

"Women don't ride on the back of my bike," I said. "Unless I'm in a relationship with them."

Her eyes thinned. "Aren't you two in a relationship?"

"Kind of," I said. "But not really. It's complicated."

I rang Jess' doorbell. The door opened, revealing a half-dressed Jess. Dressed in cut-off sweat shorts, a lace black push-up style bra, and nothing else, she held the door open.

"Get in here," she whispered.

I tore my eyes away from Jess' boobs and waved at the neighbor. "Nice to meet you."

Before she could respond, I stepped inside. Jess turned toward the hallway. Her hair was straight and much longer than I expected it to be – draping over her shoulders and down to the middle of her back.

"I've got to finish my makeup," she said over her shoulder.

I looked around the living room. "I'll wait in here."

"You can wait in my room while I get ready, silly. It'll just be a few minutes."

Her boobs were boiling out the top of her bra, and I wasn't certain I could be in her presence without becoming aroused to the point of making a fool of myself. To date, I'd seen her dressed, or not at all.

I gestured toward her loveseat. "I'll just wait in here."

She crossed her arms and huffed out a sigh. When she did, her boobs heaved. My cock responded with a noticeable twitch.

I shoved my hand in my pocket and pressed the heel of my palm against it, hoping to deter any further erection developments.

I turned away. "I'll just--"

She grabbed my wrist. "Come on."

Reluctantly, I followed her into the bedroom. While I sat on the edge of the bed, she sat on the floor and did her makeup in front of a full-length wall mirror.

With her back to me, she talked as she worked. I listened intently and responded as need be, all the while gawking at her boobs in the mirror's reflection. Within seconds, I had a full-fledged hard-on.

Embarrassed, and not sure how to conceal the rock-hard chunk of flesh, I fidgeted with her decorative pillows. After opting to smash one into my lap, I looked up.

She was buttoning her blouse.

"Does this bra look silly with this top?" she asked.

"I uhhm. I don't think so," I stammered. "Why?"

"The top is sheer, and the bra is black."

"Looks fine to me."

"I don't like it," she said.

Before I had a chance to argue, she was standing before me without her top. Then, her bra hit the floor. She covered the majority of her boobs with her biceps, but there was a lot to cover. Little, if anything, was left to the imagination.

My slowly recovering male anatomy went stiff as a stone.

She pulled open a dresser drawer and snatched a nude bra from the selection of neatly arranged undergarments. When she did, I got a glimpse of the side of her boob.

I was forty-seven years old and had a raging hard-on that was derived from seeing a girl's boobs. A girl who I knew I wasn't going to have sex with. I felt like I was in high school again. Watching her stuff her massive boobs into her bra was like witnessing a train wreck.

I simply couldn't look away.

She put on her top, making eye contact with me several times as she buttoned it. Her innocence, in my eyes, faded away. It was replaced with a streak of orneriness. After she buttoned the last button, she looked right at me.

"Ready?" she asked, her mouth twisted into a taunting smirk.

"Sure," I said. "In just a minute."

"Let's go now." She yanked the pillow from my lap.

Her eyes locked on the denim tent my cock was pitching. "Oh. Wow." She looked up. "Everything okay?"

"I'm not used to watching someone get dressed," I said.

"Sooo," she said, drawing the word out for a few seconds. "You still want to go?"

"As soon as I can stand," I said.

"Are you sure?"

I didn't want to go. I wanted to undress her, toss her on the bed, and have my way with her. But. I knew it wasn't in our friendship's best interest.

I sighed. "Yes."

The look of disappointment that covered her face was enough to thwart any more blood flow to my nether region. In a few seconds, I stood.

"I'm ready if you are," I said.

With her face washed with disappointment, she stepped to my left side and gripped the inside of my bicep. "Let's do it."

She was nothing short of remarkable. I couldn't help but wonder, however, how long I could continue our relationship without making sexual advancements.

I further wondered just how long it would be before she either did the same or threw in the towel.

When we pulled into the donut shop, Chico's bike was parked on the sidewalk in front of the building. He lived in the same area as Jessica did, which was only a few blocks away.

"That's one of the fellas," I said with a nod.

"It's okay if we go in?" she asked.

I'd made it clear with her that the club's business was private, and not to ask questions. As a matter of respect, I'd shared very little, if anything, about any of the men, including their names.

Teddy was the only exception, and he gave his approval.

"It'll be fine," I said. "Don't ask him anything. I mean, if he talks to you, you can participate in the conversation. Just don't ask about the club. Use your best judgement."

"Okay," she said.

I had faith that she wouldn't do anything to embarrass me.

I walked inside with her attached to my left elbow. As soon as we cleared the door, Chico looked up. His sunken eyes were bloodshot, and I could see it from thirty feet away.

"Ay, chihuahua!" he announced. "Miss Yessica!"

"What do you want me to do?" she whispered. "He's scary."

He was wearing a bandana, which was folded into a three-inch wide strap and stretched across his forehead. When combined with his goatee and deep summer tan, he resembled a Chicano gang member who'd ridden into town from Los Angeles.

"He's harmless," I assured her.

He stood, almost falling over in the process. Obviously drunk, I suspected he hadn't been home since the night before. After steadying himself, he opened his arms.

It was common for bikers, us included, to greet one another with a hug. When I began to walk in his direction, he coughed out a laugh.

"Not you." He nodded toward Jess. "I wanna hug her."

Wearing a smile that I expected was false, Jess gave him a hug. After they broke their embrace, Chico slapped the top of the table with his fingertips. "Have a seat, Yessica."

Jess glanced at me.

"You don't need his approval," he said. "Sit down."

She sat down across from him. "You look sad."

"I am," he said.

"Why?"

"Because where I live, girls that look like you don't exist. They're all fugly."

She wrinkled her nose. "What's fugly?"

"Fucking ugly," he said. "Fugly."

She laughed. "Oh."

"Go get your drinks, 'Mano," he said. "I'll protect her while you're gone."

"I'll be right back," I said.

There was an unwritten rule that held true with all motorcycle clubs. One man didn't mess with another man's woman, nor did he treat her with disrespect, regardless of what he thought of her.

I knew Jess was in good hands with Chico, whether she realized it or not.

I returned in a few minutes, coffees in tow. When I did, Jess was laughing out loud at a story Chico was telling. Although I shouldn't have been, I felt a little jealous seeing her have such a good time with him.

So far, I'd separated Jess from my MC brethren. For no other reason than protecting the club was why I told myself I'd done it, but

I now wondered if I was being truthful in that reasoning. As she caught her breath from laughing, I felt my blood pressure rise.

I set her cup of coffee down in front of her and took a seat at her side.

I clenched my coffee cup with both hands, almost smashing it in the process. "What's so funny?"

"He was telling me a story about when you ate some Thai food," Jess explained. "He said you ended up in the hospital after almost bleeding to death from a ruptured hemorrhoid."

Of all the stories for him to tell, he had to tell her that one. I pushed my coffee to the side and glared at him.

"Why don't you tell her the story about when you tried to eat that oyster, El Vato?"

"Because it's not funny."

"I think it's funny."

He folded his tattooed arms across his chest and shot me a glare. "I don't."

"Let's let Jess decide."

"Let's not."

"I want to hear it," she said.

While Chico shot a laser sharp glare in my direction, I began to tell the story. "We rode down to Corpus Christi and ended up in this dive of a bar that served fresh seafood. Chico had been drinking since about six am, and it was six in the evening. King ordered oysters on the half shell. Chico got up and went to the bathroom, and when he got back, he decided he wanted to try one. There was only one left, but King agreed to let him have it. Being a Kansas native, he hadn't had 'em before. So, he picked up the shell, looked at it, and then looked at King. 'How do you eat one of these fuckers?', he asked. King explained that you just suck it off the shell, chew it once, and swallow it. So, Chico gave it a try. After rolling it around in his mouth for five minutes and almost barfing two or three times, he eventually swallowed it."

Jess stared at me intently. After a few seconds, she squinted. "That wasn't funny."

I looked at Chico, and then at her. "The story's not over."

She smiled. "Oh."

I smiled at Chico, and then continued. "Chico reached for his beer, took a drink, and then swallowed hard again. 'That wasn't so bad', he said. I looked at him and grinned. 'Surprised you kept it down,' I said. 'Why's that?' he asked. 'Because,' I said. 'I barfed that same fucker up about five times while you were in the bathroom.' Ol' Chico hopped off his barstool, and turned toward the bathroom, but he didn't make it. He puked it up right on the floor, and then slipped and fell in the puke before he could get to the bathroom."

"Oh, my God," Jess said. "That's awful."

"It was worse than awful," Chico said. "The bad thing was that shithead here really didn't eat it. He just said he did. Found out later that it was a joke his Pops had told him, and he played it on me to see if it would work. We ended up getting kicked out of the bar."

She wrinkled her nose. "That's awful."

"What was awful was that little fucker coming back up," he said. "Shot out of there like a little oyster rocket."

"Okay," Jess said with a laugh. "Enough about hemorrhoids and oysters. Let's talk about something else."

"I'm single again," Chico said. "We can talk about that."

Chico had just gone through a divorce and had been screwing a waitress from one of our hangouts. The problem with him was that when he was drinking, he would screw whoever was close enough to grab. My guess was that he got caught with his hand in the cookie jar.

"What happened?" I asked.

He shrugged. "She got pissed."

"About?"

"She said I was a whore."

"I'll be damned," I said dryly.

He looked at Jess. "Got any friends?"

"My neighbor," she said. "She likes bikers."

"She'd be perfect for you," I said, laughing inside the entire time.

"Get something set up. Introduce me to her," he said.

Jess grinned. "Okay."

"I like this chick," Chico said.

I reached for my coffee. "Makes two of us."

We sat and talked for hours. All the while, I mulled over the differences that would exist if Jess and I were in a sexual relationship. The risk, I decided, would be exposing myself to being hurt again.

I realized Jess had done nothing to indicate she couldn't be trusted. From a statistical standpoint, however, the odds were against her. It would just be a matter of time before she realized I was too old for her, too brash for her, or simply too set in my wicked ways.

She would come to one of those realizations, though.

It was as inevitable as the tide.

CHAPTER TEN

Two days had passed since we saw Chico at the donut shop. I'd been busy finishing a project with Teddy. Although Jess had asked to meet on both days, I simply didn't have time to do so.

On the evening of the second day, I agreed to go to dinner. For the first time since I met her, Jess was not her joyful self. Seeing her in such a somber mood troubled me. I desperately wanted to fix whatever was wrong and have her return to her normal state of being.

"Are the kids okay?" I asked.

She looked up from her bowl of noodles. "They're fine."

"Are you busy at work?"

She shrugged. "I've been pretty busy, yeah."

"You're okay on money? You don't need anything?"

I wasn't in a position to be giving anyone money, but I'd certainly give her my last cent if I needed to.

"I'm doing good."

"You don't look like it," I said. "Something's wrong."

She twisted her fork through the noodles while she stared blankly at the bowl of soup. After a moment, she looked up.

"Are we in a relationship?"

I gave a nod. "I'd say so, yes."

"An actual *relationship*?"

I didn't like where the conversation was going. In response, I did as I always did when I was asked a question I preferred not to answer. I answered it without necessarily answering it.

"What we have is a relationship, yes."

She released her fork. As it slipped into the bowl, I realized exactly what was wrong.

"We've been seeing each other for months. Months. You've introduced me to your friends. We've been hanging out together. We run here, we run there, and we goof around together. But, you haven't made a pass at me. Do you think I'm pretty?"

"You're gorgeous," I said. "Breathtakingly so."

She twisted a strand of hair with her finger. "Am I sexy?"

"You are. Very much so, to be honest."

"Why haven't you taken the next step? We haven't even kissed."

My heart wanted me to lean over the table and kiss her. My mind wouldn't allow it. The two struggled with one another for a moment, with my mind winning the argument. I often wished I wasn't as strong-willed and stubborn as I was, but change wasn't an option.

I swallowed heavily, and then met her gaze. "I'm not ready to be in a relationship."

She released the strand of hair and gave me a look. "You're not ready?"

"No, I'm not."

"When will you be?"

"I don't know," I said, choking on the words as I spoke.

The thought of losing her crushed me. The risk associated with being in a relationship with her was far too much for me to make a move in that direction. With our eyes locked on one another, I sat silently and wondered what a future without her would be like.

"Let me think about it," I said.

"Think about this," she said. "I don't want to be friends with you.

I like you far too much. I want to be in a relationship with you. I want more. I want to be your lover. If we can't agree to give *that* a try, I need to end this. Before I get hurt."

And there it was. The "L" word.

She needed a lover.

I'd placed myself in some extremely awkward situations over the years. Barfights, gunfights, drug deals, knife fights, riots, beatdowns, stabbings...I'd seen it all. Through it all, I'd never been truly scared. Fear was an emotion I didn't seem to be in touch with.

Yet.

I feared allowing myself to love Jess would produce nothing more than pain. I further feared walking away at that moment would cause pain that I wasn't prepared to deal with. I'd placed myself in a position where I couldn't win, and the outcome, either way, scared me to death.

I'd hurt enough in my lifetime. Walking away from her at that moment would undoubtedly cause pain, but nothing compared to what I'd feel if I allowed myself to love her, and then lost her.

My head spun.

"Let me think about it," I said.

She pushed her chair away from the table. "I want to go home."

I gestured toward her soup. "You haven't eaten a thing."

"I can't eat," she said. "I'm too upset."

Hurting her was the last thing I wanted to do. Nonetheless, my simple existence was causing her pain, and I could see it.

"Alright." I tossed fifty dollars on the table and stood. "Home it is, then."

CHAPTER ELEVEN

Certain that I didn't want to expose myself to the possibility of being hurt, but uncertain that I wanted to let Jess go, I chose to discuss matters with the only people I felt I could trust. The problem was that none of them shared my odd set of moral beliefs.

Teddy's eyes followed me as I paced the floor of the clubhouse. Bones and Chico stood at his sides.

I paused and glanced at each of the men. "Well? Let's hear it."

"Why don't you just fuck her," Bones said. "That's what she wants."

Chico chuckled and shook his head. "He can't. He's a fucking weirdo. He's got to be in a relationship with her first."

"That's not weird," I said. "It's respectful."

"It's not respectful," Chico said. "She's a woman. Women want dick. You've got a dick. It's simple mathematics. You're good at math. Do the math. Give the poor girl some dick."

"To give her dick, I've got to be in a relationship. I can't do that."

"Won't," Teddy said flatly.

I looked at him. "Won't what?"

"Won't be in a relationship. You can. But, you won't. Don't say *can't*. You can."

"Since when are you an authority on relationships?" I asked.

"I'm not an authority on anything," he said. "But I know you well enough to know you can do anything you set your mind to. You could be in a relationship with her. You're not willing to."

"I might be willing to. That's why we're talking. I'm trying to decide."

"Chico said she's hotter'n fuck," Bones said. "Decision's easy, far as I'm concerned."

"Her being *hotter'n fuck* doesn't make it okay for me to do something I wouldn't normally do. I either need to commit to her or walk away."

His gaze fell to the floor. "Commit?" After a moment, he looked up. "I hate that word. Women say *cunt* is the 'C' word. I say the "C" word is *commit*. It's impossible to commit to anyone."

"It's not impossible," I said. "But, there's a risk involved."

He crossed his arms over his chest. "Risk? What's the risk?"

"Getting hurt."

A laugh shot from his lungs. "You? The man who volunteered to go to the joint? You're worried about getting hurt?"

I was like an M&M. I had a hard outer shell, but I was soft and sweet in the inside. As difficult as it was to admit, I was extremely sensitive. When life caused me to deal with emotions, however, I shut down and refused to do so.

The combination of having a delicate inner self and either being unwilling or incapable of dealing with my emotions caused me to be far more precautious than most men.

"It's not that I'm worried about it. I'm just not willing to take the chance."

"If you're not willing, you're not willing," Chico said. "Let me know if you're walking away, though. I'll take over where you left off."

I spun around. "You're not going to fucking touch her," I growled. "Not now, not ever. Understood?"

He shrugged.

"Under-fucking-stood?" I barked.

"I got it," he said.

I glared at him. "You better."

My heart wanted one thing, and my mind clearly wanted another. After months of seeing one another, the thought of losing her was unbearable. Exposing myself to another painful breakup, however, loomed over my desire to be with her like a black cloud.

I needed to decide and relying on my MC brethren to assist me wasn't in my best interest. The decision was mine to make, and mine only.

My risks were as follows: if I committed to be in a relationship, it might work out, and it might not. If it didn't, I'd lose Jess, and that loss would crush me. If I walked away now, the loss would be painful.

But it wouldn't be as painful as the loss if I allowed myself to love her.

I glanced at each of the men.

My decision was made.

"I've got some shit to do," I said. "I'm out of here."

"What are you going to do about Jess?" Chico asked.

I stretched my leg over the rear fender of my chopper and lowered myself into the seat. "I've only got one love." I patted my palm against the gas tank. "And, I'm getting ready to ride her out of here."

I flipped the ignition on, hit the *start* button, and gave each of the men a nod.

CHAPTER TWELVE

I no more than pressed the doorbell, and Jess opened the door. She was dressed in a pair of oversized sweats and a loose-fitting tee shirt. Her hair, for the first time since we'd met, was an absolute disaster.

She wasn't smiling.

In the background, I could hear her children playing.

I craned my neck to get a view of them. In response, she pulled the door closed, leaving only her head poking through the opening.

"Did you decide?" she asked.

I swallowed heavily and gave a nod.

"Well?"

"I'm not in a position..." I swallowed heavily, again. "I can't commit to be in a relationship with you."

She broke my gaze. Her lips pursed. After inhaling a long breath through her nose, she looked up.

"Okay. Don't text me, don't call me, don't come by. Respect me enough to grant me that, will you? You're a remarkable man, Scott. You truly are. But, you're a remarkable mess. Goodbye."

With those words, she shut the door.

I hadn't cried since the last time I'd disappointed my father enough to cause him to spank my ass. I was twelve at the time. Since that night, I hadn't so much as shed a single tear.

On the evening I left Jess, a tear may have escaped me. I'd later claim there was something in the air that night. I'd never know for sure. The summer night's air dried whatever it was as I rode toward the eastern horizon.

When the sun rose, I'd covered three hundred and fifty miles.

My eyes were dry, and my heart was filled with a pain that was new to me.

A pain so intense it was crippling.

CHAPTER THIRTEEN

The summer was over, and fall was in full swing. I'd walked away from my job with Teddy and was living off the funds I had set aside to purchase a home. I had no desire to work, to mingle with outsiders, or to ever go back to the donut shop where Jess and I met.

Nights were spent on my motorcycle, and days were spent at home. Be it from not working, or as a result of missing Jessica's company, I had fallen into a state of depression.

My only escapes were music and riding my motorcycle, neither of which provided much comfort.

Convinced I'd made the right decision, and that the pain I was feeling was confirmation that I had no business in a relationship, I swore off women completely.

I sat in my parent's living room, staring blankly at the television. I had no desire to watch it. I hadn't had a television in five years and doubted I'd ever have another. My home was also void of any access to the internet. My phone was my only link to modern-day technology.

"So, what's going on?" my father asked.

"Same old shit," I responded. "Riding the bike and hoping winter never comes."

"How's that pay?" he asked in a sarcastic tone.

I shifted my eyes to meet his and rolled them dramatically.

"Something you need to be aware of," he said. "Sooner or later, you're going to run out of money."

"I'll be alright."

"You won't be alright forever. Not to poke my nose where it doesn't belong, but you need to pull your head out of your ass, Son."

I looked at him and raised my brows. "Excuse me?"

"Your head," he said. "It's up your butt. When that happens, it's too dark for you to see what's going on around you. Pull it out so you can understand just what it is you're doing. From my vantage point, you look like a damned idiot. I have the luxury of knowing that's not the case. Pull your head out of your ass, Son."

I didn't always agree with my father, but his observations were typically spot-on. I didn't have to agree with him, but I needed to consider what he said.

I shifted my eyes to the television. "I'll have a look at it."

"If you get confused," he said. "There's another dead giveaway that you're head's in your sphincter."

"What's that?" I asked, my tone deadpan.

"It stinks," he said, equally flat in expression.

I chuckled. "Thanks for the hot tip."

"Anything I can do to expedite getting you back to normal."

I had no idea what normal was. It was different for everyone. I certainly wasn't my usual self, I knew that much for sure. Knowing my father could see the changes in me was disappointing. I didn't like disappointing my father. I hadn't done so since I was a child. Even then, I doubted he was truly disappointed.

Throughout my legal matters he supported me one hundred percent. Although my mother didn't agree with me not accepting the offer of probation, my father did. Admitting to guilt was something he never would have done. There was no doubt I was my father's son. I saw a lot of him in my decisions and actions throughout my legal battle.

We had always been close. During my prison sentence our relationship changed. We became best friends. Every week, without fail, I received a letter from him. They were written on Sundays, the day we normally met.

Often, he'd scribe two letters, as he was unable to get everything he had to say stuffed into one envelope.

Through the course of the letter writing, he told me he was proud of me.

I beamed with pride upon reading that letter.

Fluent in Spanish, he taught me slang. He further educated me on Spanish customs, culture, and what was perceived as disrespectful. All of this was done through his letters. It was truly a step back in time for me to write a letter asking a question, and to wait two weeks for him to receive it, and then respond.

His assistance allowed me to communicate with men who were either unwilling or incapable of communicating with me otherwise.

Early in my incarceration, I met a man from the state of Chiapas, Mexico who simply went by the name Chiapas. He spoke no English whatsoever. With my father's assistance, I learned to communicate with him. Soon, we became friends.

I learned that he was going to be taken to the border and released after serving his prison sentence. He had every intention of returning to his home state, but it was several thousand miles away from the border. The journey, he explained, would be on foot.

Upon finding out they were going to simply drop him off at the border, my father took it upon himself to deposit money into Chiapas' account.

Chiapas was elated to the point of being in tears when he received it.

When I advised my father that it was a federal offense for him to deposit money into another inmates account, he simply stated the federal prison system was comprised of a bunch of *fucktards*.

With winter now approaching, I wondered if it would be feasible that I ride my motorcycle four thousand miles to the Guatemalan border and see him. Mexico's warmth would be a nice change of pace.

Still staring blankly at the television, I broke the silence. "I think I'm pissed that winter's coming."

After a few moments, he peered over the top of his Kindle. "Instead of bitching that you can't ride your bike, you ought to thank God for the car you've got."

"I feel free when I'm on the bike. When I'm in the car, I feel like I'm confined."

He lowered his Kindle. "You've been out for what? Three years?"

I nodded. "Give or take."

"You're a free man whether you're on that motorcycle or in the comfort of your car."

"I don't feel free."

"Prison was a drop of rain on the windshield of life, Son. Don't let it become any more than that. Separate yourself from that part of your life and move on. If you dwell on it, they've beaten you."

"I'm trying," I said. "It isn't easy."

He spit out a laugh. "You've never been prone to taking the easy way out of anything. Stop whining and lift your chin a little."

"I'm not whining."

He went back to reading. "It's cold outside and I can't ride my scooter," he said in an exaggerated whine.

"It's not a scooter," I snapped back. "It's a chopper."

"Fuck you. It's a scooter."

"It's a goddamned chopper."

"It's a piece of purple shit."

"It's black with purple flames."

"It looks like a girl ought to be riding it. Surprised those degenerates you ride with allow it in the clubhouse." He lowered his Kindle. "They don't make you park it outside, do they?"

"Go to hell, Pop."

"As long as I've got to look at you wear that long face you're wearing, I'm already there," he said.

My father had an odd way of getting his point across. Hearing him say those words caused me to realize the hell I was putting him through.

He'd aged considerably during my incarceration, and even more so since my release. Although he claimed his time at home was much easier than the time I spent behind the walls, I doubted that was entirely true.

I had no intention of causing him any more pain, stress, or agony.

Living as a hermit was slowly killing me. I needed to get my life in order. Settling down with a woman and living a conventional life was the answer. I knew I could survive being in another relationship.

I doubted, however, that I could endure another breakup.

CHAPTER FOURTEEN

With a look of disgust etched on my face, I peered through the window and into the parking lot across the street. Although winter was nearly over, a blanket of snow covered the asphalt for as far as I could see. A late winter storm had dumped six inches of the foul substance on the city while I slept.

Growing angrier with each passing minute, I sipped my coffee and glared at the blinding snow. When the cup was empty, I picked up my phone and dialed Teddy's number.

"As soon as they scrape the streets, I'm out of here," I said.

"They're out of money."

"Who's out of money?"

"The city. Said on the news that they're out of salt, and that they've spent their allotment for road maintenance. We've got to wait for it to melt."

My car had two inches of ground clearance and was incapable of driving through as little as an inch of snow. Until the roads were clear, I was stuck.

"As soon as it melts, then."

"Where you headed?"

"Somewhere warm."

"About out of money, ain't ya?"

"I'm close," I said. "But I've got enough to drive to the coast. I'll sleep in the car."

"How long you going to be gone?"

I was at wits end. I needed a change in my life. Grasping at straws, I felt warm weather might snap me out of my current state of mind.

"As long as it takes," I responded.

"Want company?"

"No, Brother. I need to go this one alone."

"Keep me posted on what's going on?"

"Always."

"Alright, then."

Four days later, the snow had melted entirely. After counting what money remained, I realized that I was six hundred dollars away from being destitute. Nonetheless, I packed my bag, got on the elevator, and went down to the parking garage.

In the past three and a half years, I'd acquired several motorcycles. Although I only rode the chopper with regularity, I kept the others as trophies of my successes, riding them when an urge to do so developed. In the last year I listed them as collateral on a loan, using the money to pay bills and survive.

A loan which was due in thirty days.

Without sleeping, I drove to Atlanta. I intended to go south on highway seventy-five, then on to southern Florida. The trip, so far, cost me one hundred and fifty dollars in gas, and a few dollars for gas station burritos.

By my calculations, I could easily make it to the coast of Southwest Florida. I wondered if the warm weather would encourage me to get a job, and if I might stay until summer arrived.

In midtown Atlanta, and tired beyond compare, I pulled into a gas station to get a cup of coffee. It was Saturday night, and the parking lot was packed. I parked in a lot that separated the gas station from an adjoining bar and sauntered down the sidewalk.

Upon returning to my car, I noticed someone had placed a bright yellow boot on my left front tire.

The devices were used to prevent a car from being driven.

Furious, I glanced around the parking lot for any sign of who may have attached it. In my search, I noticed a sign that I'd not seen before.

NO PARKING. VEHICLES WILL BE TOWED AT OWNER'S EXPENSE

I tossed my cup of coffee down onto the ground.

"Mother fucker!"

"That your BMW?" a voice from behind me asked.

I spun around. A man dressed in a pair of navy pants, boots, and a matching jacket looked back at me. He was clutching a metal clipboard.

"It is," I said. "Are you the one that put that fucking thing on my wheel?"

"I sure was."

"Take it off."

"That'll cost you three hundred bucks."

"Fuck you," I seethed. "Take it off, or I'll whip your ass."

He pulled a radio from his belt and raised it to his mouth. "If you take another step, I'll have the cops here in five minutes. You'll go to jail, and your car will be impounded."

I had roughly four hundred and forty dollars to my name. If I gave him three hundred, I'd have enough money for gas to get home.

"Son-of-a-fucking-bitch," I muttered. I reached into my pocket. "Give a discount for cash?"

He shook his head, and then nodded toward my car. "Put the cash under the windshield wiper, and then go over and stand by that telephone pole."

I glared. "Seriously?"

"After that outburst? Yeah, I'm serious."

I did as he asked.

He removed the boot and gave a nod. "Have a nice night."

I got into the car and counted my money. After a quick calculation, I realized I *barely* had enough money to get home. I certainly didn't have enough to return to Kansas *and* to eat.

It was over.

For the first time in my life, I'd been defeated.

Admitting it was exactly what I needed. I opened my sunroof and peered out into the night's starry sky.

I know I don't talk to you as often as I should. Nonetheless, my way of thinking got me here. I need your help, and I'm not afraid to admit it.

I need one thing, and one thing only.

Guide me.

Please.

It's all I ask.

Then, I lowered my head and drove home.

CHAPTER FIFTEEN

With an eviction notice in one hand and my phone in the other, I listened to what my loan officer had to say.

"If you can pay the interest, we can push the principal out another six months."

"I can't pay the interest."

"Can you pay a portion of it?"

I had less than five dollars. I laughed to myself. "No, I can't."

"If you can't we're going to have to come pick everything up. We could call it a voluntary repossession though. That'll help you out, once you get back on your feet."

She'd been my banker since I was in my mid-twenties and was well aware of what I'd been through. There were limitations to what she could do for me, though. The thought of losing all my vehicles, less the chopper, tasted bitter. I didn't like it. I didn't like it at all.

I swallowed a lump of pride and cleared my throat. "If you could give me a little loan on my chopper. I could use that to--"

"We can't loan money on the chopper," she said. "It's already on this note."

I straightened my posture and widened my eyes. "What?"

"We put it on *this* note. We had to. It was the only way we could get to the principal you wanted to borrow."

My heart sank. I'd had the motorcycle for over a decade. When I was arrested, the motorcycle, my cars, my SUV, and everything else of value was confiscated under a civil action lawsuit.

Per federal law, when a crime is committed, a lawsuit can be placed against any merchandise the defendant owns, claiming that it was the product of ill-gotten gains. The burden then falls on the owner to prove the merchandise was purchased with legitimate funds. The process isn't as easy as one might think.

That particular lawsuit was entitled *The United States of America v. (1) Big Dog Chopper*.

The ATF filed it to simply prove a point. Although they later dropped the lawsuits against all my other merchandise, they maintained suit against the chopper.

I won the lawsuit, proving the motorcycle was purchased legally. Despite that victory, the ATF agent kept possession of it, and used it as a bargaining chip – hoping to coerce me to plead guilty. When I didn't, he simply *lost* the motorcycle.

The judge ordered that it be returned. A search of the ATF's warehouse determined it was somehow misplaced. A subsequent search of their records indicated it had mistakenly ended up in Kansas City on the ATF's auction block.

As difficult as it was to believe, I managed to find out about it on the day of the auction. Speaking to the manager of the auction house while I drove, Teddy and I sped to Kansas City with the judge's orders in hand.

Upon providing a copy of the judge's signed order, the motorcycle was returned to me.

I'd proudly ridden it over the years, all the while considering it a trophy, of sorts. Proof of my only victory over the agency that ruined my life.

"Come get it," I said. "Come get everything."

"Scott. I know what the chopper means to you. Maybe we can--"

"Nope. Come get everything. I got myself into this situation. The only way to prevent me from doing this again is to learn a valuable lesson. Come get 'em."

"Are you sure?"

"Positive."

"Scott. I'm so sorry. Maybe I could just loan you some of my money. You could pay me back--"

"Appreciate the offer, but I can't. I need this, really. Come get 'em."

"I'll get the paperwork processed. Again, I'm sorry."

"Don't be."

"If you don't mind me asking, what are you going to do?"

"I'm going to write a book," I said.

"What?"

"I'm going to write a book."

"Seriously?"

For the twenty years that I'd worked in the construction industry, I belonged to a society of mechanical engineers. For sixteen of those twenty years, I sat on the board of directors. During that time, I wrote a monthly article for their magazine.

My articles won several awards. I'd never tried to write a book, but I'd always joked about it. With my back to the wall, and my wallet empty, it was time for me to put up or shut up.

I'd never been one to shut up.

"Yes," I said. "I'm serious."

"What's it going to be about?"

When I was twenty-one, I left my girlfriend at the time to go to basic training in the Marine Corps. Upon returning to Wichita, I went to visit her.

Her father answered the door. His face was expressionless. "She left something for you," he said. "Wait here."

In a moment, he returned. After handing me an envelope, he started to push the door closed.

"Is she here?" I asked.

His face contorted. "You have no idea, do you?"

I could tell by the look on his face that something was wrong. "About what?"

"She committed suicide."

With those words, he shut the door. The envelope contained a poem. I carried it in my wallet for years. To recover from the loss, I placed the poem – and my wallet – in storage. From that day on, I never carried a wallet.

With the phone cradled against my cheek, I reached into my left pocket and rubbed the money clip I'd carried since retiring the poem.

"It's going to be about suicide," I said. "Hopefully it'll make a difference in someone's life who's considering it."

"That's amazing," she said.

"We'll find out in time," I responded.

A few days later, the bank picked up my BMW, and all of my motorcycles, the chopper included.

It was exactly what I needed to fuel me to crawl out of the rut I'd allowed myself to sink into. When the last truck left, a motorcycle strapped to its wooden bed, I placed my laptop on my desk, opened it, and I began to tell my story.

CHAPTER SIXTEEN

Over the next several months, I slept very little. Working twenty hours a day on the manuscript of what would later be my first novel, I drank coffee, ate ramen noodles, and typed with two fingers and two thumbs.

The story was fiction but contained many truthful elements from my life. Told from the points of view of five different people, four of which were high school students, the tale unraveled along a winding road of mystery, misery, and mischief.

The four students were all tied together by friendship. Each of them had their own set of problems, most of which were common among high school students. One of the students, a girl, chose to befriend an online blogger and confide her problems in him.

Seeking advice she felt couldn't obtain from her overly strict parents, she spoke to the blogger through email, text, and, eventually, by phone. The blogger, whose name was simply The Fat Kid, spent all his time in the coffee shop, pecking away on his laptop.

After losing his girlfriend to suicide, he spent every waking hour attempting to help anyone he could through his blog. Unbeknownst to those he helped, he was running from the realization that his girlfriend's suicide wasn't his fault.

I typed the last paragraph, read it, and grinned. It was the perfect ending. Somehow, I'd managed to write a seventy-thousand-word manuscript.

In celebration, I called Teddy.

"It's done."

"What's done?"

"The book. I just finished it."

"Good," he said. "Now, sell it. I'm tired of paying your rent."

"I need to get it edited and everything. Then, I'll see what I can do. Up for a cup of celebratory coffee?"

"Be there in a minute."

Thirty minutes later, we pulled into the coffee shop that I used to frequent regularly. At that time, I hadn't been there in well over a year. As we entered the parking lot, I laughed at the fact that nothing had changed.

The same regulars were still seated in their normal places. Through the glass, I could see the college professor I had dubbed the Nigerian Nightmare. He pecked away on his computer, undoubtedly working on a school project.

Seated along the south exterior wall, the six Bulgarian's glared at passing traffic. Over the years, we jokingly called them the Bulgarian Mafia. None of them worked, they always had money, and they wore matching Adidas track suits from yesteryear.

I opened the door to the truck and stepped into the parking lot. "Some things never change."

"Looks just like it did last time we were here," Teddy agreed.

After getting a cup of coffee from a barista with porcelain-like skin, we took a position alongside the Bulgarian Mafia.

Svetli, the leader of the group, looked me over. His hair was closely cropped, and he wore a neatly-trimmed goatee. Beneath the opened jacket of his track suit, he wore a stark white wife beater.

"Scaht. Vehr the fahk you've been? Yuri says you write book.

Vaht the fahk?"

I nodded. "I just finished it."

"Vaht the fahk. Vaht it be about?"

"Nothing, really," I responded. "About a guy who hangs out in the coffee shop."

"No shits?" He shrugged. "Bring me copy, no?"

"After I get it edited, I will."

"Who for edits?" he asked.

"I don't know. I need to find someone."

"Call the fahking Jew," he said. "He is for edits, no?"

My eyes narrowed. "The Jew?"

"The fahking Jew," he shouted. "The Jew with the little car. The fahking Jew."

It was difficult – if not impossible – to determine the state of mind of any of the Bulgarians. They always seemed angry. They often shouted, rarely smiled, and stern was the only facial expression they wore.

"Little car?" I asked. "What little car?"

"The fahking convertible," he bellowed.

He looked at Demo, who was his right-hand man and second in command of the group. "Vaht the fahk is convertible?"

"Solstice," Demo answered without looking up.

"Oh," I said. "Lawrence."

Svetli tossed his hands in the air and looked at me as if I were an idiot. "Lawrence. The fahking Jew."

"I didn't know Lawrence was an editor."

"He's fahking editor. He is for edits."

I raised my coffee cup. "I'll give him a call."

That night, I called Lawrence. I learned he was a freelance editor, and that he had time to edit the manuscript. After borrowing another three hundred dollars from Teddy, I hired him to edit the book.

Then, I waited on pins and needles for him to give his opinion of my ability to write.

CHAPTER SEVENTEEN

A week later, Lawrence provided the printed copy of the manuscript to me. Hand-written remarks littered it from beginning to end. I flipped through the pages of red penciled notes, scanning them lightly before turning to the next page.

"What'd you think?" I asked.

"I'm reluctant to tell you the truth," he said.

"Why?"

"Because, I've got fifty unfinished manuscripts littering the floor of my apartment."

"Really?"

"No differently than the plumber that has the leak, or the contractor that has the home in need of repair, I'm the editor that can't seem to write a complete manuscript."

"So, what'd you think?" I asked again.

"The story is fantastic. Absolutely fantastic. It sends a great message, is fast-paced, and kept my interest throughout. I don't know who you think your audience is, but it has quite a bit of cussing."

"The Fat Kid's got a mouth on him, doesn't he?"

He chuckled. "He sure does."

"So, you liked it?"

"I loved it. You're one hell of a storyteller. Your writing needs some work, though. You do have great style and prose, for what that's worth."

"Where do I go from here? After I get these corrections made?"

"I've got a friend in New York that's a literary agent. I could send it to her if you'd like."

My heart skipped a beat. It was exactly the break that I needed. "Would you do that?"

"Sure."

A week later, two rounds of edits were completed. The manuscript was then sent off to his friend. I waited with baited breath to hear what she had to say.

Two weeks later, she called.

"The book doesn't really fall into YA, and it's definitely not mid-grade fiction," she said. "Your protagonists are between sixteen and seventeen, but there's too much cussing. It might be able to be marketed as NA, but the NA audience isn't going to like the subject matter. It's too juvenile."

"What's NA?"

She chuckled. "New Adult. The protagonists are between the ages of eighteen and thirty."

"And YA must be young adult?"

"Yes."

"So, what are you saying?"

"For me? It's not marketable. You can self-publish it. It's a great story, it's just not marketable to a major publisher."

"What can I do differently next time?"

"Well, that's why I called. Have you ever written a romance novel?"

"I've never written an anything novel. The manuscript you have is my first stab at this."

"Impressive," she said. "I want you to write a romance novel for adults."

I chuckled. "I'm a tattooed biker who's been to prison. Romance? Really?"

"You have an uncanny ability to shove your ideas down the readers throat and make them like it. That talent can't be taught. Your style and prose scream romance. My guess is if you write an adult romance, it could be a bestseller."

"A bestseller?"

"I think that's a realistic possibility."

"I'll write one, then."

"Send it to me when you do."

"I will."

"Thank you, Scott. It was a pleasure talking to you."

"Likewise."

Disappointed about my manuscript not being marketable, but eager to begin my romance venture, I self-published *Broken People*.

As soon as the book was made available on Amazon, I called my father. For as long as I could remember, he had a book in his hands. He read two or three books a week, not favoring any one subgenre.

He simply loved the escape reading provided him. My guess was that it was comparable to what riding the motorcycle gave me.

He eagerly agreed to read it.

I let the men in the motorcycle club know of the book's release, but very few of them read books, and none of them read on Kindle, which was the only way the book was available at the time.

The next afternoon, I called to see how my father was coming along. Personally, I loved the book, but I realized my opinion was prejudiced. I wanted my father's view, because I knew he wouldn't sugar coat the truth.

"Can I talk to Pop?" I asked.

"He's busy, Honey," my mother replied.

"Put him on the phone, Mom."

"Honey, he's tied up. He said not to bother him."

"What's he doing?"

"He's finishing your book."

"What's he think of it?" I asked excitedly.

"I'll let him tell you when he's done."

"Tell me," I demanded.

"He told me not to, Honey."

I forced a sigh. "Whatever."

"Wait a minute, it looks like he's done."

I could hear her walking through the house. "It's Scott," she said. "He's calling about the book."

She fumbled to cover the mouthpiece. After a moment, she got back on the phone. "He'll call you back in a little bit."

"Put him on the phone, Mother."

"I can't," she whispered. "He's crying."

My father was the toughest man I'd ever met. I'd stood up to any man who ever opposed me, and I couldn't imagine standing up to him. To think that the book I'd written could cause him to cry satisfied me and bothered me both.

"Have him call when he can," I said.

Thirty minutes later, my father called. "I'm proud of you, Son," he said as soon as I answered.

"Thanks, Pop. Did you like it?"

"I loved it."

"Really?"

"It was a great book. One of the better stories I've ever read. Damned good piece of literature."

"Really?" I asked excitedly. "You're not just saying that?"

"I might be slightly biased, but it's a damned fine book, Son. Damned fine. I laughed till I damned near peed, you had me flipping pages to find out what happened to that girl, and there wasn't one place where I wanted to skim through what you'd written. All in all, it was a great piece of work. Brought a tear to my eye in the end. Maybe in the middle, too."

"Sorry about that," I said.

"Don't be. Any book that can bring that kind of emotion out in a man like me earns it. I'm excited for you, Son."

"Why's that?"

"Because I know you've found your calling."

"Do you think so?"

"I know so. Now get your nose to the grindstone and get to work. Damned books aren't going to write themselves."

"Thanks, Pop."

"Talk to you soon."

The book received immediate praise from family members, other authors, and readers. One reader, an award-winning author from India, praised the book, stating that it prevented him from committing suicide.

Elated at the comment, I sent Jessica a text message. At the time, I hadn't made any effort to communicate with her in over a year.

Hope you're doing well. I wrote a book. Just thought I'd let you know.

She responded immediately.

I asked that you leave me alone. I'm in a relationship. Please respect me by not contacting me again.

The cloud I was floating upon crashed back down to earth.

Some things, I decided, were simply not meant to be.

CHAPTER EIGHTEEN

Three months quickly passed after the release of *Broken People*. In that short period of time, two things of significance happened. The first was that I realized I wasn't going to pay the bills with my income from my first novel. Despite the favorable reviews, sales were dismal, at best.

In eight weeks, I'd made a little over five hundred dollars.

The second thing that happened was that I met someone. A female someone. She was pretty, satisfied with me being financially inept, and was extremely attracted to me. I decided to toss inhibition to the wind and give a relationship a try.

Four weeks later, I learned that she was unhappily married. Her husband worked nights, freeing her up to visit me in the evenings. While I worked during the day, she spent her time with him. Upon learning the truth, I escorted the double-dipper to my door, guided her through it, and locked it behind her.

It was all the confirmation I needed. Women, in their entirety, were evil.

I sat on the other side of that locked door for two months, writing my first romance novel. The book's Hero, a man named Erik Ead, was modeled after me. The heroine, Kelli Parks, was modeled after a woman who I considered to be perfect for him.

Jessica.

I wasn't sure of Jessica's preferences in the bedroom, but I did know enough about her to make some educated assumptions. The adult romance industry was all abuzz at the time over EL James' *Fifty Shades of Grey*. The book was about a relationship between a Dominant male and a submissive female. Its pages were filled with scenes that included the use of dungeons, paddles, whips, and leather restraints, amongst other things.

I happened to be a Dominant male but had always considered women to be my equal. Whipping, spanking, and depriving women of equality wasn't something I could ever do. I wasn't willing to write a book about it, either.

I wrote the book about a man who was Dominant, but treated his respective other with care and admiration, despite her naturally submissive tendencies. Out of the bedroom they were equal. Once inside the bedroom, he was in charge.

Having commitment issues and not trusting women, the book's Hero didn't believe in relationships. The heroine was beautiful and playful but didn't completely trust men. There was a significant age gap between them, with her being younger. Their no-commitment relationship worked well for them. As the book progressed, he became less of an asshole, and she blossomed into the woman he had hoped for.

I left the last chapter of the book up in the air, closing it with a happy-for-now ending. My hope was that if the book succeeded, I would write two or three more, continuing their relationship throughout the series.

As soon as the book was completed, I sent it to the literary agent.

She called the next day. "Holy mother of God," she said. "You took my breath away."

"Did you like it?"

"I loved it. The sex was off the charts. The relationship arc was perfect. The only problem is this: your Hero is a dick."

"I know. But by book three, he'll be better. His character arc is slow. You see, he's--"

"You've got to change it. Soften him up. If you do, I can guarantee you I'll get an offer from my connections at Random House."

Most people in my shoes would have eagerly made the changes. I, however, wasn't most people.

"I've got to keep it the way it is?" I said.

The phone went silent.

"Michelle?" I asked. "Are you there?"

"What do you mean you've got to keep it the way it is?" she asked.

"The book's written," I said. "The characters are who they are. I can't change them. It'd be like rewriting history. That's already happened."

"Uhhm, I've got a newsflash. It's fiction."

"I know. But, in my mind the characters are real."

"So, you're not going to change it?"

"I'm sorry, I can't."

"Self-publish it," she said. "You'll do well. Write me another. Make sure the Hero isn't a horse's ass."

"Okay. Thanks again."

I self-published *Baby Girl*. Immediately thereafter, I contacted reviewers on Goodreads, an online book review site and asked them to consider reading it. Several did, and the reviews were mixed. While one reviewer would give a five-star review, the next would either refuse to finish the book, or give it a one-star review.

The huge disparity in rankings created interest. That interest caused people to read it. Most of the readers reviewed it, and their reviews continued to be either in the *love* category, or in the *hate* category.

With *Baby Girl*, it seemed there was no in between.

I watched the book's ranking climb the charts. The second Saturday night following the book's Tuesday release, I fell asleep while watching my sales chart on Amazon's publishing platform. It was too early to tell for sure, but it appeared I may be able to pay a month's rent with income from the book.

The next morning, the phone's buzzing woke me. Confused, I picked it up and stared at the screen. My father was an early riser but having him call me at six am was out of the ordinary. His heart was failing, and he'd had no less than four surgeries to repair it. In the end, they gave him a defibrillator and wished him the best.

Assuming the worst, I answered the phone.

"Congratulations," he said.

"On what?"

"Writing a bestseller," he said.

"Huh?"

"Your smut," he said. "It's number one."

I leaped from the bed. "What?"

"It's the number one bestselling Erotic Romance novel. It's number one in a few other categories, too."

"No shit?'

"I shit you not."

"Holy crap," I exclaimed.

"I'd second that," he said with a laugh. "Looks like you found your niche."

"I don't even...I don't..." I was so excited I was at a loss for words. After fumbling mentally for a moment, I continued. "Thanks for calling."

"Yeah, big shot like you probably needs to call his manager or agent or something, huh?"

"Whatever," I said with a laugh. "Last night it looked like I might be able to pay a month's rent. Teddy bought me another case of Ramen noodles. I'm good for a month, but I won't get the income from this one for another two months. It's not what you think."

"I'm just shittin' ya," he said. "I'm sure proud of you, though."

"Thanks, Pop."

"I want to read this one, too."

"Don't!" I screeched.

"Why not?"

The book contained sexual elements I wasn't completely comfortable having my father read. The thought of him believing for one minute that Erik Ead was a resemblance of me made me extremely nervous.

"I'd just prefer you don't read this one. Can you not?"

"Is it important to you that I don't?"

"I'd prefer you didn't. It's just. It's. It's different. It's basically porn without pictures."

"There's no story to it?"

"There's a story, but it's mostly sex."

"I'll leave it alone, then."

"Thank you."

"Well, mister author, I've got shit to do. Can't sit here and chew the fat all day. I'll talk to you soon."

"Okay, Pop."

After hanging up, I searched for my book on Amazon. Just as my father said, it was ranked number one in several categories, including Erotic Romance. At that moment, at least, my book was outselling *Fifty Shades of Grey*.

I quickly went to my Amazon publishing page to check my income.

I'd made enough to pay a month's rent, and to give Teddy back a good portion of the rent he'd paid for me. I was far from out of the doghouse, but I was undoubtedly making strides in the right direction.

I hadn't left my house in two months. My only option for food was Ramen noodles. I ate them for breakfast and dinner, skipping lunch on most days. My books were being published in my building's lobby, using their internet service to submit them. I was living the life of a hermit, surviving on one-tenth of my previous income, no longer owned a car, and didn't have a motorcycle for the first time in my adult life. If I needed to go anywhere, I had to walk.

Yet.

I was filled with gratitude.

CHAPTER NINETEEN

Convinced I could live the rest of my life without a woman in it, I was living vicariously through the actions of my book Hero, Erik Ead. His relationship with Kelli was exactly what I would have with Jess if I wasn't such an idiot, or so I told myself.

I doubted that would be the case in real life, but it was okay to dream.

I began writing book number two of the *Baby Girl* series. The process for me was different than for most authors, or at least I suspected that was the case. I didn't use an outline for my books, preferring the *fly by the seat of your pants* method of writing. It gave my characters the freedom to live life. In doing so, it infused my stories with the same passion that life possessed.

As the book unfolded, I fell in love even further with the characters. The series was based in the city I lived in. Erik and Kelli went to the restaurants that Jess and I had frequented. They had the relationship I yearned to have, but fully realized I never would. In the bedroom, their hunger for one another was exactly what I suspected Jess and I would share.

I finished the book in three weeks, and then published it. Afterword, I talked to the literary agent, Michelle.

"I see you finally got a Facebook account," she said. "Do you have Twitter yet?"

I considered myself a private person. As a result, Facebook, Twitter and Instagram were platforms I chose not to use. After Michelle explained I must use social media to succeed in today's world, I reluctantly opened an account for each.

I also started a blog.

I was an anti-social butterfly, but I was making strides in the right direction. To log in to any of the accounts, I had to go through the trouble of walking to the elevator, riding it downstairs, and going into the lobby. The inconvenience of doing so kept my social time to a minimum. After I finished writing, I'd get online for an hour or so.

It was usually at two am.

"I've got Facebook, Twitter, and a blog," I said.

"Good. Use them."

"Okay."

"Congrats on the success of *Baby Girl*, by the way. Let's hope this one does just as well."

"I'll keep my fingers crossed."

"Write me a book about a cop," she said. "A dirty cop."

"I'll see what I can do."

We ended the call, with me agreeing to write her a dirty cop book as soon as I was able. It seemed once I was in the groove to write, doing so was second nature. Instead of losing my writing mojo, I quickly wrote a romantic comedy of sorts, entitled *The Alpha-Bet*. The protagonist, Christy Cross, was an alpha female, and a drunk. She had a tremendous sense of wit, and an insatiable appetite for sex.

In a drunken stupor, she bet her best friend that she could screw her way through the alphabet before summer's end.

I published it before the ink dried on *Baby Girl II*.

Baby Girl II went on to be another number one bestseller. *The Alpha-Bet* wasn't far behind. My check from Amazon at the end of the month was enough to pay my rent, pay Teddy a portion of what I owed him, buy another case of Ramen noodles, and purchase a five-hundred-dollar car. It was a far cry from the BMW I was accustomed to, but over the course of the last year, I'd learned to love the taste of humble pie.

When everything was paid, I had roughly a hundred dollars left to last me the remainder of the month.

Elated at my successes, I quickly began writing Baby Girl III.

I struggled mentally with how to end the *Baby Girl* series. It wasn't so much that I didn't know how to end it as much as it was not wanting it to end. I knew I would write another series. Developing two characters I enjoyed as much as Kelli and Erik, however, would be a difficult task.

While I fumbled with writing a scene, my phone dinged, indicating a text message had been received.

When I opened the text message window, I saw a phone number I didn't recognize. Upon reading the text message, my throat tightened.

My heart paused.

Then, I struggled to breathe.

CHAPTER TWENTY

The text was broken into two messages. I devoured the message as if I were starving.

In many respects, I was.

Scott, this is Jessica. I don't know if you remember me or not, but we used to hang out a lot. If you're up for it, I'd like to get a cup of coffee. I think about you a lot.

My heart palpitated.

I fumbled to type a response.

I'd love to get a cup of coffee. How have you been? I think about you quite

I paused, read the unfinished message, and backspaced until it was gone.

When are you thinking? I've been pretty busy lately, and getting away from here is difficult, at best

Once again, I deleted the message before finishing it. Then, I typed another.

Jess, I'd love to meet you for coffee. I'm guessing you're out of that relationship. Otherwise you'd

I highlighted the message and deleted it. Then, I typed a simple response.

Sure

I read it, grinned, and pressed *send*.

Her response was immediate.

What time works for you?

I looked at my watch. It was fifteen minutes past noon.

12:30?

Again, her response was instantaneous.

Okay

To get there in fifteen minutes, I needed to pick a spot at a halfway point between us. It didn't take much time for me to decide.

Donut Whole? I asked.

She sent me a smiley face in response.

I jumped in the shower, shaved my head, and got dressed. After hopping into my jalopy, I sped down the street and screeched into the parking lot with two minutes to spare.

Jess was standing outside of her Mazda Protégé.

It was late fall, but the weather was warm that day. She was wearing fun pants, heels, and a sleeveless top. Seeing her caused me to choke on my breath. Whatever weight she felt she needed to lose when we'd first met was long gone.

Her cheeks were gaunt, her skin was tan, and her hair was bigger than ever. I parked my car, took a long admiring look at her, and reached for the door handle. I had no idea what her intentions were, but I hoped we could reconcile a relationship of some sort.

I got out of the car and opened my arms.

She rushed to me, all but knocking me down in the process. When we hugged, I lifted her from the ground and turned in a circle. After lowering her to her feet, I took a step back and looked her over.

"You look great," I said.

"So do you." She gestured toward my Craigslist SUV. "I like your new car."

"First things first," I said. "Are you single?"

She nodded. "Yes."

"I'm sorry about that text I sent you," I said. "I was excited about the book and I wasn't thinking. It was selfish of me."

"It's okay," she said. "Things between us ended right after that, anyway."

"Not because of that text?"

"No. It just. I thought things might work out with him, but they didn't." She looked away, shook her head, and then met my gaze. "He wasn't you. You were all I ever thought about."

"I thought about you a couple of times," I said, stretching the rubber band of truth to the point of failure.

She looked remarkable. Finding it difficult not to stare, I gestured to the entrance. "Should we?"

She smiled and turned toward the building. I wanted her to take her usual position at my left side, but she didn't. Wearing a smile she couldn't see, I followed her inside and to the counter. After ordering, we took a seat at the very same table where we met for the first time.

"How have you been?" she asked.

I inhaled a long breath. "I've been better. You?"

"I've got a new job. I'm doing hair close to where you live, I think."

"Downtown?"

"In Old Town," she said. "In between First and Second."

"You're a block from me."

She smiled. "I thought I was." She sipped her coffee for a moment, and then looked beyond me. "I like the salon. It pays good. I'm pretty happy with everything. I've been working out and stuff, too. I feel really good."

"You look great."

"So, what about you?" She looked right at me. "Tell me what you've been up to."

"I've been through quite a bit since we saw each other last."

She looked me over and smiled. "Like what?"

I didn't want to tell her of my struggles with everything, but I felt

I needed to. "The bank repossessed my car and my motorcycles, including my chopper."

Her smile vanished. "I'm sorry."

I shrugged. "It's okay. I've been writing books, but it's not what you'd think. I'm making enough to pay my rent, but not enough to buy groceries. Right now, I've got a hundred bucks, and I got paid two days ago. It's got to last me a month."

She smiled. "How about you let me buy lunch?"

I shook my head. "I'll buy."

She laughed. "I know better than to argue with you."

We walked across the street to a sandwich shop. When we stepped inside, I noticed Teddy sitting in the center of the restaurant with a female friend of his. Upon seeing Jess, he jumped up and ran to her.

Teddy was dressed in his typical flannel shirt and was wearing his winter beard. Sprinkled with gray and nearly to his chest, the mass of hair growing from his face was a tangled mess.

"I was afraid I'd never see you again," he said.

"Same here," she responded.

"What are you two doing?"

She looked him over and smiled. "Eating lunch."

"Will I see you again?" he asked. "Are you sticking around?"

She looked at me.

I glared at Teddy. "Go get some business of your own, you nosey prick."

He flipped me the bird and went back to his table.

After sharing a great lunch of soup and sandwiches, we walked across the street. As soon as we reached our cars, she checked her watch, and then gasped.

"I've got to get to work."

I looked her up and down, and then gave a nod. "It was nice seeing you."

"I read that book after you sent me that text." She smiled a guilty smile. "Broken People. Sasha read it, too. It was really good."

"Thanks."

"Well, I better get going," she said.

I opened my arms. She took a step toward me, and I took one toward her. We held each other for some time before breaking the embrace. I'd hugged her hundreds of times, but that time it felt different.

Reluctantly, I released her.

She gave a finger wave and turned toward her car. It was the same vehicle she'd driven in high school, a Mazda Protégé with three hundred thousand miles on it. Jess may have been beautiful, but she was humble while being so.

I got into my SUV and stared at the brick wall of the building. I had mixed feelings about our meeting. My heart was filled with emotion but acting on it wasn't as easy as I'd hoped it might be.

Thirty minutes later, I was sitting in front of my computer. Uncertain of what I truly wanted, I began to type.

The paragraphs turned into chapters, and the chapters formed into a story. As it unfolded, my heart filled with even more emotion. That night I wrote nearly fourteen thousand words while listening to my playlist on loop.

When I stopped, I realized I wanted what Kelli and Erik had.

A fairy tale.

I Googled the definition of the word.

fairy tale ferē tāl/ noun - a fabricated story, especially one intended to deceive.

I laughed to myself, saved my day's work, and went to bed.

CHAPTER TWENTY-ONE

In the week that followed, I finished writing Baby Girl III. During that same period of time, Jess and I shared a few text messages. I found it rewarding to communicate with her, even if it was without seeing her.

I also found it confusing. My head and heart were once again at battle with one another.

I read the manuscript, struggling with the ending being too cliché. Eventually, I decided readers of romance wanted just what I'd provided. A fairy tale. Something that allowed them to escape from reality. A story that caused them, if even for only a fleeting moment, to believe in love.

My books were sprinkled with my personality, my experiences, and my desires, but they were simply a series of lies assembled in a manner that told a story. I read the manuscript again. I came to the realization that I was not only satisfying my readers with an escape from reality, I was further satisfying myself.

I had found a way to fulfill my own desires. Forcing myself to believe, for that same fleeting moment, that love truly existed. I had the luxury of knowing that love was nothing more than a word that was spoken in an effort to manipulate another being.

The human heart was easily influenced. My experiences with relationships stood as proof of the complications associated with believing the elements in the stories I told could be perceived as being truthful.

I'd taken the relationship challenge on half a dozen occasions, and each time it failed miserably. I attributed those failures to my keen sense of human nature, and my ability to smell the stench of manipulation and lies from a mile away.

While in mid-thought, I received a text message from Jess.

Driving to St. Louis to drop off kids at my mom's. Be back this weekend. :)

It didn't matter if she was in St. Louis or San Diego. Our relationship was now two-dimensional and consisted of nothing more than text messages. It was lesser than it was before. My heart had been teased with a glimpse of her. Now confused on what we had, and more confused on what I wanted, I found it difficult to focus on anything for longer than a few minutes.

I took three dollars from my month's funds, walked around the corner, and bought a cup of coffee. The coffee shop, Espresso to Go-Go, was new to the city. The owner, Warren, enjoyed his customers as much as he enjoyed hand-crafting them a cup of coffee. I found his Taoistic approach to living life fascinating. In the Baby Girl series, Kelli and Erik met at this very coffee shop on their first date.

"How's the writing?" he asked as I stepped to the counter.

"Good, thanks."

"Usual?"

I nodded and reached into my pocket.

He shook his head. "This one's on me."

"Thank you."

He smiled. "I appreciate you putting this place in the book."

"You're in the last book, too."

"That's awesome."

He handed me the cup of coffee. "Here you go."

"I've got a question for you," I said.

"Shoot."

"Do you believe in love?"

He pointed to his wife, who worked at his side, running the cash register. "Twenty years."

"Do you think we just settle, though? Most people?"

"I'm sure some do," he said. "Others wait long enough to find it."

I looked at her, and then at him. "How'd you know? How'd you know she was the one?"

They responded in unison. "The first kiss."

I smiled and raised my cup of coffee in mock toast. "That's cute."

Certain that they'd rehearsed that response over the years, and that they'd convinced themselves the kiss was truly the point in time where their love for each other was revealed, I didn't press the subject any further.

I took a seat and sipped my coffee.

"Where's uhhm. Where's the girl that was coming in here with you?" Warren asked.

I chuckled. "Found out she was married. Told her to kick rocks."

He pursed his lips and shook his head lightly. "I don't know what's wrong with people."

"I do," I said. "They want a moment's satisfaction, and nothing more. It's the internet's fault. It's driven us to have expectation of getting what we want *right now*. You're one click away from whatever it is you desire. Need a bag of almonds? *Click*. A bicycle? *Click*. Nobody goes Christmas shopping any more. They just *click, click, click*. Shit, there's dating apps where you swipe your thumb across the screen to get a date. My oldest son's friend was showing me. It's ridiculous. I think commitment is a thing of the past. Before you know it, there'll be the 'one-click dick'. Just click the button and Jeff Bezos will send you a man with ripped abs and a foot-long schlong."

He looked up from wiping down his espresso machine. "I'm sure that day's coming."

"I'll give it some thought." I chuckled. "I might write a book about it."

When I was half finished with my coffee I walked home. During that walk, I thought about Warren's response to my question about love. I'd written such ridiculousness into my books regarding kisses.

A kiss never lies.

It was one thing to write about it.

Believing it, however, was another thing.

CHAPTER TWENTY-TWO

Friday evening arrived, and I continued to struggle with the release of Baby Girl III. One thing I quickly found out about being self-employed was that there were no weekends. Every day was the same. They were all opportunities for me to develop another bestselling novel, but only if I was making an effort to do so.

My phone beeped.

I swept my thumb across the screen. A message from Jess appeared.

My last client cancelled. Busy?

I typed my response.

Not so much.

Want to hang out? she asked.

If her last client cancelled, it meant she was across the street, at her salon. In the past, I hadn't allowed women into my house unless I was in a relationship with them. Keeping women away from the place I lived eliminated any confusion as to what my intentions were.

The northern side of my loft was constructed of windows. From three feet off the floor to the top of the sixteen-foot high structure, the sixty-foot long wall was made of glass.

I peered through the window, and down at the busy street. I lived in Old Town, which was Wichita's party district. The streets were lined with restaurants, bars, nightclubs, and a movie theatre.

My building was in the center of it all.

The city was crawling with the early night crowd that was hoping to get a seat at their favorite restaurant or club before it became so packed they couldn't get in. I had no desire to manipulate my way through the crowd and meet her anywhere.

Nor did I have any desire to drive through the traffic. In a moment of weakness, I typed my response.

Come here

Where's here? she asked.

I gave her my address, further explaining how to get past the security system. I then gave directions on where the elevator was. Then, I sat at my desk and watched out my third-floor window for her to arrive.

I smiled as she walked from the parking lot to the front door. She possessed a certain elegance in her gait, especially when she wore heels. Watching her walk was akin to watching a miracle unfold.

In a few moments, she knocked on the door.

I opened the door. She was wearing a pair of jeans and a white top that had a chevron pattern printed on it. The top fit her as if it were made for her. The jeans were cuffed perfectly, the bottoms hovering two inches over a pair of leopard print heels.

She looked adorable.

I waved toward the living area. "This is it."

She peered past me, focusing on the wall of windows. "It's huge."

I moved to the side. "Come in."

Gingerly she stepped through the door. Using the same delicate steps, she slipped between me and the corridor's wall, making eye contact with me as she walked past.

The sweet smell of her perfume tickled my nostrils.

I reached for her shoulder, stopping her from going any further. Our eyes locked. Without warning, I pushed her against the wall and kissed her deeply. Her purse hit the floor with a *thud*. She wrapped her arms around me and returned the kiss, matching my passion completely.

For a period of time that I couldn't accurately describe, we were tangled in that passionate kiss. Our hands fumbled to touch places we had held sacred from one another. We continued to kiss until my mind was aflutter, and then I broke the embrace.

She looked at me with wide eyes and a face washed with hope. She wiped her mouth on the back of her hand, and then smiled.

"What was that about?" she asked, wearing an ear-to-ear grin.

"It was a test," I replied.

"Did I pass?"

She certainly did. The kiss was everything I wanted it to be, and so much more. It was the kiss novels were written about. The kiss that caused men to become weak and women to fall in love. The kiss that said what no words were able.

The kiss that answered the question my mind was afraid to ask, but my heart yearned to know.

As I gazed at her with admiring eyes, I realized I had a decision to make.

One that could expose me to far more risk than battling the ATF in court. One that had the ability to either drive me to a lifetime of celibacy, or a lifetime of reward.

I simply needed to commit to take that risk.

CHAPTER TWENTY-THREE

In the forty-eight hours that passed following the kiss, Jess and I spent every moment that she wasn't working with one another. While sitting at my desk rereading the manuscript, a smile formed on my face.

I sent Jess a text.

Get a sheet of paper and a pen.

In a few minutes, she responded.

I've got them both. Now what?

Wearing a smile, I typed the next message. *I need you to write something down and take a picture of it. Only write it if you truly believe it.*

Okay, she responded.

I typed the next message and pressed send.

Scott Hildreth owns me

In a matter of seconds, my phone beeped. Much to my satisfaction, the message contained a picture. Holding my breath, I opened it. In the most delicate of written script, the yellow page of paper had four words written on it.

SCOTT HILDRETH OWNS ME

I smiled and typed another message. This time, a question. I doubted she'd fully understand, as it was a line from my Baby Girl series of books.

Who owns you Baby Girl? I asked.

Her response came quickly and made me wonder if she had, in fact, read the book.

You do, she responded.

At that moment in time, Jess became my Baby Girl.

She simply didn't know it yet.

CHAPTER TWENTY-FOUR

The seating area of my home was fitted with two large couches and a love seat. With Jess' hand in mine, I guided her across the floor and gestured to the loveseat with a wave of my free hand.

"Have a seat. Relax."

She sat and flashed a crooked smile.

Nervous, I sat down beside her. Instantaneously, I stood. I wasn't accustomed to being nervous, and it surprised me that I felt the way I did. I decided it was further proof that I was doing what was best for both of us.

"Do you want me to get up?" she asked.

I rubbed my sweaty palms on the thighs of my jeans. "No."

"Are you okay?" she asked. "You look sick."

"I'm fine."

She crossed her legs, and then looked up. "What are you doing?"

"I've got some things I want to say, and I'm trying to think of how to say them."

"I do that a lot," she said. "Just blurt it out. It works for me. It might not come out right, but I'm sure we'll figure it out."

With my eyes fixed on the tips of her shoes, I nodded. Then, I met her gaze. "I want to be in a relationship with you. Starting right now."

"A relationship?" Her eyes shot wide. "A relationship? Like a *real* relationship?"

I gave a crisp nod. "Yes."

Her excitement diminished. Her nose and brow wrinkled at the same time. "Like what we had?"

"No. An actual relationship. We'd be lovers."

She leaped from her seat, and then quickly sat down as if she'd done something wrong. "Oh, my God. Really?"

"Yes."

"You're talking sex and everything, right?"

"Yes. But there are rules."

Her eyes gleamed. "Like Kelli and Erik?"

"You little fucker," I said with a laugh. "You read it?"

"I read it at my mom's house. When I took the kids. I didn't realize you'd released another book since Broken People until we met at the Donut Whole. After you said you'd written some more, I looked on Amazon and found it."

It surprised me that she'd read the book. I found the fact that she wasn't telling me how ridiculous it was to be comforting. Being in a vanilla relationship wasn't something I wanted to do, and I doubted I'd survive any length of time attempting to do so.

"Not *those* kind of rules," I said. "These are a little different."

"But you're Erik," she said. "Or he's you. You walk like him, you talk like him, you use the same expressions and phrases. He even asked Kelli the exact same questions you asked me on the night we met. He makes her walk on his left, too."

"You're right. He's modeled after me." I looked her over. I didn't want to influence her response, so I asked the question without preceding it with an explanation. "Was there anything in the book that scared you?"

She shook her head. "Nope."

"Are you sure?"

She grinned. "Positive."

My level of excitement shot through the roof. She was truly a one of a kind woman, and exactly what I hoped she'd be.

"The type of relationship that Kelli and Erik had is what I prefer. Trying to do anything differently would be a stretch for me. Naturally, I'm exactly like Erik. I've been that way since I was old enough to even desire a woman's company. Maybe since I was seventeen or so."

Her face was painted with surprise. "Oh. Wow."

"Does that bother you?"

"No," she said. "It excites me."

"Because you think it would be cool? Or fun?"

"No. Because I feel just like Kelli did in the book. I'm kind of like you, I guess. I've always been attracted to older guys, and I like it when they take charge. I like being told what to do, and then doing it. In the bedroom, you know." She smiled a hesitant smile. "Not in the kitchen."

"That's perfect," I said, my tone infused with excitement. "What you've described is exactly what I need to be completely comfortable in a relationship. If we agree to do this. I want you to know a few things about me."

She rubbed her hands together feverishly. "Okay."

"I'm a very caring man. I'll never let anything happen to you. I'll always protect you and the children. I'll put you first and myself last. Always. I'll never do anything to hurt you, mentally, physically, or emotionally. I'll never raise a hand to you. But, I can be an asshole. No. I *am* an asshole. In one respect, at least." I tilted my head to the side and raised my brows. "You can't ever tell me what to do."

"Okay."

"I mean ever. You can ask me. You can make suggestions. But, no matter what, don't ever tell me what to do when it comes to living life. You can tell me to pick up my clothes or that the grass needs cut, but not 'Scott, you need to live your life like X.' It's a fault I know I possess. I've got to make my own decisions, or at least think I am. It might seem weird, but it's a big deal to me."

Worry washed over her. "What happens if I slip up? Is it over?"

I chuckled. "No. If it happens, I'll simply remind you that you. Maybe when I do, you should try and remember that simply rephrasing what you want to say will work better with me. Saying 'Scott, have you ever *considered* living like X?' But, if you slip up, it's certainly not a deal breaker."

"Oh. That's easy." She grinned. "Is that it?"

"No, there's more."

"Okay." She relaxed against the back of the couch and crossed her legs again. "I'm ready."

She seemed excited and comfortable at the same time. It was nice to see her so at peace with herself.

"If we agree to do this, it'll be no different than if we were married. It's going to be you and me, and that's it. I'm committed to you, and I expect you to be committed to me. The only thing we won't have is a piece of paper saying we're married. In my mind, at least, we will be."

"I'm fine with all of that." She looked at me like she wanted to eat me. "You don't understand. You're all I've thought about for the last few years. It wasn't easy getting over you. I never really did, to be honest."

I didn't bother telling her I felt the same way.

"So, you're okay with everything?"

She nodded, and then flashed a smile. "Yes."

"There's one last thing."

"A contract? Like Kelli and Erik?" she asked excitedly. "A list of what's okay and what isn't? Lines that can't be crossed? Like the night they were at Stearman Field?"

I laughed. "No."

She scrunched her nose. "What is it, then?"

"For the first thirty days that we're together, we're going to spend every day together, if possible. We're going to try to make ourselves sick of one another. We're going to kiss, lay in bed naked, run through fields of sunflowers hand-in-hand, sleep together if we can, and wake up together. But, one thing we won't do is have sex."

Her eyes bulged. "What?"

I shook my head. "No sex for the first thirty days."

"Why?" Her eyes went thin. "What did I do?"

"You didn't do anything. That's my rule. Take it or leave it. It's not negotiable."

She looked me up and down, and then locked eyes with me. "You're serious, aren't you?"

I crossed my arms. "I sure am."

She laughed. "I knew there had to be a catch."

"Well. Are you in, or are you out?"

She smiled. "I'm in."

I extended my arm and clenched my fist, holding it over her lap.

She looked at it, and then at me. "What's that for?"

"Pound it," I said.

"Why?"

"It's our agreement," I explained.

Her brows knitted together. "A fist bump?"

I gave a crisp nod. "It's as good as a written contract where I come from."

She twisted her mouth to the side and made a fist. Then, she pounded her knuckles against mine. "There," she said. "You're all mine."

"You just made a deal with the devil," I said.

"What does that mean?"

"You'll find out," I said with a laugh. "In thirty days."

CHAPTER TWENTY-FIVE

Jess and I had been in a relationship for a week. We'd seen each on every occasion her schedule would allow. Even though only seven days had passed, I was convinced the fear I'd struggled with regarding relationships wasn't going to apply with Jess. I had an odd sense of comfort that she and I were going to make it to the bitter end.

If she could last the first thirty days, that is.

After making out on the couch for half an hour, she pushed herself away from me and stood.

"This is ridiculous," she said. "We're not in high school."

"Twenty-two days to go." I struggled not to smirk, but I didn't succeed. At least not fully. "It allows us to be in the relationship for all the right reasons. Our decision isn't influenced by sex. People have sex first, and then they're staying together because they like to fuck. I think we should be together because we like each other. The fucking comes afterward. Fucking first is going about it backward."

She gestured toward my crotch. "I wonder if that thing even works."

I arched an argumentative eyebrow. "Excuse me?"

"Your you-know-what. I bet it's messed up. Broken. Noodley, or whatever."

"There's not a goddamned thing wrong with me," I said matter-of-factly.

She looked me over. Then, she met my gaze. "Prove it."

"Believe me, in twenty-two days you'll be begging me to stop."

"I doubt that," she said snidely.

"You will. I can assure you."

"Maybe you met your match," she said.

"When?"

She gave me a look. "When you met me, silly."

"Doubt it," I said dryly.

She scrunched her nose and then looked away. "I don't like this thirty-day crap."

"Twenty-two."

"Maybe if we didn't see each other so much." She sat at the edge of the couch and forced a sigh. "I think it would be easier. A lot easier."

I crossed my arms over my chest. "That wasn't the deal we made."

"That deal we made is ridiculous. Spend all day together and not bone? Who does that? I'll tell you who. Sixteen-year-olds. Even the Amish kids up in Hutchison bone when their eighteen."

I raised my chin slightly. "We're doing it this way. It's instrumental to the relationship's survival. We'll learn a lot about each other, and we'll be in it for all the right reasons. You'll fall in love with me, not my dick."

"Erik Ead wouldn't do it like this," she snapped back. "He'd bend Kelli over the arm of the couch and give it to her like a boss."

"I'll give it to you like a boss. In twenty-two days."

She laid her face against her palms. After screaming into her hands for a moment, she looked up. "Don't you get blue balls?"

I let out a laugh. "That's a lie."

She squinted. "What is?"

"Blue balls," I said. "It's made up. Guys say that to get girls to give it up. It isn't true."

She cocked her head to the side. "Huh?"

I cupped my hands around my mouth and made a megaphone. "It isn't true!"

"It builds up pressure," she said. "It's painful. If you don't get a release, you've got to go to the hospital and have a nurse jack you off."

I barked out a laugh. "Holy crap. You seriously believe that shit?"

"It's true, isn't it?"

"It's a complete and utter lie," I explained. "There's no such thing as blue balls."

She looked as if she'd bitten into a lemon. "Are you sure?"

"Positive."

Her gaze dropped to the floor. "That sucks."

"Why, because you can't use reverse blue-ball psychology to get me to give it up?"

"No." She looked up. "Because I've been tricked a few times by the blue balls lie."

"Well, now you know."

She dragged her tongue along the edge of her upper lip. "Don't you think it'd feel good though?"

"I'm sure it'd feel great."

She looked at my crotch. "Get it out."

"I'm not getting it out."

She wagged her index finger toward my zipper. "Get it out."

"I'm not--"

"You said no sex for thirty days, right?"

I nodded. "That is correct."

"I want to suck your dick. Blowjobs aren't sex." She waved her hand toward my crotch. "Get it out."

I gave argument, but not much. The thought of her proceeding with her proposal sounded like one hell of a good idea.

"That's probably not a good idea," I said, lying through my teeth the entire while.

She smiled. "Why not? You scared? Scared you'll give in?"

I shook my head. "I'm too strong willed to give in."

"Get it out then." She nodded toward my stiffening dick. "Prove it."

"I don't think it's a good--"

She started clucking like a chicken, flapping her arms as she did so.

There was a huge difference between being strong-willed and being afraid. I wasn't afraid, that much I knew. I unbuckled my belt, unzipped my pants, and pulled it out.

"There," I said. "Satisfied?"

"Holy crap." She stared at it for a few seconds, and then looked up. "Twenty-two days, huh?"

I nodded "Yep."

Wearing an ornery grin, she curled the tip of her index finger into her palm. "Come here."

With her seated at the edge of the couch, I did as she asked. After gripping the shaft in her hand, she locked eyes with me. "Kelli Parks was a novice compared to me."

"So you say," I said. "That girl could swallow a baseball bat."

Fifteen minutes later, I was convinced Jess was right. She could have held weekend seminars on how to perform oral sex to a man's complete satisfaction. I'd always considered myself an authority on blowjobs. Truth be known, she may have taught me a thing or two about them that I didn't realize.

My strong-willed nature crumbled. I was mere seconds from climax. With the end nearing, I closed my eyes and prepared for the fireworks that were sure to follow. She must have sensed it, because she stopped mid-stroke and pulled her mouth free.

"What are you doing?" I opened my eyes. "I was about to come."

"I know." She wiped her mouth on her arm. "I'm done."

"Seriously?" I asked. "You're going to stop right there?"

"I'm tired of doing that. It's dumb." She looked at me and smiled. "I want to bone."

"Say again?"

"Fuck. Bone. Screw. Have sex." She pointed at my rigid cock. "Put that." She pointed between her legs. "In here."

"I will," I assured her. "In twenty-two days."

She shot from her seat. Her eyes did little to hide the anger that was building inside of her. She folded her arms over her chest and let out breath. "You're not going to do it?"

I shook my head. "Nope."

She cocked her hip. "Seriously?"

"Your little tricks won't work with me, Jess."

"You'll let me give you a blowjob, but I can't have any dick?" she seethed. "What kind of a crappy deal is that?"

I stuffed myself back into my pants and buckled my belt. "It was your idea, not mine."

She grabbed her coat from the arm of the couch. "I'm leaving," she huffed.

"Don't leave mad."

"I'm not mad," she replied. "I'm horny. You're not going to fix it. So, I'm going to take care of it myself."

She put on her coat, turned toward the door, and then glanced over her shoulder. "And, you can't watch."

CHAPTER TWENTY-SIX

I needed to publish Baby Girl III but couldn't seem to wrap my mind around the concept of releasing it. My focus was Jess, and I expected it would be for some time. Nonetheless, I sat in front of the computer and pecked at the keys.

The eastern sky began to turn orange. The four-story building across the street blocked horizon, but it didn't obstruct the sun's glow in the sky.

I enjoyed rising early, often as soon as four am. It allowed me to watch the sunrise and the sunset each day. To give away one of God's gifts by sleeping through it had always seemed ridiculous to me.

After the sun cleared the top of the adjoining building, I shifted my focus back to my work.

A knock at the door caused me to damned near piss my pants. I'd heard similar knocks in the past, and they'd always been the precursor to me being arrested.

I moved into the third-floor loft for many reasons, the primary reason being security. My experience with the federal government taught me a considerable amount about their practices, policies, and procedures.

During the trial, I learned that over the course of the ATF's investigation, one of their agents moved in across the street from me. At the time, I lived in one of Wichita's most affluent neighborhoods, in a five-bedroom, five-bathroom home. My location didn't prevent them from infiltrating the neighborhood.

The agent drove a car like mine, but it was black. He waved every morning when he left for work, and every afternoon when he returned. I didn't know it at the time, but when he was at home, he listen to my conversations with a parabolic microphone.

Those conversations allowed the ATF to obtain a search warrant that gave them permission to fit my home with a listening device. A GPS locator was then put on my car.

The thought of those types of things happening to me again sickened me.

So, after my release from prison, I moved into the loft. The building had a security system. To get inside the front door, a code was required. Then, to get to anyone's condo, the visitor would have to know exactly where their respective home was located.

The parking garage was also secured with electronic gates and a code. It was outfitted with security cameras. From my third-floor vantage point, no one could sneak up on me without me seeing them first.

The twelve-inch thick concrete walls and two-inch thick glass prevented anyone from listening in with a parabolic device.

In short, living there gave me a sense of security. One that I now believed to be false.

I slipped off my stool, tip-toed toward the door, and tried to mentally prepare for what was on the other side. With a racing heart and frayed nerves, I took one cautious step after the other.

Then, the knock came again.

BAM! BAM! BAM!

It was a few minutes past sunrise. Regardless of the time of day, there was only one type of person who knocked like that, and they'd been trained to.

A cop.

When I reached the door, I peered through the peep hole, fully expecting to either see a badge or nothing at all.

Much to my surprise, I saw neither.

What I did see, however, surprised me.

It was Jess, and she looked like a hobo.

I pulled the door open. "What the fuck's with the cop knock, little girl?"

"Thirty days is up, asshole," she said, stomping past me as she spoke. "Get undressed."

CHAPTER TWENTY-SEVEN

After making it through the thirty-day no-sex test, Jess had the courage of a Marine that had just completed basic training. She didn't realize that I'd been somewhat reserved since the day she met me, but she was about to find out.

I doubted I'd ever admit it, but I was in love with Jess long before we met the second time. I was simply too afraid to admit it. I now felt like we'd been in a relationship for years. A relationship without sex.

I turned to face her as she made her way across the living room floor. "I told you that you made a deal with the devil. Now you're going to find out what I meant."

As she walked toward my bedroom, she raised her hand in the air and waved it from side-to-side. "Blah, blah, blah."

"When do you have to be to work?" I asked.

She stopped at the foot of my bed and kicked off her flip-flops. "I took the day off."

She dropped her purse on the floor and took off the loose-fitting jacket she wore. Beneath it, she was wearing a wife beater and no bra. Before I made it to the bedroom door, her sweat pants were on the floor at her feet.

Now standing in her panties and a sheer ribbed tank top, she slid a hair tie from her wrist and pulled her golden locks into a ponytail.

"Good thing," I said. "Because when I'm done with you, you're going to need to get one of the fellas in maintenance to wheel you out of here in a wheel barrow."

She faced me. "What does that mean?"

"You won't walk out," I said.

She rolled her eyes. "Promises, promises."

I stepped into the bedroom. "Can you count?"

"Uhhm. Yeah. I might be blond, but I'm not dumb."

"Up until today, how many orgasms have you had during the course of sex?"

She scrunched her nose. "From the first time I had sex until the last time? All of them bundled up?"

"No, dork. In one sexual session. How many?"

Her gaze dropped to the bed. After a moment, she looked at me. "I dunno. Maybe like one and a half. One good one and then one of those stupid little things that make you kind of shudder."

I chuckled. "One and a possible, huh?"

She seemed confused. "Yeah. I'd say so. Why?"

"Well, little miss smart ass. Today, you're going to count 'em. Every damned one of 'em. That's your assignment."

"Shouldn't be tough," she said, wagging the fingers of her right hand in the air. "I've got five fingers right here."

I pulled off my shirt and tossed it at the foot of the bed. "You'll need your toes for this little adventure."

She shot me a look. "Whatever."

"You ready to start this little adventure?" I asked.

"There's one thing. My Mirena got messed up and I got an infection. They had to remove it."

I had no idea what she was talking about. The look on my face must have warned her. She continued without me asking for further explanation.

"It's an IUD."

My stare of confusion continued.

"Birth control," she said. "I'm not on birth control. We'll need to use a condom."

"I don't even know how to operate one of those things. Condoms are for guys who fuck prostitutes. If I'm having sex with you, it means I'm committing to have children with you. That's how it works. It's all by God's design."

She looked at me as if I were insane. "You want children? You've already got three. I've got two."

"I'm committed to you, and to this relationship. I told you once, in my mind, we're married. So, yes. I'm ready to have children with you."

She slumped her shoulders in defeat. "Okay."

I changed my tone of voice to what my mother called my *voice of authority*, and what my children called my *mean voice*. "With each orgasm you have, you'll shout out the number. Understand?"

She simply stared back at me with wide eyes.

"Do. You. Understand?" I said, barking out each word as if it were a command.

"Yes," she responded. "Yes, Sir."

"If you do not, I will slap my right hand across your ass to remind you."

She swallowed hard. "Okay."

I pulled off my sweats, tossed them aside, and reached for her ponytail. With her hair gripped firmly in my hand, I pressed my mouth hard against hers and kissed her like it would be our last. Her knees went weak during the kiss, and when they did, I bent her over the bed.

I didn't need to go thirty days without sex to know I wanted to spend my life with Jess. I'd done the exercise for her. I felt I'd loved Jess for quite some time, but simply wasn't willing to admit it. The instant I penetrated her, I was certain I loved her.

What we shared during that instant was unlike anything I'd ever experienced. My heart swelled with emotion. Dumbfounded by the feelings that rushed through me, I paused. I was right where I needed to spend the rest of my life, that much I was sure of.

After clearing my head of thoughts of my love for her, I forced myself to come to the realization that the day's sexual adventure was going to be about her, and not me.

So, using her own words, I began to give it to her like a *boss*.

Thirty seconds later, she shouted.

"One!"

I continued at the same pace. It wasn't slow and steady, nor was it rough. It was a predictable rhythm that allowed her to anticipate my strokes, yet firm enough that she was well aware of who was in charge of the situation.

To help her along, I pressed my hips firmly against her ass cheeks, turned her head to the side, and kissed her deeply. Halfway through that passionate kiss, she bellowed out the number *two* into my open mouth.

I picked her up and laid her onto the bed. "Open the blinds and look down at the parking lot," I said. "Tell me if you see any cops on horses."

She was struggling to catch her breath. "Cops on horses?"

"Cops on fucking horses, Jess. You know what a cop is, right?"

"Yes, Sir."

"And, a horse?"

"Yes, Sir."

"Look for em. Let me know if you see any."

She opened the blinds and peered out into the street. I climbed onto the bed, gripped her waist in my hands, and guided myself into her. Upon penetrating her fully, the breath shot from her lungs.

"Do *not* turn around," I said in a demanding tone.

I knew Jess well enough to know simply gazing through the glass and into the morning traffic while we had sex would be enough to drive her sexual senses wild. From the passerby's vantage point, they could see nothing.

Jess, on the other hand, could see everything. And, all the while, she'd wonder who was watching.

While she looked for something that didn't exist, I pounded myself into her with great passion.

"Three!" she howled.

Five minutes later, she shouted again. "Four!"

I continued until she got to number six. When she did, forty minutes had passed since we started. Taking her shaking legs into consideration, I rolled her onto her back and gave her a short rest.

Once again struggling to catch her breath, she looked at me with wide eyes. Her face was covered with concern.

"You're...not even...breathing hard," she panted.

I gestured toward the exercise equipment in the corner of my bedroom. "I spend plenty of time in that corner making sure I'm in good shape."

At the time, I weighed one hundred and eighty-eight pounds and had six percent bodyfat. I was the epitome of good health. Additionally, my will was so strong that I could have sex for as long as I wanted without reaching climax. It wasn't always fun to go forever without a release, but if need be, I certainly could.

On that day, I had a point to prove, and I intended to do just that.

I swept my hand over her cheek and kissed her lightly. "Are you okay?"

She nodded. "I'm okay."

"Are you sure?"

"I'm good," she said. "That was crazy. I've never had four orgasms in one day, let alone at once. That was insane."

I let out a laugh. "We're far from done."

Her eyes shot wide. "Huh?"

I pushed her left leg to the side and nestled my hips between her thighs. "Ankles to your ears, my dear."

In a matter of seconds, she barked out numbers five, six and seven. After changing positions, she coughed out eight and nine.

Number nine, for whatever reason, drained her level of energy to nothing. While she stared blankly at the ceiling, I walked to the kitchen, got a yogurt, and a bottle of water.

"Eat this, and drink this," I said.

She exhaled heavily. "My leg's got a huge cramp in it. That was insane," she said. "It sucked the energy right out of me. Like, drained me."

"The protein and calcium will make you feel better," I said. "The little bit of carbs it has will give you enough energy to continue."

She swallowed the spoonful of the coconut yogurt and then looked at me with eyes that were filled with fear. "Continue? I need a nap. Aren't we done?"

I laughed a sinister laugh. "Not even close."

She glared at me. "Really?"

"Your little mouth got you into trouble, Kelli," I said.

"Oh Lord," she said.

I nodded. "Oh Lord is right."

At one o'clock that afternoon, she shouted out *seventeen!* When she did, there was no doubt in my mind that I'd proved my point, and that she'd had enough.

As we laid side-by-side in the bed, her muscles quivered. "Don't touch me. Don't even talk to me," she said. "Just be quiet and let me enjoy this."

"Catch your breath," I said. "Then we'll go take a shower."

"Shhh. Don't talk."

We laid silently at each other's sides for some time with her simply staring up at the ceiling. Eventually, she tilted her head to the side. "I really need to pee," she said. "But I'm sure I won't be able to walk over there."

"I'll carry you."

She shifted her eyes to the ceiling. "You're insane."

"I warned you," I said.

"When?"

"I said you made a deal with the devil."

"I thought you were joking," she said.

"I don't joke."

"Ever?"

"Rarely," I responded.

She looked at me out of the sides of her eyes. "I'll remember that."

"After that shower, we'll get started again," I said.

She gave me a bug-eyed look.

I kissed her and then smiled. "That, my dear, was a joke."

CHAPTER TWENTY-EIGHT

I modified Baby Girl III to include a chapter of Kelli counting orgasms no differently than Jessica did. After reading the manuscript one last time, I published it, satisfied that it was exactly what I wanted it to be.

In the time that followed, we saw each other daily. I couldn't imagine life any other way. Her presence was exactly what I needed. For the first time in as long as I could remember, I felt like my life was complete.

Furthermore, for the first time in my life, I was certain I had found love. Having found it, I was further certain everything I had in the past was nothing more than me settling. Jessica's existence provided me with something I couldn't explain. It was as if her simply being at my side gave me the last piece of my life's puzzle, completing an unfinished picture that had been missing a chunk for my entire life.

Looking at my life with her in it, I could see my future with clarity. In the past, it had been jumbled and incomplete.

She was my missing puzzle piece.

She had shielded her children from me – and me from them – since we met the first time. During the days, they were at daycare. Her daytime schedule at work varied considerably and the time we spent together was primarily during the day, when her calendar allowed us to.

A few hours in the morning before she went to work was typical. She would also walk to my house from work when she had a break, which was oftentimes an hour or two during midday. Then, in the evening, just before the children were released from daycare, she would stop by for a few minutes.

We typically chose a weekend evening to spend together, with her opting to get a sitter for a few hours. Her children were an important part of her life, and she cherished them. Although I was anxious to meet them, I wanted to do so when she was comfortable, and not a day sooner.

A week or so after the thirty-day mark, she discussed having me meet the children. Eventually we chose the upcoming Saturday, deciding we'd all go to lunch together. The weather was supposed to be unseasonably warm and should be a great day for us all.

On the Friday that preceded the weekend in question, she called, frantic.

I learned during the course of that conversation that the sitter she had been using was the mother of her children's father. The father, her former abusive boyfriend, had been out of the picture in respect to the children and their care. His mother, unbeknownst to me, continued to have contact with them despite her son's lack of involvement in their lives.

On that night, however, her ex *was* in the picture. In fact, he was creating complications with her dropping the children off.

I'd seen tears seep from the corners of Jess' eyes on a few occasions. She had cried in my presence on the night we met, and on one other occasion, when we parted ways. I had not, however, *heard* her cry. I hadn't experienced the emotion of feeling the need to care for her, and not being able to do so.

Hearing her blubber on the phone that night crushed me.

He didn't touch her, nor did he threaten her. He simply argued with her about the children, when they could or couldn't be dropped off, and at what point in time they needed to be picked up. Furthermore, he was a drug user and a drunk, and he had a gun with him in his car. She feared for the children, for their safety, and for her own if she opposed him.

In the picture or out of the picture – at that point – no longer mattered to me. Her former lover was creating problems with her, the children, and in turn, me.

The temper I desperately tried to keep at bay exposed itself. When I got off the phone with Jess, I paced the floor of the loft. Anger leeched from my pores. The more time passed, the clearer it became. It was out of my control. At that moment, there was nothing I could do to fix what I felt was broken. The anger soon turned to rage.

Furious, I called Chico.

"Got a little issue, Brother," I said. "Something that needs taken care of."

"You alright?"

"No."

I could hear the fellas in the background. It wasn't out of the ordinary for them to meet at the clubhouse on Friday nights in the winter months to barbeque or simply hang out and drink beer.

"Who do I need to cut?" he asked with a laugh.

"Jess' ex," I said dryly.

"What the fuck happened?" he asked, his tone elevated with anger.

I'd previously explained the problems Jess had with her ex to the fellas, and what she'd endured throughout their relationship. I further explained that he was out of the picture, and that as long as he didn't reappear, I'd do my best to forget it ever happened. Although by Kansas law he had no legal right to see the children, he was their father.

"He reappeared."

"Good or bad?"

"With him, it's all bad. Just seeing him makes her shake. She curls up into a ball for a few days afterward. You know how women are after something like that."

"When can we talk?" he asked. "In private?"

"Clubhouse?" I asked. "Tomorrow?"

"Miñana it is, 'Mano. I'll bring the Big O."

Big O was our six-foot-eight gentle giant. He was muscle from head to toe, but not the typical meathead from the gym. He was quiet and had a keen sense of humor. When it was time to administer an ass whipping, he promptly transformed from a joke-telling gentleman to a monster.

"Probably a good idea," I said.

I saw Jess later that night for a few minutes. She wasn't her normal self, nor was I. Seeing her in such pain wasn't something I was willing to do ever again. I knew if I must, I would sacrifice myself to give her a moment's relief.

The next morning, upon waking, I called my father.

"Saw you got another one published," he said. "Congratulations."

"Thanks, Pop. I didn't call about books, though."

"Just finished my second cup of coffee, and I've got a belly full of bacon and eggs. I'm all ears," he said.

"Remember the guy I told you about that used to see the girl I was seeing a while back? The girl that had the gun put in her mouth on the first date?"

"How could I forget a fucktard like that? Yeah, I remember you telling me about her."

"Well, I'm seeing her again. For real this time."

"This isn't about her, is it?"

"Why do you say that?"

"You started the conversation asking me about him. What's going on?"

"He's raised his ugly head."

He cleared his throat. "Didn't touch the girl, did he?"

"Not yet, but it's only a matter of time."

He exhaled. "What's your plan?"

"Don't have one yet."

"Bullshit," he snapped back. "I raised you, Son. I know better. What's your plan?"

I forced an audible sigh. "I'm headed to meet Chico and The Big O at the clubhouse."

"Damn it, Son. I don't know that I can make it through another three years of you being in the joint."

"So, what do I do?" I barked. "Stand down? Seriously, Pop? Would you do that?"

The phone fell silent. "I doubt it."

I laughed. "You *doubt* it?"

"I'd probably start with feeding him his teeth," he said.

"Sounds about right," I replied.

"Cocksucker puts his hands on a woman, he needs to be taught a lesson," he said, his tone rising as he spoke. "God damn it, Son. Be careful."

"Will do."

"I love you, Son."

"I love you, Pop."

"Keep me apprised of the situation?"

"Sure will."

"Bring her by, will ya? You mom and I would like to meet her."

"Will do, Pop."

"Remember what I said," he said.

"Which part?"

"Man puts his hands on a woman, he needs to be taught a lesson."

"Been hearing that one since I was a kid," I said. "Hard to forget."

"Talk to you soon," he said.

"That's my plan," I responded.

In an hour, I was at the clubhouse. Chico, King, and the Big O were all drinking coffee. The flesh surrounding Chico's eyes was dark and swollen from exhaustion. The pile of clothes in the corner gave hint that he'd been sleeping in the clubhouse for a few days.

I explained the situation to them, including the problems that Jess had had in the past. I further explained that her ex carried a gun under the seat of his car. Big O hadn't met Jess yet, but it didn't matter to a man like him. He was a protector and took pride in stepping in when most men would step away.

"Chico and I will let you know what happens," Big O said.

I cocked an eyebrow. "Excuse me? I'm coming with."

His eyes went thin. "No, you're not."

"The fuck you say," I snapped back. "This is my responsibility."

He folded his arms over his chest and shot me a stern look. "Your responsibility's the girl. If you come with us, you might end up in the joint. Again. You've been there twice already. The next time could be life. You take care of the girl, and we'll take care of this."

"Goddamn it O," I pleaded.

He grinned a sly grin and flexed his eighteen-inch bicep. "I got this."

I looked at Chico.

"Tell her I want to fuck her neighbor," he said with a laugh. "And that I said hi."

I looked at King. He nodded toward The Big O. "He's got a point. Next time, they'll keep ya."

I shifted my eyes to O, hoping he'd reconsider. "I'd be more comfortable if you'd just let me come with. I'll stay out at the street. You guys can--"

He spit out a laugh. "Stay out at the street? That'd be the day." He slapped his open palm against my bicep, all but knocking me over in the process. "Like I said. I. Got. This."

Filled with emotion, I bit into my quivering bottom lip and gave a nod. "Appreciate ya, Brother."

He looked at Chico. "Ready?"

Chico gave a toothy grin. "Let's roll."

What happened was never discussed. Big O simply laughed when I asked, saying he didn't want me to be a conspirator. I do know, however, that starting on that day, Jess was never once contacted by her ex, nor were the children at risk from the dangers he'd exposed them to in the past.

CHAPTER TWENTY-NINE

Jessica's children both had birthdays in the last two months. The boy, four, and the girl, three, were adorable. They were, however, products of being raised in a broken home and not having a father figure in their lives.

Any request she had of them was met with a scowl, and immediately followed with a *no*. While we were seated at a restaurant's booth, waiting for our food order, they climbed over the backs of the seats and into the adjoining dining area.

"Get back here," Jessica said.

Landon turned around, looked her in the eye, and responded. "No."

"Landon!"

"No!"

Lily soon followed, climbing beneath the booth and crawling toward where Landon was.

Jess looked at me. Clearly embarrassed, tears welled in her eyes. "I don't know what to do."

"Is this partially because I'm here?" I asked.

"No," she said. "This is how they act. I told them to be on their best behavior. This is pretty much it."

I blew out a long breath. "It can be fixed, but it'll take time. Time and discipline."

"Not beating them?"

I laughed. "Absolutely not. Children, in many respects, need to feel like they're in charge. You give them choices, let them make the decision, and then let them see how their choices affect them. Additionally, there has to be a set of rules that need to be followed. Boundaries, if you will. If they follow, there's reward. If they do not, there are consequences."

"What kind of consequences?"

"Time out. Losing snacks. Taking something they feel they're entitled to. In time, they'll realize they have boundaries. Now?" I pointed at Landon, who was taking the silverware from someone's table. "Now, they have none."

"I'm embarrassed," she said.

"Don't be." I leaned over the table and kissed her. "We can fix this."

We cut our meal short, choosing to leave before the children had a chance to cause Jess much more grief. Disappointed, the children screamed at the top of their lungs as we left the restaurant. As we each carried one of them in our arms through the foyer, a familiar voice caused me to stop and turn around.

"Pop?" Alec asked. "Is that you?"

With Landon flailing in my arms, I faced my eldest son. "What are you doing here?"

"Going to a movie with the guys."

I gave a nod toward his three friends. "How's it going, fellas?"

They all responded in the affirmative. Alec looked at Landon, who continued to kick and flap his arms.

I shifted my eyes toward Jess. "Alec, this is Jess. Jess, this is my eldest son, Alec."

Jess waved. "Nice to meet you. Sorry, they're a little wild tonight."

"Nice to meet you," Alec said. He then glanced at Landon and grinned at me. "Good luck with that."

With a hint of sarcasm in my tone, I responded. "Thanks."

We took the children to a movie. They acted like angels. Afterward, I stopped at a convenience store to get a drink. When the children came inside, they ran through the aisles grabbing chips and snacks off the racks. They then demanded that they be purchased for them.

Jessica reached into her purse and pulled out her wallet.

I shook my head. "Tell them to put the stuff back."

"They'll scream all the way home."

"Then they'll scream all the way home. It starts here, and it starts now. Children who act like that do not get rewarded. It's ten o'clock at night. The last thing either of them need is a bag of Cheetos or a Mountain Dew."

Reluctantly, she put the merchandise back. The children, just as she predicted, screamed all the way home.

It was the last night, however, that any such thing ever happened.

CHAPTER THIRTY

A few weeks had passed since the incident at the restaurant. Landon and Lily realized that things were different. It seemed they attributed the changes to my presence in their lives. I realized discipline was the only way to get them to listen, but felt like the bad guy, nonetheless.

I gestured to the living area of the loft. "You can play here." I then waved toward my desk. "But you cannot play over there."

"Why?" Landon asked.

"Because I said so," I responded.

He glared at me. Moments later, he was climbing on my desk. I promptly picked him up, carried him to the corner, and sat him down.

"Sit there for ten minutes," I said, using my voice of authority. "If you get on the desk again, you won't get a cookie when we visit my parents later."

It was the day that Jess and the kids were going to meet my parents for the first time. They had no real reason to be, but both he and Lily were excited.

He thrust his face into his hands and pouted. In ten minutes, I lifted him to his feet. I then lowered myself to his level and placed my hands on his shoulders. "Go play. Remember, not on my desk, okay?"

"Okay."

"That seemed to work well," Jess said.

I grinned. "It's proven to be pretty effective."

"With who?" she asked.

"My first three children."

"I keep forgetting."

We drove the thirty miles to my parent's home without incident. When we walked through the door, the smell of freshly baked chocolate chip cookies hit me like a brick. It was Sunday, and my mother always made cookies on Sundays. She loved to bake and did so daily, preparing breads, pastries, and other snacks for my father.

My father's health had deteriorated significantly over the years. Suffering from congestive heart failure, he spent the majority of his time in his recliner reading. Oxygen tubes ran along the floor from a machine to his nose. The administration of it allowed him to get up and walk throughout the small house without much trouble.

Doing much more was no longer possible.

He pushed himself from his chair. Looking down at the children, he smiled. "You must be Landon and Lily," he said.

"How do you know my name?" Landon asked.

"I know a lot of things," my father said. "I'm pretty tricky."

"Do you know magic tricks?" Landon asked.

"A few," my father responded.

My father produced a quarter and then made it disappear. It was a slight of hand trick he'd performed a million times with me when I was a child. He then reached toward Landon's face, acting as if he'd plucked the quarter from behind his ear.

Upon seeing it, Landon's eyes shot wide. "Wow."

My father handed him the quarter, and then did the trick on Lily. As the children admired their quarters, my mother invited them into the kitchen to get a cookie.

My father looked at Jess. "It's nice to finally meet you."

"It's nice to meet you, too," Jess said.

We sat and talked until my mother returned.

"Where are the kids?" Jess asked nervously.

"Watching television and eating cookies in the dining room," my mother responded.

"Thanks for asking if it was okay for them to have a cookie," I said in a sarcastic tone.

She looked at Jess. "It's okay, isn't it?'

Jess smiled. "Sure."

My mother looked at me and stuck out her tongue.

After introducing Jess to my mother, I stood. "I'm getting a cookie."

Jess stood. "Me, too."

My father looked at Jess, and then at me. After alternating glances between us a few times, he fixed his gaze on Jess.

"You either make him look tall, or he makes you look short. I can't decide which."

"He's really tall," Jess said.

"He's not *that* tall," he responded.

"He is," she said.

"His brother's wife is four-ten."

"I'm a lot taller than that," Jess said.

"What," my father said. "Five-two?"

"Three. I'm five three."

"Bullshit," my father barked.

"No, really. I am."

"In a one-inch heel, maybe."

"No, really."

"Anita!" he bellowed. "Grab the tape measure."

"What?" she asked. "Did you say something?"

My mother's hearing was terrible at best, but she refused to wear her hearing aid.

"The. Tape. Measure." He gestured toward the kitchen. "Go. Get. It."

"The tape measure?"

He raised his brows in an exaggerated fashion. "Before I die of heart failure if you don't mind."

She gave him the same look she always gave on her way to the kitchen. She returned in a moment with the rule. "Here it is."

"Measure Jess. See. How. Tall. She. Is!" he bellowed.

"Okay!" she shouted.

"Take off your shoes," My father demanded, pointing toward Jess' feet. "And get your five-foot-two ass into the kitchen."

I'd warned Jess of my father and his quirky manner of being. He wasn't putting on a show for her, it was simply how he acted.

Jess played right along. She kicked off her shoes and took a few strides across the floor. "Five-three."

"I'll kiss your little tan ass if you are," he said.

"David!" my mother hollered.

My father looked at me and winked. "She always hears what I don't want her to."

I followed them into the kitchen. With Jessica's back against the very same doorframe that I measured my children as they grew up, Jess arched her back. My mother donned her glasses, stretched out the tape measure, and stared at the numbers.

"I'm feeling faint," my father shouted from the other room. "You better hurry."

"What did he say?" my mother asked.

"He's dying. He needs you to hurry."

"Tell him to be quiet."

"Mom says to--"

"I heard her," he shouted.

"Sixty-two," my mother said.

I peered around the doorframe and into the living room. "Five-two."

He snapped his fingers. "I knew it!"

Jess looked at the tape measure as my mother reeled it back into the receiver as if something might be wrong with it.

"Jess!" my father shouted.

She peeked around the corner. "Yes?"

"Bring me some cookies, will ya?"

"Sure," she said with a smile.

"You sure you can reach them?" he asked playfully. "If not, there's a stool the kids use. It's beside the desk."

While he chuckled at his own joke, Jess got him a handful of cookies. It was rewarding seeing the progress Jessica had made since the day we'd met. Her playful banter with my father wasn't something I would have witnessed eighteen months prior.

Further proof that she was right where she belonged.

As my father ate his cookies, he and Jess chatted about everything, and about nothing. My mother sat in her usual spot at the end of the loveseat with her dog at her side, watching the Kansas Jayhawks play basketball.

When we got up to leave four hours later, my father stood and opened his arms. Jess wasn't thrilled about having people touch her. It caused her anxiety. It was a ritual in our home to hug, and something Jess would just have to get used to.

With slight reluctance, she hugged my father. I did the same. Then, we both hugged my mother. After gathering the children, we turned toward the door.

"See you next Sunday, sweetheart," my father said.

Jess looked at me.

"You don't need that idiot's approval," my father said. "You can come without him."

I gave a nod.

Jess looked at my father and grinned. "We'll see you next week."

"I'll just sit my fat ass right here and wait for you," he said. "How's that?"

She smiled. "Okay."

We opened the front door for Landon and Lily, and then gestured toward the car. As they walked through the door, my father cleared his throat.

"Hey Jess," he said.

She turned around. "Yes?"

"You should probably call the city manager. Maybe see about filing a lawsuit against the city of Wichita."

Her eyes went thin. "For what?"

"Building the sidewalks too close to your ass," he said with a laugh.

She looked at me. "I don't get it," she whispered.

"You will," I said. "Here in a minute or two."

On the way home, she did.

"I like your dad," she said. "Your mom, too."

"I think it's safe to say they like you, too," I said.

There were three more people in my life that I needed to accept Jess.

My children.

That acceptance, however, wasn't going to come easily.

CHAPTER THIRTY-ONE

My lingering fear of Jessica's ex resurfacing had vanished. I felt relieved enough to begin writing again. For several days I sat at my computer and stared blankly at the screen. I needed to start a new book and wasn't certain of who my Hero and heroine might be.

Then, it came to me. I would write a book about a man who was protective. A man who was exposed to a woman that was living under the abusive thumb of her lover. The Hero would meet her and then walk away. She would then develop the courage to leave her ex, no differently than Jessica did.

Two years later, by happenstance, the Hero would meet her again. Her ex would resurface, and the Hero's friend would step in.

In two weeks the book was complete. The Hero was, at least in my opinion, a facsimile of me. The heroine, in many respects, was Jess.

The Hero was a loner, a boxer, and a biker. He had yet to be beaten in his professional career. I named the book *Undefeated*. It, too, had ended on a *happy for now* note, with the intention of writing at least two more books to complete the series.

Days after publishing the book, I knew I'd written something very special. It was difficult to argue. The book was being discussed by readers and reviewers all over the internet. Before the book had been out a week, it hit number one in erotic romance, and remained there for roughly a week.

My father called one afternoon mid-week, out of the blue. I answered the phone, knowing a congratulatory call was his intention.

"Damned good boxing scenes, Son," he said.

"Excuse me?"

"The boxing scenes. They were breathtaking. Hard to believe you wrote those. Did some research, did you?"

"Quite a bit," I responded. "Read a few books on how to train boxers and skimmed a few about managing them."

"Well, it shows. That book was one good son-of-a-bitch."

It then dawned on me that he'd read the book.

"Damn it, Pop. I asked you not to read those books."

"No, you asked me not to read that Baby Girl shit."

"It's not shit."

"Well, that's what you asked me not to read. You failed to tell me not to read this one. Amazon recommended it, so I bought it. Glad I did," he said. "You going to write a follow-up for this book?"

"I'll see how it goes."

"Write the next one about Ripton. I'm telling you, they'll eat it up. He's funny, he's protective, and he's built like a brick shithouse. The women will love him."

"They might not love him as much as you do."

"I think you might be surprised."

"I suppose time will tell," I responded.

"I'm telling ya, I loved that scene with him and that fucktard Josh. Speaking of that, your buddies didn't chop that fellas fingers off, did they?"

"I don't know what happened," I replied. "They won't tell me."

"Probably best," he said. "Man can't get in trouble for what he doesn't know."

"I suppose."

"I like that gal," he said. "A whole hell of a lot. That's saying something, you know."

"Who? Kace?" I asked, referencing the heroine in the book.

"No, you dip-shit. Jess."

"Oh," I said with a laugh. "Me, too."

"I've got shit to do around here," he said. "I can't fuck around and blab with you all day. I'll see you and your family on Sunday."

"See you then, Pop."

"Talk to you soon."

After I hung up, I realized what he'd said. *You and your family.* As permanent as my relationship with Jess felt, it didn't seem that we were a family yet. With her living in one place and me in the other, I felt like I was in high school, dating again.

I'd been single and living alone for damned near a decade, all told. Doing anything differently would be a difficult task for me, but it was something Jess and I needed to discuss, nonetheless.

I planned on doing just that.

Soon.

CHAPTER THIRTY-TWO

I developed issues with picking up my mail when I was going through my court proceedings. At the time, it seemed every time I got the mail, there was something bad in it. Another court date, civil action lawsuit, or a six-figure bill from my attorney.

As a result, I rarely picked up my mail.

The arrangement in the building regarding mail was fairly simple. On the first floor, beside the exit, there was a mail room. Each tenant was provided a locked box, and the number on the box corresponded with their respective house number.

The boxes were large in comparison to the Post Office's PO boxes. They were able to hold small packages and a considerable amount of mail, or a medium sized box. The large size allowed me to leave my mail unattended for months at a time, which worked well with my writing schedule and my mental mail disorder.

Typically, I'd open the box, pick up the four-inch high stack of envelopes, flip through them, and pick out the important objects. What remained would then be discarded.

I looked at it this way: if anyone wanted to say something to me they could do it in person.

My bills were paid online. Neither my family nor the fellas sent me letters. Therefore, I really didn't need anything the mail had to offer me.

I found the first three and a half years that I'd refrained from day-to-day mail recovery to be extremely rewarding. Then, I had a run-in with the mailman. A head-on collision was more like it.

Early in my writing career, I was being paid by Amazon in the form of a check. I didn't have a bank account at the time. The only way I could be paid was by receiving a paper check.

In hope of finding my first check, I went to the mailbox. Upon opening it, I found an official document that was dated roughly two months prior. It advised me that the box was too full to accept any additional mail, and that the contents of my box had been taken to the post office.

My mail delivery service had then been placed *on hold*.

As fate would have it, the mailman was delivering mail at the time. I read the note, and then looked at the mailman. "You took my mail to the post office?"

"Excuse me?" he asked over his shoulder.

"My mail." I raised the cute little card he left me. "You left this card in the box."

"Oh. Yeah. Three sixteen. The box was full. When I can't stuff another piece of mail inside the box, I'm required to return it to the post office. Then the box is then declared vacant."

"You're telling me you couldn't stuff another piece of mail in this box?" I asked, my tone rising right along with my level of anger. "Not another envelope, or anything?"

He turned back to his little bucket of mail and began sorting. "It was full."

"I'm not done talking to you," I said. "I'm expecting a paycheck. I need to get my mail."

"You'll have to call the postmaster," he said over his shoulder. "They'll pull your mail, and then you can go pick it up."

At the time, I didn't have a car. Going to the post office would have meant taking a four-mile hike. It wasn't something I was interested in doing any more times than I had to.

"Don't take my mail out of this box again," I said. "I know good and goddamned well you could have stuffed another envelope in there. Hell, you could put a Jack Russel terrier in there. Or, a fucking duck. It wasn't *full*."

He peered over his shoulder. His mouth was twisted into an ornery smirk. "It was full."

"Bullshit," I growled. "If you do it again, I'll bust you in the lip."

He stood from his crouched position and straightened his posture. "If you strike me, you'll be charged with a federal offense."

Dressed in a pair of jeans, a wife beater, and a pair of lace-up leather boots, I flexed my tattooed biceps and shot him a glare. "Do I look like I'm afraid of doing a federal prison sentence? It wouldn't be my first," I seethed. "Don't fuck with my mail again."

I stomped to my loft. After calling the postmaster, I scheduled the pickup of my mail. Teddy took me to get it. When we returned, I sifted through the mounds of envelopes and found the paycheck. Then, I discarded the rest.

After obtaining a bank account, I made it a point to pick up my mail every other month. I also made sure to pick it up at exactly ten am, when the mailman was delivering the mail. It allowed me to mean mug him while he filled the boxes.

It didn't make him feel very comfortable, but it gave me tremendous satisfaction.

A few months later, I opened the box to find another card. The rule abiding mailman was unloading mail from his fancy little mail bucket at the time. I looked at the card. The hand-written date was the very date I held it in my hand.

I looked in his little plastic bucket. A wad of mail bound by rubber bands looked back at me.

I shot him a glare. "Give me my fucking mail."

"The box was full again," he said flatly.

"Give me my goddamned mail."

His tone changed to one of authority. "You'll need to call the postmaster--"

I really didn't need the mail. There was nothing in it I wanted, I simply didn't want him to have the satisfaction of taking it.

"Give me the mail, or I'll put hands on you," I said through my teeth. "That, my friend, is a promise."

"You'll be charged with--"

"I don't give a shit. You've got a decision to make," I warned. "Either give me the mail, or I'll whip your mailman ass all the way to your truck."

He blinked a few times but didn't say a word.

"What'll it be?" I asked.

After a few seconds, he gave me the bound stack of mail. With my eyes fixed on him, and without looking at the mail, I dropped it into the trash can.

"That's what I think of your mail," I said.

I laughed to myself all the way back to my loft.

Two months later, I got a notice in the mail that my driver's license had been suspended due to not paying a traffic ticket. A notice was received to return to court and resolve the issue, but I didn't get it. Apparently, it was in what I'd thrown in the trash during my fit of mailman-fueled rage.

I'd received the ticket while Teddy and I were in a movie together. I took exception to the infraction. Technically, I wasn't parked in a parking stall. I was parked along a path – a sidewalk, if you will – that would have been used by a wheelchair bound patron for egress from the building.

Parking on a sidewalk was a fifty dollar fine. Parking in a handicap stall was a one hundred and fifty dollar fine. In court, I demanded the ticket be changed to the former; parking on the sidewalk.

The court refused to change it.

So, I refused to pay it.

Now, a year later, I got another reminder that I didn't have a driver's license. It went on to say if the issue wasn't resolved within one hundred and eighty days that they would issue a warrant for my arrest.

I stomped to my loft and threw open the door. Teddy was standing at my kitchen island with a bowl of cereal in his hand.

"What's going on?" he asked.

"Fucking cock suckers," I fumed, tossing the notice on the counter.

He swallowed what he was chewing. "Who?"

"Cops. Court. All of them."

It seemed he lacked interest. He took another bite. Slowly, he chewed it. After swallowing, he drank the milk from the bowl before acknowledging that I'd so much as spoken.

"What about 'em?" he asked, deadpan.

I waved my hand toward the letter. "They suspended my license."

He put the bowl in the sink, and then turned around. "Again?"

"No, not again. Same deal. Just sent me a reminder. Said I've got six months to get it resolved or they're going to arrest me."

"Better pay it," he said.

"I'll never pay that ticket. I'll burn in hell first. I wasn't parked in a handicapped stall. I was on the same fucking sidewalk you were."

He picked the cereal from his teeth with his fingernails. "I paid mine."

"You're a pacifist," I said. "I'm not."

He picked up the gallon of milk and took a drink from the carton. When he lowered it, he grinned. "Pacifist with a driver's license."

"How many times have I told you not to drink from the carton?"

He looked at the milk, and then at me. He shrugged. "I don't know. Hundred, maybe. I forget where I am."

Teddy was like Kramer on *Seinfeld*. He, Chico, and Jess all had a key to my loft. He used his as if the residence was his own, coming in at any time of the day or night without so much as a knock. I'd often come out of my bathroom to find him standing in the kitchen eating something. I'd even got out of bed in the morning only to find him in my bathroom taking a shit.

"Dump it out, drink it, or put a big 'X' on it," I said. "I don't want to be drinking after your nasty bearded ass."

He lifted the carton and took another swig.

Personally, I detested milk. The only reason I had it was for cereal. Drinking it was impossible. Teddy, on the other hand, carried a carton of it in his truck and would drink it at room temperature.

The front door opened, and Jess walked in. "Hey, Teddy."

He grinned and set down the milk. "Jess!"

He wiped the milk from his beard. Then, he walked around the edge of the island and hugged her. "Scott's going back to jail."

She alternated glances between the two of us. "He better not be."

"He is," Teddy said. "In six months."

She shot me a glare. "What'd you do?"

"Nothing."

"Didn't pay his ticket," Teddy said.

"What ticket?" she asked.

Teddy picked up the carton of milk and took a drink. "Parking ticket."

"They won't take you to jail for not paying a parking ticket," Jess said.

"When he got mad and stomped out of court, there were a couple of others he was supposed to pay. He didn't pay any of 'em," Teddy said. "He ripped them up and made it rain. Now he says it's a *matter of principle.*"

"Fuck you, Teddy."

Jess looked at me. "What's going on?"

I shrugged dismissively. "Didn't pay a ticket. Got my license suspended. Got six months to pay it. If not, they issue a warrant."

She cocked her hip. "You don't have a license?"

"I've got one in my money clip. But, technically, no."

She lowered her chin and gave me the angry wife side-eyed glare. "Since when?"

I shrugged one shoulder. "I don't know."

"Year," Teddy said. "Maybe more."

"You haven't had a license for a year?" she shrieked.

"Probably not."

"You're not driving your car anymore," she said. "Until it's resolved."

Upon hearing her command, Teddy's eyes went wide.

I glared at her. "Excuse me?"

Teddy eyes shot to Jess. He took another quick swig of milk.

Jess cleared her throat and then raised her index finger. "If you want to continue to see me, I suggest you consider refraining from driving your car. How's that?"

"Seriously?" I asked.

"It's ridiculous," she said, her tone laced with frustration. "I'm not walking home because you get arrested and your car gets impounded. What if the kids are with us?"

"Fine," I said. "You can be my chauffeur."

"I'll do it for six months, and that's it. Then, you're on your own."

With the milk in hand, Teddy looked at her and whistled through his teeth.

I shot him a look. "What was that for?"

"God gave her a set of nuts that were so big he had to put 'em on her chest."

Teddy was right. Jess had a set of balls. I laughed to myself at the courage she'd developed but didn't show it outwardly. Seeing her growth, however, was rewarding.

Aggravating, and rewarding.

At the same time.

CHAPTER THIRTY-THREE

At Jessica's apartment, there was no courtyard for the children to play in. At my loft, there was nothing but bars and restaurants surrounding the building. The *yard* that the children were able to play in was a decorative concrete area in front of the movie theatre.

Being deprived of one of life's luxuries that most children take for granted, Landon looked forward to visiting my parents on Sundays. Regardless of the weather, he spent the majority of his time in the large backyard, looking for any living creature. Often, he'd bring bugs in the house and ask my father what they were.

Predicting the late winter weather in southern Kansas was impossible. One day it might be seventy-five degrees. The next it may snow. We'd been fortunate for a few days, having temperatures in the seventies.

The car came to a stop. Landon unbuckled the seatbelt, hopped from his car seat, and struggled to get the door opened.

"Excited, Bud?" I asked.

"I'm going to find a butterfly," he said. "A big one."

"A bit early in the season for that, but it's okay to look," I said.

Jess got out and opened his door. Landon bolted down the sidewalk and up the front porch steps. While waiting at the front door, my mother opened the door.

"Good afternoon, Honey."

Landon looked at her and grinned. Then, he rushed past her.

I shook my head. "He's excited to go bug hunting."

She cupped her hand to her ear. "What?"

"Nothing, Mother!" I shouted.

When we walked in the house, my father was explaining something to Landon. Listening eagerly while holding something in his hands, Landon nodded a few times. Then, he took off running for the back door.

"What was that about?" I asked.

"I gave him a bug catching kit."

"A what?"

"A net, a magnifying glass, and a little bug cage to keep them in."

"Now he's going to want to keep them," I complained. "I'll have a houseful of bugs."

"Better than a houseful of god damned snakes," he said.

As a child, I was fascinated with snakes. I'd trek through the neighborhood, rural areas, and fields, looking for them in their usual hiding places. Under scraps of wood, rocks, and in thick brush. It wasn't uncommon for me to return after an afternoon of searching with two or three specimens. Despite my father's demands that they be left outside, I'd often kept them in my room, as pets.

"I hate snakes," Jess said. "They're gross."

My father laughed. "This goofball used to have dozens of them in his bedroom."

She shot me a look. "Why?"

"I liked them. Snakes and lizards. In California, I'd go lizard hunting. They were everywhere."

"That's gross."

I shrugged. "I think it's a boy thing."

The back door opened and then closed. Landon rushed into the living room, clutching the bug jail in his hands. He thrust it in my father's face.

"What's this?"

My father took the cage, looked it over, and handed it back to Landon. "It's a cricket."

"What's a cricket?" Landon asked.

"It's a member of the Gryllidae family of insects. They have cylindrical bodies, round heads and long antennas."

Landon eyes thinned. "What's cylin...cylindra..."

"Cylindrical," my father said, slowly. "It means the body is round and shaped like this." He held his hands parallel with one another. "Not *this*." He formed a 'V' with his hands.

Landon gave a nod and turned toward the back door.

"Landon," my father said, raising his index finger.

Landon hesitated and then turned around.

"Find me a Caelifera."

"What do they look like?" Landon asked.

"A grasshopper."

Landon took off in a dead run toward the door. "Okay."

My father had spent a lifetime reading. Consequently, it seemed he knew everything. His IQ was genius level as a child, and he'd done nothing but feed himself with information for his entire life.

It didn't matter what the question was, it seemed he could answer it. Before the internet was available, he was my Google. I'd often call him to settle arguments with the fellas, knowing he'd have the answer for whatever question I'd toss at him.

Lily and my mother went into the kitchen to eat cookies together. Jess and I stayed in the living room with my father.

"You know where the silverware is, don't you?" my father asked.

"What silverware?"

"The fucking silverware," he snapped back. "*The* silverware."

My family had passed hand-made silverware down through the generations from the oldest son to the oldest son. For three hundred and fifty years, the passing of the silverware hadn't missed a generation.

Somehow, each man who was born the *eldest son* raised a son of his own. As my father was the eldest son, and I was his eldest son, the tradition would continue with my inheritance of the silverware upon my father's passing.

"I know where it is, why?"

"I'm going to die one of these days. You need to know where it is," he said. "I was just checking."

I knew one day that my father would die but couldn't imagine living life without him. He was in his mid-seventies and wasn't in the best of health, but he was the toughest man I knew. The thought of his life ending made no sense to me. In my eyes, he was simply to mean to die.

"You're not planning on croaking, are you?"

"Not yet," he said. "But I'll keep you posted."

I rolled my eyes.

"So, I've got a question," he said, his tone serious.

"Okay."

He raised his hand to his chin. After studying Jess for a moment, he studied me. "Are you Erik and she's Kelli?"

"God damn it, Pop," I snarled. "I told you not to read that."

"I got tired of waiting for you to write another book," he said. "I see you put Teddy's dumb ass in there."

While Jess fidgeted nervously, I blew out a long breath. "I can't believe you read it."

"It was interesting," he said. "Fascinating, really. I laughed a few times, teared up a few times, and was enlightened on a few things."

"I'm glad I could entertain you," I said in a sarcastic tone.

"You didn't answer my question," he said.

To satisfy his ornery prying, I gave a quick response.

"Yes."

With his hand still raised to his chin, he nodded a few times. He then picked up his Kindle and began to read. A few moments later, he lowered it.

"Be sure and take care of her," he said. "Just like in the book."

"I will."

"I mean it," he said, his tone harsh.

I made eye contact and gave a crisp nod. "Yes, Sir."

He looked at Jess and grinned. Then, he went back to reading.

"I can't believe he knows," Jess whispered.

"He's not stupid," I said under my breath.

He lowered his Kindle. "No, he's certainly not."

My mother walked into the living room. "What are you talking about?"

"Rice," my father said.

"What?"

"Rice!"

"What about it?" she asked.

"The rising prices," he said. "It's skyrocketing in China."

"Oh," she said. "It's pretty much the same every time I go to Dillon's."

"Give it time," he said.

My mother and father's relationship was an interesting one. Filled with humor, teasing, and my father simply being cantankerous for entertainment's sake, they'd managed to stay married for over fifty-five years.

He attributed their marriage's success to their weekly Scrabble game. On Fridays – every Friday – they played a game of Scrabble. On Sundays, I always asked who won. When my father was the victor, he proudly claimed it, divulging the score of the game. When my mother won, he'd often say he couldn't remember who the winner was.

Funny, coming from a man with a photographic memory.

"Who won on Friday?" I asked.

"We didn't play," my father said.

Jess turned toward my mother. "Who won the Scrabble game on

Friday!"

"Oh," my mother said. "I did. Seven oh two to six eighty-eight."

"Every dog has his day," my father said. "It must have been hers."

My mother looked at Jess. "What did he say?"

"He said you cheated."

"He's full of beans," my mother said. "He always has been. I beat him fair and square."

"Who won last week?" Jess asked.

"I did," my father exclaimed. "Six ninety-four to six sixty."

Jess glanced in his direction. "You can remember that, but you can't remember two days ago?"

"Selective memory loss," he said. "You stick around him long enough, and you'll develop it. It comes in handy."

Landon returned throughout the afternoon with several specimens, each of which my father promptly identified. When it was time for us to leave, we all shared a hug. Our weekly visits had Jess looking forward to the ritual, not dreading it.

"See you next week, sweetheart," my father said.

Jess smiled. "Okay."

He pointed at Landon, who was clutching his bug cage like it was filled with jewels. "See you next week, Bud."

"Okay," Landon said with a smile.

"Bye, Lily."

Lily grinned her usual grin, and then waved. "Bye."

The ride home was uneventful. Lily fell asleep while Landon admired his day's findings. When Jess pulled up to the intersection across from my building, she came to a stop. After checking cross traffic, she looked at me and smiled.

"Here you go," she said.

"This is dumb," I said, referring to her having to drive me everywhere.

"Pay your ticket," she said with a laugh.

I kissed her and then pushed my door open. "See you tomorrow."

"I love you."

"I love you too, Baby."

I walked around the car and stepped onto the sidewalk. Jess turned the corner, and then stopped.

"Scott!" Jess shouted.

I looked up. Her window was down, and she was leaning out of it. "Landon said he wants to talk to you."

She lowered his window.

I leaned against the top of the car and peered inside. "What's up, Bud?"

With his bug cage held firmly in his hands, he looked up at me. The late afternoon sun hit him in the face. He closed one eye. With the other wide open, he looked right at me.

"Will you be my dad?" he asked.

My throat constricted. My eyes welled with tears. I knew if I spoke that I'd make a fool of myself.

I clenched my fist, extended it through the window, and held it over him.

He grinned and then pounded his knuckles into mine.

I swallowed heavily and stepped away from the car.

Jess looked at me. She must have seen the emotion that was running through my veins. "Is everything okay?" she asked.

"He asked me...he uhhm...he wants...he wanted to know if I'd be his dad," I whispered.

Her lips quivered. She wiped her eyes with the back of her hand. Her lips parted slightly but said absolutely nothing. She, just like me, was at a loss for words.

I clenched my fist and extended my arm.

She pounded her knuckles against mine.

Filled with emotion, I turned away. When I got upstairs, I went through the ritual of weighing myself. I'd gained a pound since we left. I stared at the scale, recalling exactly what I ate, and wondering where the additional weight came from.

Then, it came to me.

I was carrying a child's future – and his trust – on my shoulders.

CHAPTER THIRTY-FOUR

Jess crossed her arms and held them tight against her chest. "No!"

"I don't have a choice," I explained. "We have to."

She shook her head. "No!"

"Well, I'm sure not going to get someone else to do it. You've got to."

"It's the dumbest thing I've ever heard."

"It's different," I said. "But I wouldn't call it dumb."

She gave me a side-eyed look. "It's pretty dumb."

"It's already written. I can't change it now. You know how I am. My books have to be accurate. I can't go having something in there that people pick apart in their reviews. It's got to be believable."

"Take that scene out," she demanded.

"It already happened. Hell, it's part of his personality. I can't take it out."

"You can," she huffed. "But, you won't."

"We just need to give it a quick try and see if it works. If it doesn't, I guess I'll figure Ripp's an idiot, and I'll have to delete it. If it works, I'll have to say he's a genius."

"He's *not* a genius," she said. "A genius wouldn't leave his shoes on during sex, and he sure wouldn't step on someone's head, either. That's dumb."

I pointed at the couch. "We're trying it."

She lowered her arms to her sides. "Seriously?"

"We have to. If it doesn't work, we'll stop."

She glared at me for a second. "If I say stop, you better stop."

"You know I will."

"You better."

My recent book, *Unstoppable*, had a character that was modeled after The Big O. He had a rather odd sexual appetite and chose to leave his shoes on during sex. He claimed it gave him better traction. He further claimed that while penetrating his lovers from behind, that he did so with his right leg stretched over their back.

His right foot was then placed on their head.

The shoes he wore were Converse Chucks. When he wore them during sex, he called it *Chuck fuckin'*. When he did the foot on the head maneuver, he simply called it *head steppin'*.

According to him, the sex was second to none.

Eager to find out if Ripp was full of shit, I pulled off my sweats and reached for my socks. Jess looked at me and shook her head. "Leave on the socks, Boss."

"On?"

She nodded. "Oh, yeah."

I stripped down to nothing but socks and put on my Chucks. She looked me up and down and then smiled. "You look like an idiot."

"Thanks."

"A cute idiot," she said.

I pointed to the couch. "Assume the position."

She did just that. A few seconds later, we were deep in the throes of passion. With her face buried in the loveseat, and me buried deep in her, I paused and assessed the situation.

After satisfying myself that I could perform the maneuver in question, I leaned over Jess and cleared my throat.

"Ready?" I asked.

"I guess," she breathed against the fabric cushion. "Take it easy."

I lifted my right leg over her back and placed the sole of my shoe lightly against the back of her head. As I suspected, the stretching of my leg allowed a much deeper penetration to take place.

Much deeper.

She arched her back and turned her head to the side.

"You okay?" I asked.

She blinked her eyes. "Do it," she growled.

The few minutes that followed were unbelievably pleasurable, at least for me. The experience was different than anything we'd tried in the past. My elevated level of satisfaction was undeniable.

Jess felt the same way and she wasn't afraid to express it.

"Oh, my God," she grunted. "This is amazing!"

I agreed wholeheartedly.

We continued in that position for some time, but not for as long as normal. Eventually, the excitement of it all got to us both. During the extremely climactic ending, I pressed my foot down hard against her head.

It wasn't intentional, it seemed to be more a result of simply losing my mind during climax. She didn't oppose verbally or physically, so I expected it wasn't as bad as it seemed.

In the end, we stood, staring at each other in awe.

"Well?" I asked.

"Ripton's a genius," she said.

"I think he might be."

She raised her flattened hand in the air.

I slapped mine against hers, giving her the high-five that she'd undoubtedly earned.

"To Chuck Fuckin'," she said as our hands met.

I chuckled. "Head steppin'."

Her children were staying with her mother, which left us with the weekend to ourselves. That night, we performed the head-stepping maneuver once again, and then fell asleep exhausted. The next morning, we awoke to the sound of Teddy munching on a bowl of cereal. I got dressed and wandered into the kitchen to make a pot of coffee.

"Mornin', shithead," I said.

Clutching the bowl between his hands, he grinned. "Did she do it?"

Jess stepped out of the bedroom. "She sure did."

He slurped the milk from his bowl. Upon lowering it, he arched an eyebrow. "How'd it work?"

She walked into the kitchen before I responded. "Hey Teddy."

He looked at me and then at her. "Well?"

She gave him a hug. When he released her, she turned toward the coffee pot. Her head and shoulders rotated in unison, as if her head was incapable of turning independently.

She reached for a coffee cup and winced in pain. Upon realizing she couldn't reach it, she pointed.

Teddy pulled the cup from the cabinet and handed it to her.

"Thank you." She turned toward the coffee pot in a robot-like manner. "The head-stepping thing? It was awesome."

"Don't look like it," he said with a laugh.

"This?" she asked, pointing to her neck. "This is the sacrifice I'm willing to make to ensure the accuracy of his books."

He drank the rest of the milk from the bowl. After wiping his long beard, he grinned. "Better hope he don't ever write one about murderin' people."

I shot Teddy a laser sharp glare.

"What?" he asked.

"Funny you say that," I said. "That's coming up next."

Jess faced the living room. Her head and shoulders, once again, turned in unison. "He can be your guinea pig for that one," she said. "I think I've sacrificed enough."

CHAPTER THIRTY-FIVE

I released *Unstoppable*, which was Mike Ripton's contribution to the series of boxer books. The book was an immediate hit, climbing to number one in a matter of days. It's sales quickly surpassed every book I'd written. I attributed its success partially to the wild sex scenes, but more so to the readers attaching themselves to the character's belief system.

He was a vigilante, of sorts. He stood up for the heroine in the original book, taking care of her abusive ex when he physically abused her. It seemed everyone adored Mike Ripton for his willingness to do what most would not. He stepped in when most men would step away.

Immediately following the release of *Unstoppable*, I wrote a book of murder and mayhem. The manuscript was finished quickly, taking about ten days from beginning to end. While writing the story, Jess advised me that I wouldn't be writing another book like it anytime soon. She claimed I turned into an emotional disaster while crafting the tale.

I became so immersed in my characters, that I thought like them, ate like them, and even dressed like them. While writing *Undefeated*, I, no differently than the Hero, wore a hoodie everywhere I went.

For twenty hours a day through the entire course of writing the manuscript, I wore it.

Fully aware that I spent my writing time *in character*, I agreed with Jessica regarding the torturous novel.

It was mid-morning, which was late for Jess to arrive. While seated at my perch pecking away on my next story in the boxer series, she walked in and flopped down on the couch behind me.

She hadn't kissed me.

We had a rule that we started and ended our days with a kiss. Without exception. Additionally, we always went to bed at night only after telling each other *I love you*.

Something was wrong.

I peered over my shoulder. "Everything okay?"

She was crying.

I climbed down off my stool and sat down beside her. "What's wrong, Baby?"

Her lip was quivering. Upon realizing I was looking at her, she turned away, embarrassed. I lifted my finger to her chin and forced her to face me.

Then, I kissed her.

"You've got to talk to me, Baby. I can't fix it if I don't know what's wrong."

She raised her left hand and extended her index finger. Then, she reached into her purse with her right hand. After fumbling around for a moment, she lifted her cupped hand from her purse.

She held her clenched hand over my lap.

I opened my hand.

She dropped a pregnancy test into my palm. "I'm pregnant."

I was elated. My eyes quickly welled with tears. I shot up from my seat and held the plastic proof of the child we shared between us. "Is uhhm. Is this the one I get to keep?"

She wiped her eyes, and then coughed out half a laugh. "What?"

"This pregnancy test. Is it mine?" I asked excitedly. "Can I keep it?"

She shrugged. "I guess."

I looked at the pen-like object. Two darkened lines filled the window. A smile formed on my face. "This is awesome."

She stood. "You're not mad?"

I scrunched my nose. "Mad? Why would I be mad?"

"Because I'm pregnant."

"I told you when this started that I was committed to you and to this relationship. I told you I was ready to have kids with you."

"I thought that was a line of shit," she said, wiping away tears as she spoke. "That you were just talking."

I shook my head. "I don't say things I don't mean." I kissed her, and then looked her in the eyes. "You're not mad, are you?"

Her eyes gleamed like diamonds. She shook her head. "Not at all. When I called you last night, I was hinting at this. Trying to, anyway. You didn't give me the answers I wanted, so I thought you were going to be mad."

"You were talking in circles. I hadn't slept in two days. You asked me if I was ready to *treat you like my wife*. I said *yes*. That wasn't the answer you wanted?"

She laughed and cried at the same time, smiling all the while. "I don't know what I wanted. I was scared."

I led her into the bedroom by her hand and placed the pregnancy test in the top drawer of my dresser. Then, I walked into the living room and paused in the center of what we called *the dance floor*. It was a nine-foot by twelve-foot area of the loft that was marked by an ornamental rug.

We often danced there during the middle of the day, always driven by nothing more than impulse.

While Blind Pilot's *3 Rounds and a Sound* played, I pulled her close. Then, without instruction or a spoken word, we began to dance. She laid her head against my chest. I realized she was wearing the chevron top that she'd worn on the day of our first kiss, and I grinned.

She was truly a remarkable woman. To share a child with her would be the greatest gift God could bestow upon us. My life was slowly becoming a dream, and I had her to thank for it.

When the song ended, she raised her head.

"What was that about?"

"Baby Dance," I said.

She smiled. "What?"

"It's the baby dance."

She kissed me, and then laid her head against my chest again. "Let's do it again."

We did just that, dancing once again like God was the only one watching.

CHAPTER THIRTY-SIX

My three children blamed me, at least in part, for my trip to prison. Rightfully so, they were of the opinion that I didn't have to abandon them. Despite their ages at the time of ten, nine, and eight, they saw it as a choice. They fully realized that I *could* have accepted the offer of probation and continued to live the life I was living.

I was divorced from their mother at the time, but they looked forward to our weekends together, and to the time we were able to share on their breaks from school and during the summer.

The boys, Alec and Derek, were thirteen months apart. Their sister, Erin, was a year older than the oldest boy, Alec.

Erin spent most of her time reading, while the two boys spent their time at the lake behind the house, hunting for frogs, or playing basketball. They didn't have a basketball hoop at their home, but they enjoyed playing on the one I had, often doing so until dark.

My pride prevented me from accepting the government's offer of probation. Admitting to guilt when I had no intention of commiting a crime wasn't something I could ever do. As hard as it was to explain to them, if I had to repeat the process a thousand times over, I'd do the same thing, each and every time.

After my release from prison, repairing my relationship with them began. The progression of that process proved to be a very slow one.

I now looked at our pregnancy as an opportunity for me to do what I'd longed to do with them. Another chance at an opportunity for me to be the father to my children that my father had been to me.

In the underground parking garage of my building, I sat in the passenger seat of a car I wasn't allowed to drive and talked to my daughter, who was seated on the driver's side. We'd just returned from her chauffeuring me to get a cup of coffee. A senior in high school and already enrolled in college, she was an intelligent young woman.

She was also extremely perceptive, just like her father.

She'd met Jessica on numerous occasions and seemed to like her. They got along great, laughed with one another, and spent quality time together either talking or simply listening to music.

Erin stayed with me frequently, often for several days at a time. During those days, Jessica was just as much in her life as I was. Despite what I'd witnessed of my daughter's interactions with Jess, I wanted her to give me her opinion of Jess face-to-face.

We sat in the SUV and talked privately about problems she was having in her relationship at the time. After the discussion was over, I took a long drag off my e-cigarette. After blowing the vapor out the window, I looked at Erin.

"What do you think of my relationship with Jess?"

"What do you mean?"

"I want your opinion about it. No holds barred. Give it to me."

"She's good for you," she said.

"Why do you say that?"

"Dad, it's no secret that you've lived a pretty unhappy life. I've seen you in and out of a few relationships, and you've never been happy. The only thing that makes you happy is riding your motorcycle. Now you don't even have one. But, you know what?"

I grinned. "What's that, Sis?"

"I've never seen you this happy. Ever. I like seeing you like this. All I've ever wished for is that you could find happiness. Now, it looks like you've found it. I like her a lot dad, I really do."

Fighting back tears, I hugged her. "Thanks for your honesty."

"Are you going to ask her to marry you?" she asked, failing miserably at hiding her excitement.

The thought of taking that step scared me. It was the kiss of death as far as I was concerned.

"Not just yet," I said. "I'm going to ask her to move in with me."

She raised her clenched fists. "Yaaay!"

"Yay? Really?"

Wearing an ear-to-ear grin, she nodded eagerly. "This makes me happy."

I smiled. "Me, too."

We spent the afternoon together, and then she went to see her boyfriend. Immediately following her departure, Jessica arrived. When she walked in, I was in the kitchen making a cup of coffee.

"I got everything confirmed at the doctor," she said. "I'm four weeks along, right now."

"Thirty-six to go," I said.

"How do you know how many weeks are left?"

"I've been doing some reading. Brushing up on my baby skills."

"I'm so excited," she said. "And, I'm starving."

She got a container of yogurt from the refrigerator and began to devour it. "I can't eat enough."

I rubbed her stomach. "Good. Healthy mom, healthy baby."

She scrunched her nose. "I'm going to get so fat."

"Stop it. You won't. Just take care of yourself, and everything will be fine."

She shoveled the yogurt into her mouth like she was starving. "What do you think about names?"

"I like Joey, and Taylor, and names like--"

She paused, the spoon inches from her lips. "What if it's a girl?"

"Those *are* girl names," I said. "I like cute boy's names for girls."

"What if it's a boy?"

"It better not be a boy."

She dragged the spoon around the edges of the empty plastic container. "Why?"

"I want a girl. I've already raised two boys. I can tell you, they're the shits. They develop tempers, they hold grudges."

She looked me up and down. "Oh, really? That's a shocker."

"Go to hell, Jess."

"They're just like their dad."

"It's not that. It's boys in general. You'll see as Landon grows up. Oh." I wagged my finger at her. "That reminds me of something."

She tossed the empty yogurt container in the trash. "What?"

"I want us all to live together. I want all of you to move in."

Her eyes went wide. "Really?"

"Yep. As soon as possible."

"Do you think you can handle that?"

"I know I can handle it."

"Are you ready for it?" she asked.

"I've been ready."

"You've been living alone for a long, long time." She looked around the open loft. "It's going to be a huge change."

"A change I look forward to. So, what do you say?"

"The kids love it here. Landon's going to have a heart attack. He loves you, you know."

"I love him right back," I assured her. "So, is that a yes?"

She bit into her lower lip and nodded. "I can't wait."

"Give notice at your place and tell them you're moving out. We can tell my parents this weekend. I already told Erin."

"What did she say?"

"She said she's never seen me so happy, and that she's excited."

The gleam in her eyes brightened. "That makes me happy."

"Me, too."

"Sorry I missed her," she said. "What did she want?"

"Boy problems."

"Don't you dare go beating up a high school senior," she snapped back.

"It's not that. Just regular stuff."

She grabbed another container of yogurt. "I'm going to eat this, and then I'm going to take a nap. I don't have a client until ten."

"Ten is in an hour."

She put the yogurt up. "I'll take a nap first. I can eat this on the way."

"The sixty seconds it takes you to eat one of those takes away from the nap quite a bit, huh?"

She shrugged. "A minute is a minute."

I kissed her. "And, I want to spend all of my minutes with you."

She smiled. "You should write that in a book."

"I'll make note of that."

While she took a nap, I looked at girl's names on my phone. After highlighting a dozen, I copied the text and pasted it into my notepad. I peered through the doorway of what I called Teddy's room, and imagined Landon and Lily playing in the five hundred square foot bedroom.

Things were going to change, that was for sure. Stepping on Legos in the middle of the night. No longer having privacy. Changing diapers. Sleepless nights. Sharing a bathroom. A crying baby. Jess becoming an emotional wreck. No more sex. Arguments over what was going to be watched on television.

I'd always perceived change as being a bad thing. On that day, however, I looked forward to every change that was headed in my direction.

CHAPTER THIRTY-SEVEN

Two weeks had passed since Jess and I discussed moving in together. We'd ironed out the details and decided to tell everyone of our plan. Seated at my usual spot on my parents' loveseat with Jess at my side, I clapped my hands together. "I've got an announcement to make."

My father lowered his Kindle and peered over the top of it. "Jess is pregnant."

Although everyone would undoubtedly be able to determine the date of conception after the baby was born, we had decided not to announce the pregnancy until later. Jessica's parents were extremely religious. They'd prefer we were married before we had children but could accept us living together. To them, us announcing our pregnancy prior to living together would equate to sinning, squared. Or, to the tenth power of sinning. Sinning would certainly be the crux of the problem.

Jess looked at me, and I at her. I met my father's gaze. "No. It's something else."

"You're getting hitched?"

My mother raised her head. "Who's getting hitched?"

"Nobody, mother!"

She scrunched her face. "I thought your dad said someone was getting hitched?"

"We're moving in together!" I shouted.

"Oh, Good!" My mother exclaimed. "That's so exciting. Where are you going to live?"

"In the loft."

She covered her mouth with her hands. "You don't have a yard. That's not good for the kids."

The thought of moving out didn't set well with me. Although I'd been out of prison five years, the ATF's methods of invading my private life still occupied my thoughts on a daily basis.

"We'll find some place with a yard one of these days."

"Don't wait too long," my mother said. "They won't be kids forever."

"I'll try to remember that, mother."

"Congratulations," my father said. "When are you going to ditch the life of sin and get married?"

"I'm sure that'll happen one of these days," I said. "As long as she doesn't fuck up."

"Scott David Hildreth," my mother whined. "That's enough of that talk."

I looked at my father and raised my brows. "I'm with you. I think it's selective memory loss," I said, although I meant selective hearing loss.

"What?" my mother asked in an elevated tone.

"I said Jess is secretly a macramé boss!"

"Macramé makes such great pretty wall hangings," she said.

I did a mental eye roll and shifted my gaze to my father. "That's the week's news."

"How's the writing?"

"Good. Writing another boxer book."

"How many you doing in that series?"

"As many as it takes," I responded. "Four is my guess. I hope everything keeps going as good as it is right now. That last one sold like gangbusters."

"Ripton's book?"

I nodded as I pulled my phone from my pocket. After bringing up my Amazon sales page for the previous month, I handed my father the phone. "Have a look at that."

He studied the phone for a moment and then looked at me. "What's this include?"

"The first thirty days of income from that book."

"Jesus jumped up Christ!" he shouted. "Seriously?"

I gave a prideful nod. "Yep."

"Good Lord," he said, handing me the phone.

"What?" Jess asked.

"Nothing," I said. "Ripton's book sold pretty good, that's all."

"Oh."

"Get a place where those kids can enjoy themselves," my father said. "That's paramount to their successes."

"I will, Pop."

"I planned on raising you little heathens out in California, but I think you had a pretty good life here," he said.

My longing to live in Southern California had never faded, and I doubted it ever would. I simply hadn't acted upon my desire to move there. I wondered if I ever would. Expressing my disappointments in the Midwest would crush my father, so I never told him how I truly felt.

"My childhood was as good any kid could have hoped for," I said.

Jess excused herself and went to the bathroom. While she was gone, my father and I discussed book ideas. When she returned, she looked ill.

"You okay, sweetheart?" my father asked.

"I think I'm sick," she said.

"What can I get you?" he asked.

Her eyes met mine.

Something was wrong.

"Are you okay?" I asked.

"I'm sick. I think we need to go."

"Bad?"

She shrugged. "I don't know. I've got really bad cramps."

"Probably need to poop," my father said. "Never could do that at a stranger's house. Something about the comfort of a man's own home that allows him to have a proper release."

"Do you want to go?"

She nodded.

We bid our farewells and left. The entire drive home, Jess was convinced my father was right. She said she felt that she simply needed to go to the bathroom but couldn't seem to do it.

She dropped me off at the corner with a kiss, and then went home. As I rode the elevator up to my floor, I prayed that everything was alright with our baby.

I quickly became immersed in my work, attempting to finish the third book in the boxer series. I included elements of my personal life. What Jess and I had experienced. In the end, I added a little surprise for the readers.

My phone rang. I picked it up and looked at the screen. Two hours had somehow passed since Jess dropped me off.

I picked up the phone and answered it.

"I feel like crap," Jess said.

"Get some sleep. You're pregnant. We've been running around like idiots. Go, go, go. That's all we do. Take some time off. I'm sure you're just exhausted."

"You're probably right."

"Get some sleep, Baby. I love you."

"I love you, too."

The next three days passed, with Jess feeling sick most of the time. At six weeks into her pregnancy, we wrote it off as an aggravated form of morning sickness. On the night of the fourth day, my phone rang again.

Jess was sobbing.

"What's wrong, Baby?"

Her crying was the only sound I could hear.

"What? Did it get more painful?"

The crying continued. After a moment, she sucked a few choppy breaths.

"Our...baby," she sobbed.

I leaped from my stool. "What? What's wrong? Is everything okay?"

"I uhhm. I had...I had...I'm so sorry, Scott."

"Baby? What's wrong? Is everything okay?"

"I don't know...I don't know what I did wrong," she said, her voice distant. "I'm so sorry."

"I'm sure we can fix it. What happened?"

"I had a miscarriage," she blubbered. "Our baby. I'm in the bathroom. It's uhhm...it's...I don't know what to do..."

CHAPTER THIRTY-EIGHT

The thought of Jess enduring the pain of our loss alone crushed me. By contract, she had to give thirty days' notice to move out of her apartment. The notice had to come at the first day of the month. In short, we were two weeks away from being able to give thirty days' notice.

Or, six weeks from being able to move in together.

"We need to figure out something about getting you in here," I said. "Right now."

Jess looked at me. Her eyes were distant and no longer possessed the luster they once did. "You still want us to move in?" she asked.

"What?" I gave her a look. "Why wouldn't I?"

"I'm not pregnant anymore," she said. "There's no need."

My heart sank at the thought of her believing what she'd said. Nothing could be further from the truth. At that juncture, I desired her more than ever. I no longer wanted to have her come and go when it was convenient.

I yearned for the comfort of having her in my arms every night. Of falling asleep with her at my side. Waking in the mornings with the first scent to hit my nostrils being the sweet hint of her previous night's perfume.

Seeing the content look her face wore when she slept. Playing an active part in raising Landon and Lily. Teaching them the complications and rewards associated with life. Making them aware of the mistakes I'd made in living my life, so they could live theirs without making the same choices. Watching them grow from children to teens, and from teens to young adults.

I hugged her. "Me asking you to move in had nothing to do with the pregnancy. It had everything to do with me loving you and the kids. I want you here."

Her face lit up. "Really?"

"Absolutely."

"Are you sure?"

"I can't imagine living life any other way," I said.

"I was worried you wouldn't want us here."

I stepped away, looked at her, and then pulled her close. I was angry, frustrated, disappointed, and in tremendous pain, but I was also deeply in love. I wanted love to win the battle. I *needed* love to win the battle.

"I want you here now more than ever," I said.

With the side of her face pressed hard against my chest, she responded. "I think I need you now more than ever."

I learned over the next few weeks that the pain from losing a child, even if they aren't born into this world, doesn't diminish quickly. A dull aching in my heart began with each day and didn't end until I managed to fall asleep.

I blamed myself for the loss. Something, I was sure, was wrong with my sperm. Jess did the same, blaming herself for exercising too much and not eating enough. Together, we suffered the loss, and we suffered it through every waking hour of the day.

We spent much more time than normal on the dance floor. I stopped writing. I couldn't assemble a simple sentence, much less a meaningful one.

I'd suffered the pain from loss on many occasions. I had never, however, felt the level of agony that was taking over my body on a day-to-day basis. Jess and I slipped into a state of depression, each blaming ourselves in silence for the miscarriage. Truth be known, it was neither of our faults, but it would take us months to come to that realization.

There was one thing that I felt might be able to dull the pain. Having the wind in my face and the open road ahead. For those that had never experienced the magic of riding, it couldn't be understood. To me, it wasn't a lifestyle, it was *life*.

A life I was no longer able to live.

While I laid in bed at night, I dreamed of riding. During those few moments before I fell asleep, I was convinced that the pain subsided. In my manufactured heaven, Jess was behind me with her arms wrapped tight around my waist. It was comforting to know that even in my dreams, we were together.

Comforting one another through the most trying of times.

Her smile in the reflection of the rearview mirror gave me comfort that she, as a result of that ride, had somehow managed to accept the loss.

CHAPTER THIRTY-NINE

We stood in the furniture store hand in hand, staring blankly at bedroom furniture. Jess fixed her eyes on the least expensive option, a white twin bed frame that was manufactured of particle board.

"This will probably work."

I looked at it and laughed. "It tiny, and it's cheap."

"Cheap is good," she said.

"There's a difference between cheap and inexpensive. That's cheap." I lifted it and dropped in onto the floor. "You can pick anything you want. Anything at all. Take your time."

"I can't get *anything*," she said.

I'd been paid for the release of Unstoppable. We needed two beds, dressers, and a few night stands. I certainly didn't want to squander my earnings, but the store's most expensive items weren't out of reach.

I gave her a look of reassurance. "You sure can."

"That's hard for me to comprehend," she said. "I barely make it through each month."

"Well, now we'll have two incomes and one household expense. Pick out whatever you want."

The look on her face was payment enough for the countless nights I'd worked to release books at the rate of one every six weeks. After wandering around the store for an hour, we chose two matching ornate metal bedframes and several pieces of bedroom furniture.

"This is so nice," she said. "I've never bought new furniture before. Ever."

Being able to provide for her and the children gave me a much higher degree of satisfaction than I had ever obtained from providing for myself. Excited to see the look on Landon and Lily's faces when they realized that they would no longer be sharing a mattress on the floor, I set up the delivery of the pieces and drove home.

The next day the furniture was delivered and set up. Following the delivery, it was immediately apparent that Jess was excited about moving in.

"I don't like the color of Teddy's room," she said.

"The kids room?"

"Yeah. It's uhhm. It's kind of brown-ish."

I shrugged. "Have Teddy's painter paint it."

"The bathroom, too."

I glanced in the bathroom. "What's wrong with it?"

"It's white."

"White is good."

"It needs to be a blue-ish gray."

"Fine. Have him paint it, too."

The loft was one big open space, with two large bedrooms at one end. The main body of the living area, less the bedrooms, was twenty-four hundred square feet, with no partition walls. Three concrete columns were equally spaced along the center of the space.

Each column was painted a different color. One blue, one yellow, and one red. One sixty-foot-long wall was painted purple. The others were red. Ugly brown. Navy blue. The corridor that led to the entrance was painted grass green on one side and red on the other.

She glanced around the spacious room and looked at the various colors. "I'd like to paint everything."

I huffed out a breath. "Call Teddy. Have him send the painter over. I'll work something out with him."

A week later, everything was painted to Jess' liking. The home was decorated with a woman's touch. The tops of the cabinets that had been bare for years were now fitted with ornamental metal plates and plant life.

The walls were littered with pictures, photos, and cute little sayings. Candles and lamps – two of my pet peeves – were everywhere.

As I glanced around the home and wondered just what I'd agreed to, the door swung open and Teddy walked in.

His eyes darted around the room. "Looks good."

"Thanks, Teddy," Jess said.

"Looks like a whorehouse in here," I said. "There's fucking candles everywhere."

"Smells good," he said.

The only thing good that I could smell was the hint of the soup Jess was cooking in the slow cooker. I glared at him. "Go home, Teddy."

He flopped down on the couch. "Where's the kids?"

"Daycare."

"Oh, crap," Jess said. "I've got to go get them."

When she returned, the five of us sat down to a meal of her family's recipe of wild rice soup, chicken bundles, and a salad. It wasn't Ramen noodles, but I could certainly get used to it.

Teddy plucked a crumb from his beard and poked it into his mouth. "Good grub, Jess."

She swelled with pride. "Thanks, Teddy."

I raised my fork. "I'll second that. It's delicious."

She looked at me and smiled. "Thank you."

I glanced at everyone as they ate their meal. Landon and Lily's manners had improved drastically, and they were practicing them at the table. I realized as I surveyed the people who surrounded me that my family had grown.

More importantly, on that night I realized my house had become a home.

CHAPTER FORTY

I gazed through the glass wall of windows. The area was crawling with speed walkers who were utilizing their lunch hour for exercise, joggers, and the occasional neon Spandex clad bicyclist. In the distance, the fountains in front of the theatre were spraying water high into the air.

Jess had returned to work. I was attempting to write. Neither of us had fully recovered from the loss of our child. I doubted we ever would. Masking our grief had become second nature.

We spoke to each other in passing, had no interest in sex, and spent the nights cuddling silently until we fell asleep. Something needed to change, but I had no idea how to implement it. Time, I decided, would heal our wounds.

The door swung open, and then closed. Without turning around, I lifted my chin slightly. "Morning, shithead."

"Mornin'."

I mentally followed the clicking of his boot heels along the concrete floor. The sound of the refrigerator door being opened and then closed was followed by the sound of the cabinet door doing the same.

"'Bout out of milk."

"Jess is headed to the store after work."

Teddy sat down beside me and commenced to devour his cereal.

My desk was positioned directly in front of the window. An eight-foot by three-foot slab of marble, it was more than large enough for the four barstools that were positioned in front of it.

I leaned to the side and gave Teddy a look. "Scoot over a few seats, would you?"

"Was wanting to talk to ya."

"You don't have to sit on me to talk to me. Scoot over."

He spooned the Honey Crisp into his mouth and talked over the mouthful of food. "How much money you got?'

"Fuck, I don't know. Why?"

"In case you didn't realize it, spring has sprung. It's time to ride, dude."

I returned a narrow-eyed stare. "You forget about the bank picking up my shit?"

He shoveled another spoonful of cereal into his mouth. "Nope."

"Hard to ride what one doesn't have."

"Remember Tater Salad?" he asked.

"That big goon that rents the house from you out west?"

"Yep."

"I remember him, why?"

"Lost his job a while back. Ten months ago, to be exact."

"What's this story got to do with me?"

He lifted the bowl and took a big slurp of milk. Upon lowering it, he grinned. "Owes me ten grand. He's got a job now, but he'll never be able to pay me the back rent because he don't make enough to get ahead."

To call Teddy a pacifist was giving him tremendous credit. He had a horrific temper, but he never acted on it. He, no differently than the other men in the club, seemed to rely on me to act as their mouthpiece.

"You need help kicking him out?"

He shook his head. "I'm gonna give him an option." He lifted the bowl to his mouth, finished the milk, and then set it aside. "*You're going to give him an option.*"

"Pay or get out?"

"Nope."

"Jesus, Teddy. What? You gonna whore his wife out?"

"He's got a Heritage Softail. You're going out there with me. We're taking the bike. I'll call it even. You give me five grand for it. I'll call the rest a loss. I'll never see it, anyway."

I jumped from my stool, knocking it over in the process. "Five grand for a Heritage? Does it run?"

He nodded. "Like a scalded dog. He never rides it. Bought it new."

"I'll give you five for it," I said. "Right now."

He wiped the milk from his beard and then looked at his hand. "When you want to go out there?"

"When does he get off work?"

"Three."

"Let's be there when he gets home."

He grinned. "This is gonna be fun to watch."

"Why's that?"

"You ain't seen him in five years. He's about Big O's size. A little shorter though."

I shrugged. "He gets between me and that Heritage, and I'll be on him like shit on a wheel."

That afternoon, we waited with Tater Salad's wife in the garage while he was on his way home from work. An oversized four-wheel-drive truck pulled into the driveway and came to a stop. When the door opened, a two-hundred-and-twenty-pound man with a shaved head spilled out of the opening.

He was wearing slacks and a dress shirt, but it did little to hide the bulging biceps that were beneath the powder blue cotton fabric.

After giving me a lingering glance, he shifted his eyes to Teddy. "What's going on, Teddy?"

"Here about that money you owe me," Teddy said.

He gestured toward me. "What's he here for?"

Teddy shrugged.

"I'm going to cut to the chase," I said. "You owe my man Teddy ten grand. You don't have it. He needs it. Under Kansas law, he could evict you. He doesn't want to. But he needs that money to start a construction job that starts Monday. It's Thursday. In my opinion, you have one option."

I nodded toward the Harley that was parked beside the weight training equipment. "Go get the title to that bike, sign it on the back, and hand it to him. I'll ride the bike out of here, and you'll be paid in full."

He looked me up and down. "What if I say no?"

His teenage daughter walked into the garage. "Hi dad."

"Go back inside, Terra."

"What's going on?"

"Go inside. I'll come inside here in a minute."

Tater's wife escorted Terra inside the house. I looked at him and raised my brows. "If you refuse, you, your wife, and that daughter of yours will be out in the street trying to decide what to do with all your belongings. A week or so later, you'll be hit with a lawsuit. Attorney's fees will be about a grand on top of the ten you owe Teddy, and then you'll have to pay his attorney's fees as well. All told, you'll be twelve grand out of pocket and homeless."

He looked at the Harley. "Shit. I've had that bike ten years. It's part of the family."

"I know plenty about that," I said. "My chopper got repossessed a little over a year ago. No differently than you, I was jobless, and couldn't pay for it. Getting that thing taken from me was the best thing that ever happened to me. A turning point in my life if there ever was one. It caused me to take a long hard look at me and what was wrong in my life."

"I'm guessing you're going to end up with it, then. Is that right?"

I nodded. "I'm paying him for it. Like I said, Teddy needs that money."

He folded his arms over his chest. His gaze fell to the driveway. He was almost there, he simply needed a nudge.

"I plan on turning it into a show bike. Fishtail exhaust, air ride suspension, chrome spoked wheels, black paint, and as much chrome as Harley will sell me for it. I'll text you pics as it's coming along." I pulled the contract I'd drafted from my back pocket. "I'll just need you to sign this, and then Teddy will sign it. It shows you're caught up one hundred percent. It'll be a good feeling to get that debt off your shoulders, won't it?"

He took the sheet of paper and opened it. After reading it, he looked up. "Show bike, huh?"

"Slice at that custom shop downtown will do the paintwork. Silver and purple hand-painted old-school stripes. Stretched fenders. Hand-stitched solo seat. Big ape-hanger handlebars. I'm planning on going Cholo-style. Like the bikes out in SoCal."

He grinned. "That'd be badass."

"Need a pen?" I asked.

He shook his head. "Got one in the truck."

With some reluctance, he signed the contract, and then produced the motorcycle's title. After he handed me the keys, I looked at Teddy.

"Jess said I couldn't drive my car, right?"

"Yep."

I grinned. "She never said I couldn't ride a bike."

Tater Salad looked at Teddy. "What's he talking about."

"Fucker ain't got a driver's license. Told his Ol' Lady he wouldn't drive his car until he got it resolved. Never said nothing about a bike, though."

Tater looked at me. "Better take it slow. Cops in this town are sons-of-bitches."

I lifted my leg over the rear fender, lowered myself into the seat, and started the engine. After agreeing to leave the bike at Teddy's house, I rode it there and parked it.

When he opened the garage door, my jaw hit the floor. My one-of-a-kind BMW was sitting in his garage.

"What the fuck?" I gasped.

"Forgot to tell you," he said with a low laugh. "Bought it from the bank at auction. Thought I'd keep it in the family."

I looked the car over. Short of being covered in dust, it looked just the way it did on the day they picked it up.

"It's dirty," I said.

"Never drive it. Probably never will. I'll just keep it. You can come visit it any time you want."

I shook my head. "Love ya, Brother."

He stroked his beard and nodded toward the motorcycle. "When you telling Jess about this?"

"When it's done," I said.

"You seriously going to do all that shit to it?"

"Starting tomorrow."

My means of recovery from the loss we'd suffered was sitting in Teddy's garage. I was sure of it. The ten-minute ride to his house was hint enough to provide me with hope. Jess had never been on a motorcycle before, but I had my suspicions that she'd enjoy it.

In a few weeks, I intended to find out.

There was one thing I had to take care of first.

CHAPTER FORTY-ONE

With Jess at my side, I stood in front of the counter and mentally prepared to explain my situation. The woman on the receiving end of the conversation was a few days from retirement and had advised us that her departure party was scheduled at the end of the day.

I made comment about her beautiful snow-white hair and grinned.

She smiled in return.

Then, I placed my suspended driver's license on the counter between us and began to explain. "If you look up my name, there'll be several infractions, and some pretty significant fines and fees. I'd like to get those resolved, but there's a catch."

She reached for my license. "Let's have a look."

After a moment, she shifted her gaze from her computer to me. "Your driver's license has been suspended."

"I'm well aware."

She glanced at the screen. Her eyes widened slightly. "A warrant is scheduled to be issued next month."

"I'm privy to that, too."

"Are you wanting to pay for everything today?"

"That's where the problem comes into play," I said.

She alternated glances between Jess and me. "What problem?"

"There should be four violations, all dated within a few weeks of one another, one of which is a parking ticket. Parking in a handicap stall."

She reviewed the information on the screen. "That's what it shows."

"Here's the problem. I will not pay the parking ticket. In fact, I can't. Not today, not ever. I didn't park in a handicap stall. I parked on a sidewalk. I'll pay an additional fine, I suppose. Or an additional fee. You can shuffle it around however you like. But, I want a detailed printout. If there's a line item for a parking ticket, I won't pay it."

Jess leaned in front of me. "He's stubborn," she whispered.

The woman grinned. "This is my last day. Let me see what I can do."

After several failed attempts, she called over her supervisor. She explained the situation to him. He poked a few keys on the computer, swiped his ID through a reader, and then typed something on the keyboard.

"That should do it," he said.

She looked at the screen and smiled. "How does speeding, illegal lane change, and eluding an officer sound?"

Those were the three tickets I'd received a week before the parking ticket. It had been a shitty day, and I was in a bad mood. When the officer tried to pull me over, I decided I'd simply speed through traffic and outrun him. A few miles later, his friends were waiting for me.

It was a long night.

"Is that it?" I asked. "Nothing else?"

"Those three. The fine will be a total of seven hundred and eighty-six dollars."

"Can I look at it?"

She turned the monitor, so I could see it.

"Looks great," I said.

I paid the fine. A review of the receipt showed nothing of the parking ticket. Technically, I didn't pay the parking fine. In short, I'd won the battle. I folded the receipt, put it in my pocket and looked at Jess.

"I've got something I want to show you."

"What?"

"Give me your keys," I said. "I'll take you there."

Fifteen minutes later, she stood in front of the finished bike and smiled. "I love it. It's pretty. Are you thinking about buying it?"

"It's ours."

She spun around. "What?"

"They just finished building it for me."

She studied it, and then looked at me. "It only has one seat."

"On that kind of bike, you use a suction cup seat on the rear fender," I explained.

She chuckled. "Just like Erik did with Kelli."

"That's right."

She tilted her head to the side and gave me a look. "He didn't have a big seat on his bike because it didn't look cool."

"Sounds about right."

She faced me. "Do you have a suction cup seat?"

"They've got one inside."

"I suggest you buy it," she said. "Because I'm not sitting on the fender."

After buying the seat, I gave her instructions on how to ride, where to place her feet, and the precautions she'd need to take with the hot exhaust.

It was Jessica's maiden voyage on a motorcycle. It was also the first time I'd had a woman on the back of my motorcycle in many, many years. She was a natural rider. Short of her hands wrapped around my waist, I didn't realize she was behind me.

I crept along the highway's on-ramp. "How's a hamburger sound?" I asked over my shoulder.

"You're not stopping already, are you?"

"No. I was going to head to Stearman Field. An hour away, give or take."

"Stearman Field that Kelli and Erik rode to?"

"That's the one."

"I'd like that."

I twisted the throttle, speeding up to merge into traffic. In checking the rear-view mirror, I saw Jessica was wearing a look of content that I hadn't seen since our loss. An hour later, when we pulled onto the runway at Stearman Field, my face was plastered with the same look.

I realized I'd never forget what happened. Nor would I ever be completely free of the lingering pain.

The ride on that day, and on the many days that followed, slowly began to cleanse my soul. The therapeutic properties of riding were undeniable. We spent that summer on the bike as much as possible.

I released the boxer book I'd been working on and didn't release another book for four months. It was hard to write when I was riding. My followers and devoted fans didn't understand why I took the break from writing. I never shared with them the tragedy that Jess and I suffered.

When the summer was coming to a close, the MC started to plan the year's poker run. One night, Jess and I rode to a planning party at a local biker tavern. It was to be the night that she finally got to meet everyone in the club.

I knew the night would be a special one for many reasons. When we arrived, Jess looked at the sea of motorcycles parked in the lot.

"Holy cow," she exclaimed. "They're all inside?"

"It's going to be wild," I said. "Not everyone is with us. Just pay attention to who's wearing kuttes."

"Okay."

We got off the bike and walked inside. Just through the door, The Big O stood. Jess hadn't met him yet. She knew nothing of his involvement in ridding her of the thorn that had been in her side for years.

She simply knew that one cold winter's day, her ex disappeared from the picture. He was still around, and I knew it. I further knew he'd never step foot within a hundred yards of her, thanks to O.

He opened his arms and grinned an ear-to-ear grin. "You must be Jess."

I'd told her enough stories that she knew just who he was. As if they were long lost friends, she rushed to him and gave him a hug. The top of her head came to just over his belly button. As he held her, he looked at me and gave me a wink.

Three chapters of our MC were gathered in the bar that night. Back slapping, hugs, wild stories, and beer drinking were aplenty. As Jess and I sat and listened to one of the brethren's stories, King and his Ol' Lady sat down at our side. I stared at them in shock but knew not to express myself verbally. In the years that I'd known him, I'd never seen a woman within fifty feet of him.

After introductions, I looked at him and smiled to myself. Even things that are etched in stone, I decided, have the capacity to change. On that night, mysteriously, they did.

When Jess and I returned home, we made love. It was the first time we'd done so in a long, long time.

We hadn't recovered, but we were on our way.

One mile of open road at a time.

CHAPTER FORTY-TWO

To describe the excitement level Jessica's parents felt regarding our relationship could easily be done with one word.

Nonexistent.

They had no idea of Jessica's past experiences with her ex. The countless times she'd filed protection orders. The domestic violence reports. The stabbings. The death threats. The visits from Wichita Police to stop him from beating her. The file listing his trips to jail was several inches thick. Her parents knew nothing of any of it.

As with most abuse victims, she was embarrassed and blamed herself. She feared telling them the truth, so she told them nothing.

It seemed they knew everything of me, however.

"He writes pornography," her mother said. "His books depict relationships with unwed couples having sex."

"They're books, mother," Jessica said. "Just books. He treats me with respect. He's good with the children."

"We don't like the idea of you being with someone like that," her mother replied. "He's got tattoos."

Clinging to their belief that she would one day have a spiritual awakening and break off the relationship with me, they'd never taken the time to meet me. After our physical relationship began, their contact with Jessica diminished to a once a month phone call, at best.

Each of their attempts to contact her were met by Jessica's praise of how the children's attitudes and manners had improved. She explained how she felt loved, respected, and safe. She also reiterated during each call that our relationship sat firmly on a solid foundation of respect and love.

Eventually, they felt the need to drive to Wichita and point out my deficiencies in person. I wasn't thrilled about being criticized from afar – or in person – by anyone who spewed the Bible's scripture as if they'd written it themselves.

Hoping that they'd somehow find a way to accept me for who I was and not what I appeared to be, I agreed to the meeting. The next weekend, Jessica's mother, father, younger brother, and one of her younger sisters arrived in Wichita.

We met for an early evening dinner at *The Anchor*, a local bar-restaurant that was situated within a few blocks of where we lived. It was typically filled with hipsters, artists, and musicians who enjoyed the eclectic fare offered on the often-changing menu.

Jess, the children, and I walked from the adjoining parking lot to the lot her father had parked in. Jess looked like she was ready for a fashion show, as usual. The children were wearing their typical late-summer attire; Landon wore shorts and a tee shirt. Lily, a dress.

I wore a V-neck tee, jeans, and the Chuck's used for what had become Jessica's favorite sexual position. Upon exiting the car, her father looked me up and down, pausing for an inordinate amount of time to take in my full sleeve of tattoos.

An aeronautical engineer and former Air Force pilot, he now worked for Boeing as a Program Manager on the F-16 Program. His military career as an officer didn't include obtaining the tattoos often sought by Marines or Army infantrymen.

Although he may not have realized it – or believed it – my choice to use my body as a canvas didn't make me any lesser of a man. I had no intention to prove my worth to him. I would simply be myself. He could then base his opinion of me on fact, not fabrication.

I extended my hand. "Pleasure to finally meet you, Sir."

With a smile and a nod, he accepted my hand, gripping it firmly in his. "Terry."

"It's a pleasure, Terry."

I faced her mother. She looked at me and gasped. It wasn't intentional, it was more of a reaction to what she'd seen. She was appalled at my appearance. There was nothing she could do to hide it.

With bulging eyes and shaking hands, she stared at me.

Feeling that a handshake would exceed the extent of her desire to touch me, I chose to not to shake her hand.

Instead, I opened my arms. "Come here, Lisa," I said with a smile. "It's Lisa, right?"

Hoping to be saved from the situation, she glanced at Jess. Well aware that there was nothing she could do to prevent me from proceeding with the awkward embrace, Jess simply shrugged.

Lisa's face distorted into a fearful scowl.

It was all the invitation I needed. I took a step in her direction, wrapped my arms around her, and pulled her close.

"So nice to finally meet you," I said.

"Nice to uhhm...nice to meet, you, too," she stammered.

I held her for just long enough to make her mildly uncomfortable. Then, as a group, we went in the restaurant. Surrounded by tattooed hipsters and artists adorned with no less than a dozen facial piercings, I felt right at home.

We ate dinner together, talking about everything from airplanes to AC-DC. After the table was cleared, the waitress brought the bill.

"How do you want this split?" she asked.

I handed her my bank card. "All on one."

Her father shook his head. "We can split it up. I'll gladly pay for-."

"You're our guest for the weekend. Let me treat you as such," I said.

He alternated glances between Jessica and me, then grinned. "Thank you."

The next day they came to the loft. While Lisa seemed appalled by the living space, Terry was nothing short of fascinated.

"It reminds me of the flats in Europe," he said. "Only much bigger."

"For now," I said. "It suits us just fine."

Lisa wrinkled her nose, surveyed the space, and picked apart every facet of the arrangement.

When the weekend ended, Terry offered a smile and a congratulatory remark. Lisa, on the other hand, offered nothing but a scowl followed by a side-eyed stare as they walked to their car.

I looked at Jess as they drove away. "Much better than I expected."

"Me, too." She waved at her sister and then offered a consoling look. "My mother will take time."

"She'll eventually accept me," I assured her. "She doesn't have a choice."

"What do you mean?"

"Any time she sees you, she'll see me. Eventually, she'll accept me. It might take time, but it will happen."

"When I go there to visit, you're going to come with me?" she asked excitedly.

"Of course," I said. "We're a family."

At that moment, the splinters of amber that were sprinkled throughout her brown iris glistened with a brightness I'd yearned to see for months.

And the depth of her beautiful eyes returned.

CHAPTER FORTY-THREE

My motorcycle was normally parked beside my Craigslist SUV, which sat in my assigned parking stall in the underground parking garage. In the other assigned stall, Jessica's vehicle was parked.

On a Sunday evening, I moved the SUV into the parking lot to make room for me to work on the motorcycle. Parked beneath the basement lights, I adjusted the carburetor, set the tire pressures, and checked every nut and bolt for tightness.

The MC's poker run was fast approaching. Jessica was excited to participate. I was equally excited for her to attend. Our turnout for the event normally exceeded a thousand bikes. Expressing the feeling associated with hearing the rumble from a thousand motorcycles was impossible.

Witnessing it was breathtaking. Participating in it was a life changing experience.

When the mechanical work was done, I waxed the painted surfaces to a high gloss. After polishing the chrome to a mirror-like appearance, I admired my work.

Satisfied the bike was ready, I went upstairs and ate dinner. The next morning, Jessica took the children to daycare. An hour later, while I was drafting my upcoming novel, *Finding Parker*, she returned.

She handed me a cup of coffee. "Where's your car?"

"It's in the parking lot,"

"I saw it out there last night," she said. "But it wasn't there this morning."

"What do you mean?"

"I mean it's not there."

The SUV, a Chevy Tahoe, would be an easy vehicle to steal. All General Motors products were. A screwdriver was all that was required to drive one of them away.

I knew all too well what the risks were in having a GM vehicle that was desirable to thieves. In my twenties, I had a highly-modified Oldsmobile Cutlass. After spending thousands of dollars getting it painted, installing a high-horsepower engine, and reupholstering the interior, it was stolen.

The theft left me feeling vulnerable. It reminded me that despite my honesty, not all men are honest. My intimidating personality, the permanent scowl I wore, and the sleeve of tattoos did nothing to deter a thief that had no idea who he was stealing from.

A month later the vehicle was recovered in Harrisburg, Pennsylvania. Having it returned did nothing to diminish the feeling of helplessness I suffered in having it taken.

Upon getting the car home, I promptly sold it.

Then, immediately following my release from prison, I traded a motorcycle for a Chevy Suburban. The extensively modified four-wheel-drive resembled a monster truck. Fitted with a lift kit and forty-four-inch tires, the vehicle wasn't something I wanted, but it was more valuable than the motorcycle by thousands of dollars.

The trade would allow me to sell the Suburban for three thousand more than the motorcycle, coming out much further ahead than if I'd simply sold the motorcycle outright.

The massive truck was far too large to fit beneath the garage door opening of the underground garage, so I parked it in front of the loft, in the busy street beside the bar.

The next morning when I went to work, the vehicle was gone.

I rushed to the remote farmhouse of the three-hundred-pound thief who traded it to me. Certain that he had traded the vehicle, kept a spare key, and later returned to take it back, I pounded on his door filled with a plan to administer vengeance.

He answered the door wearing nothing but boxer shorts. As he wiped the sleep from his eyes, I began my verbal assault.

"You motherfucker," I howled, my right hand resting on the knife that was clipped to my right pocket. "Did you really think you could steal that truck without me coming here to get it? Where the fuck did you put it?"

The look on his face hinted that he had no idea what I was talking about. The ten-minute-long conversation that followed confirmed it.

He hadn't taken the vehicle.

I apologized and left feeling foolish and, once again, vulnerable.

It was found in Wal-Mart's parking lot a year and a half later.

Now facing what would be my third vehicle theft, I looked at Jessica and shook my head. "I'm sure you just missed it."

"Missed it?"

"You drove past and didn't see it."

"I'm not an idiot, Scott."

I didn't think she was an idiot. I simply thought she was blind. I went downstairs. Upon entering the parking lot, my mouth fell open.

Someone had stolen my vehicle.

Again.

In talking to the maintenance men, I learned the vehicle was parked out of the field of view for the security cameras.

I returned to the loft feeling the same vulnerability I'd felt the previous two times. Having one's vehicle stolen leaves the victim much more than carless. The cowardly act left me feeling, at least on that occasion, weak.

"Well?" Jess asked.

"Someone stole it."

"How?" she asked. "The parking lot is gated. You need a clicker to get past the gate."

"They make remotes that will break the code to the gate."

"Who does?"

"Companies that cater to thieves."

"That's dumb."

It was dumb, but it was true. Frustrated, I sat at my stool and called the insurance company. Then, I called the police.

"What are you going to do for a vehicle?" she asked.

"What's your dream vehicle?" I asked.

"One of those four-door Jeeps? Why?"

"Get on the internet and find the one you want," I said. "That's what we'll do to replace it."

"Really?" she shrieked.

"Really."

Two weeks later, I flew to Phoenix, Arizona and picked up the exact vehicle she wanted. When I returned home, her appreciation was expressed in the form of tears.

To me, it was nothing more than a vehicle with a removable top. To Jess, the Jeep was a way of life.

It was her motorcycle. A means of cleansing her soul of the horrors from her past.

From that day forward, her hair was never the same.

CHAPTER FORTY-FOUR

I refrained from telling my followers on social media about Jessica. Considering the input from a few followers who knew about my relationship with her, I decided to take their recommendation to heart.

You can't tell the book world you're in a relationship, I was told. *If you do, you'll fail.*

I entered the Indie Author world about the time it was getting started. I saw C. D. Reiss, Meredith Wild, and Vi Keeland as inspirations, but there was one clear difference.

I was a man.

According to those few followers who were *in the know*, part of my success, if not all of my success, was based solely on me being a man. At the time there were very few Indie Authors, and even fewer male romance authors.

My sole income was what I received from writing books. The thought of causing my own failure filled me with fear.

One evening during the previous winter, a friend in the industry had told Jessica and I her beliefs.

The women who read your books want to escape through the

stories you write. Furthermore, that escape is enhanced by you being a male author. You can be in a relationship, but you can never announce it to your followers. Shoving that in their face would lead to complete failure.

I believed her. Jessica did not. Based solely on my fear of failure, I put my foot down, assuming the person who had spoken with us based the knowledge on nothing but statistical fact. So, for the eleven months that Jessica and I were in a physical relationship, I kept it a secret. I felt I needed to consider the advice of anyone who may be able to assist in my continued success. I chewed my lower lip while attending online functions and acted as though the woman I loved didn't exist.

Over the course of that time, Jessica's heart was breaking. I didn't realize just how much I was hurting her. After a few tear-filled discussions one evening, I understood to what extent my selfish decision had affected her.

When I sat back and took a long look at myself, I saw a man who was willing to lie for the betterment of his career. I'd always considered myself to be brutally honest. My actions were in clear contrast to my beliefs. As I worked on completing the manuscript of *Finding Parker*, I stayed off social media entirely.

Upon completing the manuscript, Jessica offered to make the cover for the book. In addition to being a licensed cosmetologist, she'd gone to college to be a graphic designer. To date, my book covers were rudimentary at best. Jessica fashioned a cover that put my previous covers to shame.

We decided to tell the book world of our relationship when I released the cover. I was either going to sink or swim. I had no idea which one it might be.

I rolled the dice. I released the cover of the book on my Facebook page. In doing so, I told the world of my relationship with the woman I loved. The post was 'liked' by someone. And then, another. And another. Minutes later, a hundred people had liked it. Then, several hundred. The number escalated to over a thousand.

I realized something on that evening.

Jessica – and our relationship – were widely accepted by the book world.

Nervous, I released *Finding Parker*. It was my first release in almost six months. The book was a contemporary romance novel about a college graduate who was an orphan. He developed a friendship with a wealthy and very eccentric man who acted as a father figure to him.

Through that man, he found himself in a very unique relationship with a girl.

The book didn't have my trademark elements of wild sex and violence, nor was it sprinkled with expletives. It was soft and tasteful. It could be read by high school students in the classroom. It did, however, appeal to a broad audience. An audience which I hoped included my followers.

Because of the depth of the father-son relationship in the book, I dedicated the book to my father.

The book was an instant success.

To me, *Finding Parker* was proof that I could succeed without tricks, lies, or lure. To Jessica, it was the point in time where she became part of two of the three worlds in which I lived. The only one she may have felt excluded from was the world of the motorcycle club. She had met the men, but she had yet to attend a function where she rode with them.

She wouldn't have to wait long to feel accepted in all three worlds.

CHAPTER FORTY-FIVE

Despite being late in the summer, the weather had taken a turn for the worse. It was fifty degrees and cloudy, with a chance for rain. Even for a seasoned rider, the day wasn't a good one to spend eight hours on a motorcycle seat.

After checking the weather forecast on my phone, I peered through the wall of windows and into the cloudy sky. "Probably not a good idea for you to go on this one, Baby. Sorry the weather went to shit."

She stepped through the bedroom door. With her hair up and a bandana tied across her forehead, she looked like an Ol' Lady of a one-percenter.

"I'm going," she said. "I don't care what the weather's like."

I gestured toward the cloud-filled sky. "Look."

"There's windows in the bedroom. I've seen it. I'm going."

I shrugged. "Okay."

We rode the forty minutes to the clubhouse. After eating breakfast and having a cup of coffee with the fellas, we waited anxiously for the event to start.

She scanned the countless motorcycles that were neatly parked for as far as the eye could see. "Does everyone leave at once?" she asked. "This will be a mess."

"We'll be up front," I said. "Leading the group. Side by side, there will be two columns, until everyone's out."

Her eyes widened. "That's a long line of bikes."

"Miles and miles," I said.

"What about traffic?"

I gestured toward the four Sheriff's cars that were parked at the side of the lot. "They'll lead us out of town. After that, we're on our own."

The corners of her mouth curled into a smile. "This is so exciting."

Half an hour later, the cool morning air was thick with the rumble from the exhaust of that very sea of motorcycles. Most found the sound deafening.

It sounded like comraderie to me.

Various motorcycle clubs, nationalities, and ethnic groups converged in one place. For a day, they set differences and past arguments aside. They rode for a cause. On that year, to raise money for suicide awareness.

The police cruisers pulled out of the parking lot. King raised his hand high in the air. "Let's roll."

Side by side, we exited the parking lot. We followed the police escort for the first few miles. Then, with a wave of their respective hands, the officers freed us of our confines.

Parked cars lined the highway, as if pulling over for a funeral precession. Children waved. Mothers cringed. Fathers dreamed.

Within an hour, contrary to the forecast, the sky cleared. We rode for seven hours that day. Jessica never complained once. In fact, she was disappointed when the ride ended.

Afterward, we ate the traditional barbeque. Men told stories of their experiences during the days' events, and of past events and rallies. We attended a silent auction and waited on the announcement of who won the poker run. Although Jessica believed it would be us, we didn't win anything except a beautiful day of riding.

One by one, and in small groups, the motorcycles left the lot. All that was left was the men of the MC.

"Anyone up for some moonshine?" King asked.

"I'll try some," Jessica responded.

King raised his clenched fist. "Stearman Field!"

We rode to Stearman Field. After lining the runway with Harley-Davidsons, we sauntered inside and sat as a group. Seated at half a dozen large tables, we sat with the sun in our faces. We talked, laughed, and drank our way into the evening.

Jess learned on that day that family isn't always bound by blood.

Sometimes it's chosen.

When the sun began to set in the western sky, I looked at Jess. "Need to get home pretty quick. Babysitter's expecting us."

She finished her moonshine lemonade and wiped her mouth. After slamming the empty Mason Jar onto the table, she looked at King and grinned.

He smiled in return. "Atta girl."

Jess glanced at me. "Okay. I'm ready."

She stood. She stumbled. She steadied herself against the table. At five-two and one hundred and thirty-five pounds, she had no business matching drinks with the fellas. But, she somehow managed to.

"She'll fall off the back of that bike, Scott," Big O said with a laugh. "Let's get some bungie straps and we can wrap them around you two."

"You're not going to tie her to me," I said. "She'll be fine."

"She's as drunk as a monkey," he said. "She'll fall off the back when you gas it at a light."

"She's a biker's Ol' Lady." I raised my index finger. "She'll ride without aid or assistance."

Jess shot a playful glare to each of the men. "She sure will."

We made it home without incident. As I tucked Jess into bed, I couldn't help but grin. "Did you have fun?"

She flashed a drunken smile. "Best. Day. Ever."

Then, she fell asleep.

That day, whether she realized it or not, she was widely accepted by the men in the club. She had met the presidents of other MC's, loners, weekend riders, admirers, and even a few men who I'd had problems with in the past.

She did so without embarrassing me, putting me at risk, or making a fool of either of us. She was accepted with open arms by all. She had also gone toe-to-toe with some of the best drinkers the Midwest had to offer.

She was now a part of all three worlds in which I lived. I admired her as she slept. In a moment, my mouth curled into a prideful grin.

There was only one more step I needed to take.

The next day, we sat along the southern exterior wall of the coffee shop. Landon and Lily sipped their Frappuccinos. I sat beside Svetli and watched the cars pass. Hiding beneath her hat and sunglasses, Jess was seated at my side. As she recovered from the previous evening's alcohol intake, I stole admiring glances when she wasn't looking.

She was undeniably beautiful. Beneath the surface of her skin, however, was the most beautiful part about her.

Her willingness to accept me wholly and without reservation. Her wit. Her willingness to place the children first, and herself second. She was ambitious, had a great work ethic, and loved her job. She was nurturing. Genuine. Kind. Honest. Compassionate. She was also predictable, which brought me tremendous comfort.

I had no idea women had the capacity to be predictable.

I glanced at Landon. He was instructing Lily on how to remove the lid to her drink and lick the whipped cream from the inside.

I looked at Jess. Nursing a hangover, she was gazing at the passing traffic through her mirrored Aviators.

"Got a question for you, Baby," I said.

She turned her head to the side. "I hope it's an easy one."

"I hope so, too."

She pulled the glasses down the bridge of her nose and looked over the tops of the lenses. "I'm ready."

"Do you want to get married?"

She swallowed hard, and then choked on her response. "I mean yeah. I want to someday."

"Let me rephrase that." I cleared my throat. "I want to marry you. Will you marry me?"

She removed her glasses. "You're asking me to marry you? Right now?"

I smiled. "I am."

"Yes," she blurted. "Absolutely. I will."

I clenched my fist. "Let's make it official."

She glanced at my hand and met my gaze. "Seriously? On the day you propose to me?"

Stone-faced, I held her gaze.

She made a fist. As she pressed her knuckles to mine, she smiled. "I don't know why I'd expect anything else from you."

On that afternoon, with the assurance of a fist bump as her only proof, we became engaged.

CHAPTER FORTY-SIX

We sat side by side on my parent's loveseat. Although I made a constant attempt to erase the smile that was plastered on my face, I came far from succeeding. Jess also wore an ear-to-ear grin, making denying of our excitement impossible.

Without looking up from his Kindle, my father spoke. "When are you going to make your e-books into paperbacks? I'd like to have that book you dedicated to me in paperback before I die. Is that a possibility?"

"Should be available in days."

He grunted. "I'll believe it when I see it."

"I'm serious. Jess just finished formatting it."

He lowered the Kindle. After glancing at Jessica and me, he picked up his glasses. A thorough look followed.

"What the fuck's going on with you two?" he asked.

"What do you mean?"

"Both of you look like guilty idiots. Cats that ate the proverbial canary."

I looked at Jess and shrugged. "Nothing going on here."

He glanced over his shoulder. "Anita! Get your ass in here."

Wearing her apron and covered in flour, my mother rushed in the living room. "What is it, David?"

He waved his hand toward us. "Look at these two fools. What in the hell's wrong with them?"

"Well," she said. "They're not idiots."

He forced a sigh. "Look at your son and his respective lover and tell me what in the hell is going on."

She wiped her hands on her apron. "Looks like they're sitting on the couch."

He scowled at her, and then scowled at us. "You two know something that I don't. Lest you forgot, young man, I don't like being in the dark."

I stood. "Mom, Dad, we have an announcement. We're getting married."

My father grabbed his Kindle. "It's about goddamned time."

"This is so exciting," my mother gasped. "When?"

"We haven't decided."

"Where?" she asked.

"We haven't decided that, either."

"Sounds like a line of shit, to me," my father said dryly.

"We're getting married, Pop. Seriously."

"Don't see a ring."

"We did a fist bump," Jess said. "At Starbucks."

He pulled off his glasses and squinted. "A what?"

She clenched both her fists and pounded them together. "Fist bump."

He shot me a glare. "That's what you and your cronies do before you go pull each other's puds, isn't it? That's not a way to secure a woman, you idiot."

"Works for us," I said.

He rolled his eyes. "Congratulations."

"David Wilson Hildreth!" my mother shouted. "That sure didn't sound very sincere."

"I'm happy they're engaged. I'm not happy about how he did it."

"It doesn't matter," my mother said. "What matters is their love for one another."

He raised his Kindle. Frantically, his finger flipped across the screen. He turned it to face me. It was clearly a page from a book, but I couldn't read it.

"Erik Ead didn't pound Kelli's fist," he said. "He put a ring in a coffee cup."

"That's a book," I said.

"A book *you* wrote," he complained.

"Well, we're engaged. That's the news of the week."

"Who won Scrabble?" Jess asked, hoping to change the subject.

He laid the Kindle on the end table. "I don't remember."

"What?" my mother asked.

"Who won the Scrabble game?" Jess shouted.

"Oh," she said. "I did. Six sixty-four to six-twenty."

"Six-twenty?" Jess asked. "Isn't that a low score for you?"

"Bad night," my father replied, gesturing to me. "Proof that dipshit here isn't the only one that can have a brain-fart."

We watched bits and pieces of a golf tournament and talked for a few hours about everything except marriage. When it was time to go, my father stood and opened his arms.

Jess gave him a hug.

After he broke their embrace, he clenched his fist and extended a shaking arm. "I'll be honored to have you as an official member of the family."

Jess pounded her fist into his. "Thanks, Pop."

CHAPTER FORTY-SEVEN

I considered myself a damned good cook. My grandmother on my father's side grew up in the south. Her cooking was a reflection of it. She taught me how to cook as a child. My mother, who learned to cook from my father's mother and her mother, was a fabulous cook. She, too, taught me to cook.

Jessica's cooking put mine to shame. She took pride in everything her hands touched, and the food she prepared was indicative of that trait.

When asked what we needed to bring for Thanksgiving dinner, my mother replied *pecan pies*. I was thrilled. Pecan pie was not only my favorite Thanksgiving Day treat, it was also my son Derek's.

Jess had already won the heart of my daughter, but the older boys were different. Much different. They were respectful to her, but the love my daughter expressed wasn't matched by her two younger brothers.

Jessica's homemade pies were going to win their hearts, and their stomachs. I was sure of it. On Thanksgiving morning, Jess did her magic. When she removed the pies from the oven, her heart sank.

"They're like pie soup," she said.

Inexperienced at pie preparation, I stared at the watery concoction. They looked perfect. The consistency, however, was comparable to my mother's clam chowder.

I poked a pecan with the tip of my finger and submerged it in the syrup. "I'm sure they'll be fine when they cool."

Holding the pie tin with oven mitts, she shook it from side-to-side. "They're like Jello."

"Maybe cook them a little longer?"

Jess agreed. She cooked them until they were on the verge of bursting into flames. When she removed them from the oven, the pecans were blackened. Yet. They were still soupy. We dismissed it as a fluke and took them to the dinner, nonetheless.

"I just wanted to make the boys happy," she said during the trip.

"Derek will still eat it. Alec? Probably not. He's a lot like his father. He'll see it as being different. He hates change."

"I know," Jess said. "That's what worries me."

We ate Thanksgiving dinner with my father, mother, brother, sister, and their respective spouses. My three older children weren't in attendance for dinner, as they ate with their mother that year. They did make it for dessert, though.

Nervous, Jess cut the pies. Kind of. As much as one can cut soup, that is. Derek devoured the pie, claiming that it tasted as good as any he'd ever eaten, despite the consistency. Alec, on the other hand, took one bite and decided he was too full to continue.

Jess didn't say it, but I was sure she was devastated.

She had been accepted by the three worlds in which I lived. She hadn't, however, been accepted by the three children I fathered prior to meeting her. Until that happened, I felt our lives would be incomplete.

We sat in the breakfast nook and talked with the three older children about college, graduating high school, and about life. When the evening was over, Erin, Alec and Derek made their rounds, hugging everyone before they left.

Erin and Derek hugged Jess.

Alec did not.

He simply bypassed her.

I told myself it was unintentional. I didn't say anything at that moment about it, nor did I mention it later. I hoped Jess didn't realize it had happened. In a family that passes out hugs the way most families pass the potatoes, I was sure she did, though.

During the thirty-mile drive home that evening, she gazed out the side window of the Jeep. The rural area was primarily fields of hay or crops of some sort. It certainly wasn't anything interesting enough to stare at.

With her eyes fixed on the fields of nothing, she spoke.

"Alec didn't hug me."

"He didn't?" I asked, although I knew the answer.

"No."

Alec was six-foot-six. Compared to Jess, who stood five-foot-two, he was a giant.

"He probably didn't see you," I said jokingly.

She faced me. "Derek hugged me. He's almost as tall as Alec."

She was right. Derek was almost six-foot-five at the time. "I don't know, Baby. I'm sure it was an oversight."

She tried to smile but couldn't. Her gaze went back to the fields of grass that filled the northern horizon.

We never spoke about what she was thinking that evening. We didn't have to.

I knew.

My oldest son was a mirror image of me. No one could tell him what to do. His temper had the ability to place him on the verge of lunacy. He was stubborn. He was set in his ways. He detested change. Lastly, he didn't trust women.

At all.

I hoped in time he'd somehow find a way to trust Jess. When that day came – if it came – I prayed that his acceptance of her soon followed.

CHAPTER FORTY-EIGHT

Despite Jess' hatred toward cats, we'd adopted two from the Humane Society, Chuck and Taylor. Chuck's decision to piss on Jessica every night while we slept earned him a trip back to the shelter.

Taylor spent her days sleeping in my lap while I worked, often remaining motionless for four or five hours at a time.

When Christmas came, everything changed.

"Do cats always act like this?" Jess asked.

Taylor was mid-tree, slapping at a Christmas ornament.

"Pretty much," I said.

"Cats are dumb."

It was our first Christmas together as a family. On Christmas morning, when the kids awoke, visions of my childhood promptly returned. Landon and Lily ran to the tree, surprised to see there were more gifts under the tree than the previous night when they went to bed.

"Santa came!" Landon shouted.

Lily, as always, agreed in the form of a toothy grin. Like her mother, she spoke very little and wore her emotions on her shirt sleeves.

Sitting side by side so close that we were touching, Jess and I sat and sipped coffee while the children opened their gifts. Then, we opened ours. The excitement in Jessica's eyes that came with each present she opened was more rewarding than I ever imagined.

After the gifts had all been opened, Taylor played with the pieces of wrapping paper while we prepared for the trip to my parent's house.

A second Christmas was enjoyed with my family. The joy on my mother and father's faces as they witnessed Landon and Lily open their gifts was rewarding. I looked around the room. Scattered about, amidst the gifts, my family surrounded me. I'd made great strides in my recovery from incarceration in the past five years, and proof of it surrounded me.

Alec played with Landon in the back yard, showing him how to properly throw a football. In the past, he hadn't so much as acknowledged Landon's presence. Having an older brother meant the world to Landon. Having another younger brother didn't seem to appeal to Alec at all. At least not until that day.

I sat alone, watching them play together for a long time. I feared joining my family in the other room would cause the development I was witnessing to cease. Derek soon joined them, and the three boys played catch together as brothers would.

Alec and Derek were both fabulous athletes. They played football, basketball, and ran in track.

As a child, I viewed sports as nothing but another means for someone to tell me what to do. I also despised failure. If I was part of a team, and the team failed, I failed. Regardless of my effort or devotion, I would have to accept that failure as mine. Succeeding at everything was my goal. An unrealistic goal, but a goal, nonetheless.

As a result of these personal beliefs and deficiencies, I never participated in sports.

Furthermore, I grew up with no desire to watch them on

television. Short of the bits and pieces I'd seen by accident while my father watched, I'd never seen a professional football game or basketball game. I had no desire for that to change.

Short of their school games, I avoided sports entirely.

In retrospect, I believed my lack of interest disappointed my sons. They never said so, but they really didn't have to. To love something as much as they did, and not have their father share that love would be difficult.

As I watched them play, I filled with resentment for not being more flexible in my beliefs. As that bitterness came to a head, I opened the sliding glass door and walked outside.

"Dad," Landon shouted. "Are you going to play?"

Landon and Lily had been calling me dad for some time. I wondered how Alec and Derek would accept it. I mentally cringed as I walked to their side.

"Sure," I said. "I'll play."

My mother didn't get her white Christmas that year. The weather was unseasonably warm that day, setting an all-time record high. As we tossed the ball back and forth in the warm Christmas sun, I decided that God wanted to give the gift of sunshine that year.

Eventually, we agreed to go in and have another helping of Christmas dinner. Landon and Derek walked side by side, tossing the ball back and forth.

Alec sauntered toward the door at my side.

"The kids never really had a dad, did they?" he asked.

"No. Not really. He was a turd. He's got half a dozen with three or four different women. Doesn't care about any of them."

"You going to adopt them?" he asked.

Jess and I had discussed it. We'd talked to an attorney and were getting our things in order, so I could do just that. Surprised, that he asked, I looked at him.

"I'm planning on it."

He nodded and gave me a pat on the shoulder. "Good."

Alec was a man of very few words. What he did say, he meant with all his heart.

"I think it'll be good for all of us," I said.

I realized, after I spoke, that *all of us* included him. I took a few hesitant steps and waited for him to respond.

"Having another brother and sister is kinda cool," he said.

He didn't say it *would be* cool, he said it *was*.

Fighting back tears, I acknowledged his statement. "I love you, Son."

He patted me on the shoulder. "Love you, Pop."

We stayed that day until the older kids had to go. Before they left, we announced that a decision had been made regarding our marriage.

In complete contrast to Jessica's mother suggesting that we get married on December thirteenth, we opted to choose February fourteenth as our wedding day. Her mother believed marrying on 12-13-14 would be cute.

I never believed much in gimmicks and wanted our relationship to succeed based on love, not a quirky date. We couldn't think of any other day that commemorated love more than Valentine's Day, so that day was chosen.

We also decided to do it alone. In Las Vegas.

With my arm around Jess, I made the announcement. "We're getting married on February fourteenth. Valentine's Day. And, we're doing it in Vegas."

"Jesus H. Christ," my father spat.

"David Wilson Hildreth!" my mother shouted.

"That's great," she said. "I'm glad you've decided on a date. It'll be easy to remember your anniversary."

"You going to have Elvis do it?" my father asked.

"No," Jessica said. "We've got it scheduled at a church."

"You're actually going to a church?" my father asked, his tone reflecting slight interest.

"Yeah, kind of. It's a church in the casino," she said.

He rolled his eyes.

The older kids congratulated us, and then made their rounds, hugging everyone goodbye. Alec, once again, missed Jessica somehow.

I had to acknowledge his expressed acceptance of the children, and I did so. Mentally. His lack of acceptance of Jessica, willing or not, was crushing me.

The look in Jessica's eyes as they drove away confirmed it was crushing her, too.

CHAPTER FORTY-NINE

Jessica's salon was having a late Christmas party. I doubted I'd have much fun attending a gathering with twenty people I didn't really know. Hoping to extend the love and warmth of the Holiday season for one more week beyond New Year, I reluctantly agreed to go.

"Why did they postpone it for two weeks?" I asked.

"She had to. All the bars were scheduled out with Christmas parties and New Year's Eve stuff until the second week of January," she said. "She forgot to schedule it until mid-December."

I'd known about the party for a month and had dreaded its arrival. "You're sure it's okay that I dress like this?"

"She's having everyone dress down this year. She thinks it'll let everyone cut loose or whatever."

I pulled on my Chucks. "Suits me."

After the babysitter arrived, we walked across the street to the bar where the party was to be held. It was Saturday night. As always on the weekends, the bar was packed. The establishment, *The Pump House*, was an old gas station that had been converted to a bar.

Our MC often met there, and it was one of the few places I felt comfortable going. Crowds of people I didn't know had always made me anxious. If I was in a place where I felt comfortable, however, I could somehow manage to relax.

Pleased that the party was being held in a familiar location, I opened the door and guided Jessica inside. After she passed through the door, she paused.

She took position at my left side, gripped my arm in her hand, and smiled. "Let's go."

The bar's entrance gave no view to the inside of the establishment. A short corridor hid the patrons entirely. As we walked down the hallway, I imagined a night of Jessica drinking with her co-workers while I repeatedly told them why I chose to refrain from partaking in liquor.

The scene would be slightly uncomfortable for me. Not terrible, but I'd be uneasy. I was sure of it. While the sound of R.L. Burnside's *Someday Baby* blared over the sound system, I clenched my jaw and stepped around the corner.

A hundred feet in the distance, I saw Teddy.

I envisioned spending the evening sneaking away from the party and mingling with him while Jessica drank wine with the owner of the salon.

"Shit," I said. "Teddy's dumb ass is back there in the back."

"I'll be darned," Jess said.

"Where are we meeting them," I asked.

"In the back. Around the corner."

We took a few steps toward the rear of the bar. King came into view. Seated beside Teddy, he looked up and grinned a slight smile. At his side, Basher sat.

I began to fill with rage. The MC was having a gathering that I knew nothing of. After a few more steps, I saw Mainline. I looked at Jess.

"Shit," I said. "Someone's having a fucking party."

My brother came into view. Then, an old friend from school. My head spun. Something was happening, and the sight of it was confusing me. It was a gathering of people who I knew, admired, and loved, but it didn't include me.

Disappointed, I took a few reluctant steps.

Teddy stood.

"What's going on, shit-head?" I asked in Teddy's direction.

He returned an awkward grin.

I paused and surveyed the group. *What the fuck is going on*, I thought.

"Surprise!" Jessica said. "Happy fiftieth Birthday. I love you."

It took a moment for what she said to register. When it did, I wasn't very happy. Anger slowly replaced the disappointment.

As an adult, I chose not to recognize my birthdays. Having a party to celebrate being one year closer to death seemed ridiculous to me. So, I prohibited it. If anyone knew my hatred toward birthdays, Jessica knew.

So did Teddy.

My brother did as well.

I glanced up and down the length of the tables. Dozens of people, all of which I knew, and knew well, were seated side by side.

"Happy birthday, motherfucker," many of them said.

I looked at Jess.

She flashed a half-assed smile. "I hope it's okay. It's your fiftieth. It's a big deal."

"You did this?"

She bit against her lower lip and grinned. "I did."

The anger vanished. Affection and adoration replaced it.

"I love you," I said.

She kissed me. "I love you, too."

I couldn't have said when the last time was that I had a birthday party, but I suspected it was in my teens.

I spent that night with the fellas, old friends, family, and the woman I loved, telling stories, listening to lies, and reliving events of my past. When it ended, I had to admit to myself – and to Jessica – that it was the best birthday I'd ever had.

That night, I realized her love for me wasn't simply a word that was spoken.

Her love was true.

I'd never experienced the depth and honesty of the love Jessica felt for me. Filled with comfort to the point I feared I'd burst, I fell asleep that night with her held tightly in my arms.

I prayed that night that the few remaining pieces of our life's puzzle would one day snap firmly into place.

CHAPTER FIFTY

I started writing a new series, intending to make it a six-book installment. The *Selected Sinners MC Series* took place in a rural Kansas town, and was based on the lives of the members of a motorcycle club. The men in the club would all share some of the same characteristics that made my character Mike Ripton popular.

They would seek vengeance when someone committed an act that either couldn't or wouldn't be punished by the judicial system.

The first book, *Making the Cut*, did extremely well, surpassing my previous books in sales. The series would go on to win two Amazon Kindle All-Star Awards and provide me with several paid bonuses from Amazon. Thrilled at the performance of the first installment of the new series, I was eager to begin writing the second book.

My work schedule was often a matter of contention between us. I worked seven days a week, from five or six am until ten o'clock at night. I often lost track of what month it was, and rarely knew what day of the week it was. I had always been somewhat of a workaholic and being self-employed made matters measurably worse.

The only time off that I took from writing was the morning after I published a book. Jess and I would go to a small diner across the street and have a celebratory breakfast. It soon became a tradition. Jessica had fun with it, often posting photos on Facebook of the food we'd chosen or a silly pose of both of us over our empty plates.

Eager to get the second book out, I went to work immediately following the traditional breakfast. Jessica complained, wanting me to spend time with her while the children were in preschool.

I explained that I couldn't. The success of my new series was something that we, as a family, needed. If we intended to move into a place more suitable for a family, the additional income was instrumental to our being able to do so. In the wake of *Sons of Anarchy's* television series ending, it seemed women had a void in their lives that only motorcycle clubs could fill. I intended to fill that void with my books. *Capitalizing on the opportunity*, I explained.

I wrote for the next month, barely taking time to sleep. Upon completing the second book, *Taking the Heat*, I sent it to Amazon for review before publication.

"When are you going to pack?" Jessica asked. "Tonight, or tomorrow morning?"

I looked up from my computer's screen. "Huh?"

"We're going to Vegas tomorrow. To get married."

"Oh. I was going to pack in the morning."

If she hadn't reminded me, I wouldn't have known the day arrived. I fell asleep that night, exhausted from the sixty days I'd worked without a break.

The next morning, we drove the children to St. Louis. I met her mother at the door with a big hug. At that point, I'd been in her company no less than three or four times, each of which began and ended with a hug.

As we ate with her family that night, her mother asked what I was writing. I nearly fainted. Apparently, forcing myself upon her had worked. She'd done just as I predicted. She found a way to accept me.

I responded with an abbreviated version of the truth, explaining that I was writing a series about men who rode motorcycles. I purposely left out the violence and the fact they were all well-endowed.

After giving Lisa a departing hug the next morning, Jessica and I flew to Las Vegas. I was excited for us both. It was Jessica's first trip to Las Vegas, and I knew she'd enjoy the endless shopping the city of sin offered. I looked forward to the week-long vacation.

The new book was released while we unpacked our things at the hotel. We announced through social media that the book was available, and later enjoyed a nice dinner together.

Jess spent the next three days in awe of everything Las Vegas had to offer. We shopped. We ate. We shopped. We ate. We gambled. We ate. We shopped some more. We didn't, however, take time to make love.

When Saturday arrived, we got dressed for the wedding. She wore an ivory wedding dress, and I wore a tuxedo, sans the dress shoes.

Chucks seemed much more appropriate.

In my mind, I'd married Jessica long before that day. At least that's what I told myself. The ceremony did one thing, though. It solidified my relationship with her. We were now bound by vows, a contract on paper, and an agreement with God. I knew in my heart of hearts that she took the oath as seriously as I did.

Finally, Jessica was mine forever. I had a wedding ring to prove it.

We paraded through the casino, opting to eat wedding night sushi. I held my head high everywhere we went, proud that she was mine, and that I was hers. When the night ended, we returned to the comfort of our hotel room and did what we didn't seem to have time to do over the previous two months.

We made love.

It was different that night. Be it that we hadn't done so in months, or that it was our wedding night, I don't know. I did know, however that it was special. A change had taken place. A significant one.

The next morning, Jessica agreed. Something was special about it.

It simply felt perfect.

With magic in our eyes and smiles on our faces, we ate and shopped our way through the next two days of our vacation.

Beaming with newlywed pride, we returned to St. Louis. We were greeted by her parents with balloons, streamers, and some fabulous homemade cooking. After a few days of visiting, we returned home.

Within hours of our return, I was pounding away at book number three of the series. Despite the changes we'd made in our lives during the previous week, some things, I decided, simply weren't destined to change.

CHAPTER FIFTY-ONE

Immersed in my work, the next two weeks passed without realization. While struggling one morning with a difficult scene in the upcoming book, the phone rang. Aggravated, I reached for it. Much to my surprise, it was Jessica.

"When will you be at a stopping point?" she asked.

"Two weeks. Maybe three."

"Have you got a minute?"

"Sure."

"I uhhm. I took. I'm," she stammered. "I'm pregnant."

I leaped from my stool. "I figured you were," I blurted.

"What do you mean?" she snapped back. "That's your response? *I figured you were?*"

"I've been thinking you were," I said excitedly. "For the last week. It's a wedding night baby."

"Why do you say that?"

"Do the math, genius," I said jokingly. "We've only boned once in the last two months."

"I think I'm much more pregnant than that. Either that, or this one is going to be twins, or something. I'm exhausted."

She'd done nothing but sleep since our return from Las Vegas. She was also short-tempered and moody. The changes in her had me hoping she was pregnant. I had a gut feeling she was, and that the baby was conceived on our wedding night.

"Let's go to the doctor and find out," I said. "My bet is that we conceived on February fourteenth."

"Okay. I'll see you when I get home."

"I love you," I said.

"I love you, too."

The elation we'd both exhibited a year earlier was missing. I was still on my heels from our previous loss and couldn't fathom going through the same thing all over again. I had little expectation that I could live through losing another child. I doubted Jessica could, either.

Nonetheless, I was hopeful.

We spent the next two weeks joyous one moment, and fearful the next. Waiting for the axe to one day fall, we sat on pins and needles, hoping for the best, but expecting the worst. Four weeks into the pregnancy, Jess made a doctor's appointment.

Our visit to the doctor confirmed my suspicions.

Our week-long trip to the city that never sleeps allowed us to shoehorn many activities, shows, meals, sights, and events into our schedule. It only afforded us one opportunity, however, to make love.

Our wedding night.

Upon receiving the confirmation from the doctor regarding the day of conception, I clenched my fist and held it over Jess' lap.

She rapped her knuckles into mine.

The doctor grinned. "What was that about?"

"Wedding night baby," Jess said.

"That's awesome," the doctor said.

"What about the baby's health?" I asked anxiously. "Is she healthy?"

"You don't know it's a girl," Jess said.

I arched an eyebrow at Jess, and then looked at the doctor. "What about the baby's health?"

"Everything looks fine right now, but it's way too early to tell."

We explained the miscarriage we'd experienced. The doctor expressed her condolences but offered nothing to comfort us in the way of assurances that this baby would be any different than our last.

I begged for a sonogram. The doctor refused. She then placed a device on Jessica's stomach, which produced an audible heartbeat.

Hearing it was enough to convince me that this time was going to be different. There was nothing to support my belief, but somehow, I *knew*.

Two weeks later, contrary to Jessica's requests, I posted a picture of her on Facebook, and included a hashtag with the photo.

#babymomma

The book world went wild.

"What if--" Jessica began.

I pressed my index finger to her lips. "It's going to be just fine."

Having told my fans and followers, we had no choice but to tell our families. We told her parents by phone, and then made the trip to my parent's house on the following Sunday. After taking our position in the usual places, we made the announcement.

"Mother!" I shouted. "We've got an announcement."

She glanced to her side. "Okay."

"Are you listening, Pop?"

"Like Dumbo the elephant," he said. "I'm all ears."

"Jessica's pregnant," I said. "We're going to have a baby."

"Oh," my mother said. "I already knew that."

I looked back at her in complete shock. "What?"

"I had a dream. Last Wednesday. I told your father." She glanced at my father. "When was it, Dave?"

He rolled his eyes. "Wednesday."

She grinned, and then rubbed Jessica's shoulder. "I'm so happy for you."

My mother claimed to be clairvoyant. I never disputed her

claims. She had several circumstances over the years that were inarguable.

My father cleared his throat, commanding our attention in doing so. As Jess and I both met his gaze, he smiled. "Congratulations."

"It's a wedding night baby," I said.

"Gave her the wedding night dick, did ya?" he said with a laugh.

"David Wilson Hildreth!" my mother shouted.

He chuckled. "She always hears the bad, and never hears the good."

A few days later, I told the older children. Erin was excited to the point of coming home from college, and Derek was excited about having a baby brother. Alec gave congratulatory comments to us both, but his sincerity seemed lacking.

I couldn't help but wonder if the animosity it seemed Alec felt was a result of Landon, Lily, and the new baby getting what he felt he was cheated out of when I went to prison. Before I left, we were inseparable. After I returned, he never quite had the time to spend with me that he once did. Initially, I dismissed it, assuming it would change in time.

Based on his actions, I wondered if time had the capacity to heal *all* wounds. As Jess progressed through the pregnancy, I prayed for two things.

Acceptance from my eldest son, and the baby's health.

If I could somehow obtain those two things, my life – and Jessica's – would be nothing short of perfection.

CHAPTER FIFTY-TWO

With the first trimester over, and no complications noted by the doctor or Jessica, we loaded the kids in the Jeep and headed for Disneyland. I found the twelve-hundred-mile trip relaxing. I'd been on the exact same route no less than a dozen times as a child. At the end of each trip, I always returned to the coast. This time, I'd be returning to the Midwest.

If I had my way, I'd only be returning there once. I intended to talk Jessica into moving to California. Working from home afforded me an opportunity to work from anywhere. Kansas had changed drastically since my childhood. The Midwest now manufactured more methamphetamines than anywhere in the United States.

I looked at things no differently than my father did forty years prior. Distancing my children from the drugs and crime that plagued the Midwest was my main concern. Providing them with an education, doing my best to separate them from drugs, and minimizing their exposure to crime was my responsibility as a father.

As we entered California, the weather forecast changed. Los Angeles was being drenched by rain. We chose to stop in Palm

Springs, a city in the desert southwest of the Joshua Tree National Park.

We enjoyed time at the swimming pool, sunbathing, and seeing the sights the surrounding desert had to offer. While driving through the city, I pointed out several homes I'd found online that were for sale.

Each got the same response. *I don't like it here. There's no beach.*

Her response, in many respects, was perfect. Certain that once we were in Los Angeles Jess would see things differently, I waited for the weather to change. In a week, it did. We packed up our belongings and headed to Los Angeles.

Jessica's anxiety hit an all-time high when exposed to the LA traffic. The ninety mile-an-hour bumper-to-bumper traffic was more than she could handle. Before I had a chance to ask, she made clear her thoughts.

"I hate this place," she complained. "This traffic is dumb."

She was right. The traffic in LA was dumb. After our Disneyland vacation, I planned on going to San Diego. I wanted to show Jessica and the children where I played as a child. Mission Beach's Belmont Park, Point Loma, Balboa Park, the San Diego Zoo, and Sea World were on the list of places to go. I hoped her opinion of California changed once we were out of LA's traffic and away from their fast-paced lifestyle.

The children found Disneyland fascinating. It didn't seem as enchanting to me as it did when I was a child. I found myself wondering if an adult's eyes saw things differently than a child's. I wondered if my father saw the park the same way when he took us through it when we children.

One of the many sacrifices, I decided, that a father makes for his children. I feigned excitement as we went from ride to ride and from park to park. After two days, I was exhausted. I longed to return to what I had always considered my home town, San Diego.

On our way to San Diego, we stopped in Huntington Beach to meet someone who saw our trip's route on Facebook and wanted to meet us. Then, we drove to San Clemente and met with my niece, and her boyfriend.

The drive along California's Pacific Coastal Highway was breathtaking. For a few hours' time, Jess and the kids had a view of California's coast that could only be obtained along the PCH.

When we arrived at the hotel I'd chosen online, it was late that night. It was so disgusting that I didn't allow the children to take their shoes off. After a thorough inspection, I demanded that they sleep on top of the comforter.

Our introduction to San Diego wasn't off to a good start.

The next day, we drove to a resort in Mission Beach. We stayed in a room that was mere feet from the beach. The children went wild with excitement. Later, when asked what their favorite part of the trip was, they would respond, *the beach.*

We went to Point Loma and peered out at the ocean. We hiked trails along La Jolla's cliffs. The kids spent all day at Belmont Park, riding rides and eating oversized ice cream cones. They spent every evening playing in the sand on their own personal beach.

We stayed two weeks in San Diego, enjoying everything the city had to offer. At the end of it all, I asked the question.

"Do you think you'd want to live here?"

Her response was immediate.

"No."

"Why?" I asked.

"I don't like the traffic. It gives me anxiety."

We returned home from the month-long trip with the children elated, Jessica exhausted, and me feeling slightly disappointed.

That disappointment, however, didn't last long. Four weeks, to be exact.

CHAPTER FIFTY-THREE

Filled with anxious energy, I watched as the doctor rubbed the jelly-like substance on Jessica's stomach. After untangling the cord to the hand-held scanner, she glanced at the monitor.

"Are you ready?"

"I've got questions," I said.

The doctor paused. "Yes?"

I folded my hands in my lap and gave her an intent look. "What are the chances this thing doesn't work?"

"The equipment?" she asked.

"No," I said. "The test."

She looked at me like I'd asked her to kick-start a Harley. "I'm not sure what you're asking."

"You're going to look at the monitor, and then tell us your belief regarding this baby's sex. Correct?"

"Yes."

"Is it an opinion, or is it fact?"

"Scott," Jessica said, drawing my name out for three seconds longer that it normally took to pronounce it.

I glanced at Jess and then met the doctor's gaze. "Let her answer the question, Jess."

"It would be the opinion of a trained medical professional."

"An opinion. Not fact?"

"That is correct."

"I don't want an opinion, Doc. I want facts."

"Scott," Jessica repeated.

"Let me take a look, and we'll go from there," the doctor said. "How's that?"

"If you know, say something. If you don't, just keep your mouth shut."

She looked at Jess. "Is he always like this?"

"I'm afraid so," Jess responded.

A few minutes later the image of a perfectly healthy-looking baby was on the screen. I counted the fingers. *Ten*. The toes. *Ten*. From my vantage point, everything seemed to be perfect.

The doctor grinned. "Are you sure you want to know?"

Jess nodded eagerly.

"Only if you're spewing facts, Doc," I said.

"You're going to have a little girl."

I leaped from my seat and thrust my hand in the air. "Yes!"

Jess nearly jumped from the examination table. "Be quiet, Scott. We're in a doctor's office."

"It's not a library." I looked at the doctor. "Are you sure."

"Positive." She lifted her brows. "I'm guessing you wanted a girl?"

"I want two of them. Any chance there's twins in there?"

She shook her head. "I'm afraid not."

I had a gut feeling we were going to have twins, and so far, my gut feelings were one hundred percent accurate.

"Bullshit," I said. "I want a second opinion."

"Does he ever stop?" The doctor asked.

"When he goes to sleep," Jess responded.

I was on cloud nine. We were over halfway to the finish line, and everyone was healthy. The baby's size was above average. Jessica's weight was exactly where they wanted it to be. Other than Jess' constant craving for ice cream bars and grilled cheese sandwiches, everything about her was normal.

As normal as an estrogen-filled pregnant woman could be, that is.

We announced to our family, and to my followers that the baby was a girl. A few days later, as I worked on the next installment in the *Selected Sinners MC Romance* series, *Otis*, a knock came at the door.

BAM!

It wasn't a cop, I knew that much.

Jess answered the door.

"Who was it?"

The UPS man.

"What'd he bring?" I asked over my shoulder.

She lifted a cardboard box and raised her eyebrows at the same time. "I don't know."

We opened the box and found a quilt inside that one of my readers had hand-fashioned. Thrilled at the thought of a fan sending a gift for our baby, we thanked her in a private message, and then posted a photo of the gorgeous gift.

Two days later, the same knock came at the door.

Two more boxes arrived.

A knit monkey cap, and a sweater.

The next day, another box. The day after that, three or four more. Over the next three months, we received no less that one delivery a day, five days a week, that were gifts for our baby.

All from people who had befriended us on Facebook.

Clothes, hats, dresses, skirts, diapers, mittens, boots, shoes, blankets, rattles, pacifiers, silverware, cups, mobiles, toys. If we were going to need it, it eventually arrived.

I released *Otis*. The character was modeled after Big O. He and his respective other fell in love in high school. After he expressed his desire to maintain a single life, she left him and moved to another state. Ten years later, she returned for a funeral, and their relationship was immediately rekindled.

The book outsold every book I'd written to date. At the time, I'd written roughly a dozen. The book broke through the top one hundred books on Amazon, regardless of genre, and it didn't stop there. After breaking into the top fifty, the literary agent I'd spoken to on numerous occasions called.

She explained how my writing – and stories – had improved since Jessica and I began our relationship. I told her Jessica was all the inspiration I needed to write meaningful love stories.

She asked that I write a mafia book for an editor at Random House who had been nagging at her for one. She explained how going mainstream with my work would benefit me in the long run.

I agreed to do it. A few weeks later, we signed a contract.

I was officially represented by an agent.

Two weeks later, while I was at Alec's football game, she called. Amazon wanted to buy the audio rights to the entire Selected Sinners MC Romance Series.

Two weeks after that, we agreed on a price. After reaching the agreement, Jess and I had a talk. It was time for us to move out of the loft, and into a home. A place where the kids could play. A place where our new daughter could grow up with a bicycle, a scooter, and the ability to go outside and play in the grass.

If Jessica wasn't willing to move to Southern California, a home in Kansas would suffice, I decided. We enrolled Landon in a magnet school, and he was accepted. Then, we decided to move into the district where the school was located.

All we needed to do was find the perfect place.

CHAPTER FIFTY-FOUR

Despite appearing to be an idiot on the surface, Teddy was an intelligent man. Extremely intelligent. He simply didn't speak much to anyone other than me, and most mistook his quiet nature as idiocy.

They were wrong.

He attended a private Christian school as a child and continued attending such schools through high school. During middle school, he fell hard and fast for a yellow-haired girl who rode the bus with him. They played together, giggled as pre-teens often do, and eventually shared a seat on the daily bus ride to school.

She would be the first female he would ever buy a flower for.

In time, the puppy love turned to adoration. The adoration matured as they grew older, and they eventually fell in love with one another.

Head over heels for the girl with the golden locks, Teddy's days and nights were filled with thoughts of growing old with her, and of having a life that mirrored that of his parents.

His parents were as old-school as old-school could be. Sunday dinners of chicken-fried steak and potatoes, church service, and speeches declaring the value of the almighty dollar were commonplace in the home Teddy grew up in.

Being a single child, he got his fair share of each parent's attention. He ended up with his mother's empathy and compassion, and his father's work ethic. His frugality was self-taught.

What he didn't, however, end up with was the yellow-haired girl.

One day, on the bus ride to school, Teddy rode alone. Heartbroken, he simply waited for the next day, knowing the love of his life would return. But, she never did. Teddy would find out years later what happened – but talk around the school was that her parents moved away on a moment's notice.

She may have been gone, but Teddy's love for her remained. The depth of that love allowed him to live through each day without succumbing to the offers from the women who found him to be the sweet and respectful young man that his mother so proudly taught him to be.

We peered out the window of the loft, knowing it would be our last summer in the downtown area. The street was lined with modified cars, hotrods, custom show bikes, and vintage junk. Wichita's summer car show, *Automobilia,* attracted tens of thousands of people, and hundreds upon hundreds of cars.

Teddy, in addition to being an authority on motorcycles, was a walking, talking encyclopedia on all things cars.

"Let's go have a look," he said. "Last time we'll have a chance to walk down there."

The show dragged on for miles in three directions. The street beneath the loft was only the beginning. To walk the show, entirely, would take hours. With slight reluctance, I agreed.

We got on the elevator and rode down to the first floor. Side by side, we walked to the front door. As soon as I opened it, Teddy's jaw flopped open.

He took his glasses off, wiped them, and then put them back on. "Heather?" he said, his voice laced with a hint of hope.

A yellow-haired girl stood on the center of the sidewalk admiring an old pickup truck. She wore pigtails, and a sleeveless sweater. Upon hearing Teddy's voice, she spun in a half-circle. When her eyes met Teddy's, they went as wide as the saucers Teddy's mother served him dinner with.

She took long strides toward Teddy with open arms. Teddy, in turn, did the same. They met fifteen feet from where I stood, all but knocking each other down when they made contact.

He lifted her from her feet and twirled her in a circle.

She babbled an explanation of years ago, when her mother pulled her from school, and how she yearned to one day find Teddy, but that she couldn't due to circumstances that prevented her from it.

Back then, there weren't cell phones. In the absence of the internet and Google, a phone book was the only way to find someone's telephone number. Some people preferred privacy and had numbers that weren't listed in such books.

Teddy's parents were such people.

Fate, on that day, brought Teddy back together with the girl he bought the flower for.

I learned that night that she still had the flower. She kept it for over twenty years, pressed in a book filled with her life's hope and dreams.

My opinion on fate changed that night. I knew in my heart of hearts that it wasn't simply blind luck that brought those two lost souls back together.

When the night ended, Teddy confirmed his thoughts mirrored mine. The man of few words that he was, he simply looked at me and grinned a cheesy grin while he unknowingly stroked his beard. Then, he spoke.

"God provides to those who wait."

CHAPTER FIFTY-FIVE

The last load of furniture was on its way to the new home. I peered into the empty loft. I'd lived there for six years. It was my belief that the unique housing situation shielded me from the government's watchful eye and provided me tremendous comfort.

It was a comfort I no longer needed.

Somehow, the government, prison, and the ATF had become nothing but another of my life's experiences. An experience I was now grateful to have been exposed to. That series of events, over time, formed me into the man I'd become.

That man stood proud of who he was.

I took one last look, pausing at the massive marble desk where I'd penned over twenty novels. One of the fellas and I built it in place, permanently attaching it to the concrete beneath the wall of windows.

I wondered if I could write anywhere else, or if the magic of my craft was derived through the windows that gave me an unobstructed view of the world below.

I prayed that it was my mind, and not my mind's location, that provided the inspiration.

On the heels of that prayer, I closed the door one last time.

CHAPTER FIFTY-SIX

Landon's sixth birthday fell on a Thursday that year. We planned a birthday party for the Saturday following his birthday. We knew my parents would have a party for him on Sunday, so the gathering at our home was more for our family to celebrate the occasion. I let the older children know with a text message more as a matter of respect than due to any expectation of them attending.

Erin was a sophomore at Kansas State University. Alec was a freshman, playing basketball on a scholarship. Derek was a senior in high school, preparing for college, and maintaining his perfect GPA.

I prepared myself for the fact that none of them could – or would – attend. Realistically, I couldn't expect them to.

Eight months pregnant, and looking like she was carrying twins, Jess strung crepe paper streamers over the doorways. Balloons dangling from every archway followed. As Landon and Lily played around the lake that backed up to our new home, Jess waddled to the edge of the dining room and admired her handiwork.

"Looks good, Baby," I said.

"When should we call them in?" she asked.

I looked at my watch. "One?"

"What time is it?"

"Fifteen 'till."

"Okay."

A knock at the door surprised me. I knew Teddy and Heather would stop by, but we weren't expecting them until dinnertime. Since being reunited, they hadn't been away from one another for a single moment.

I looked at Jess, shrugged, and walked to the door. Opening it revealed two extremely tall men, and one smiling woman.

I stepped aside. "Come in."

My daughter hugged me and then yelled at Jess. "Oh my God. You're so cute."

"I'm huge," Jess complained. "Scott still says twins."

Derek grinned. "Where's Landon?"

"They're down at the lake."

Alec stepped through the door and patted me on the shoulder. "Afternoon, Pop."

"Good afternoon, Son."

He glanced around the house. "Nice digs."

"Thank you."

"Kids down at the lake?" he asked.

"They're playing down there, yeah."

"Come on, Dee," Alec said. "Let's go down there."

"I uhhm." The words got stuck in my throat. "I appreciate you guys making it."

Alec turned to face me. "It's my little brother's birthday. Wouldn't have missed it for the world."

Something as simple as a birthday party shouldn't have brought out so much emotion. That's what I told myself. Yet. As Alec and Derek walked down to the lake, I fought back tears. It wasn't an easy struggle. I had yet to cry since that day when I was twelve, and for whatever reason, it seemed I took pride in realizing it.

After we opened the gifts, Alec and Derek went down to the lake and played with the remote-controlled boat that Landon got for his birthday.

"I had one of these when I was your age," Alec said. "Dee and I each had one. We lived not too far from here."

"Oh really?" Landon asked.

Alec pointed toward the western sky. "Halfway to Starbucks. The house backed up to a lake, just like this."

It was the home I lived in when I was arrested. The children loved that home, and still talked about it regularly. I desperately tried to forget it. I found it strange that an object could bring such satisfaction to one, while causing another such grief.

The boys played for hours. Alec taught Landon a few tricks with the soccer ball. Football followed. Then, the fall sun set along the western horizon.

After another piece of cake and cup of coffee, the *big kids*, as Jess called them, announced their need to go.

Erin hugged Jess. "Can't wait."

Derek then hugged Jess and grinned. "I still think it's going to be a boy."

Alec patted me on the shoulder. "Nice seeing ya, Pop."

After he hugged me, he looked at Jess.

Jess waved.

He waved in return. "See ya, Jess."

The day's events made clear that as a family, we'd made progress. It wasn't perfection by any means, but we were getting close.

CHAPTER FIFTY-SEVEN

"We don't want to do a C-Section if we don't have to," the doctor said. "I need you to push one last time, Jess. Can you do that for me?"

The doctor decided to induce labor two weeks early. Her expectation, based on Jess' weight and size, was that the baby may weigh as much as twelve pounds. Still armed with the belief that we were having twins, I loomed over Jessica's right side while the doctor was wedged between her thighs.

Jess looked at me.

I extended my left hand. She took it in hers, met the doctor's gaze, and nodded.

The doctor counted down from five to one. "Push, push, push, push. Come on, Jess, you can do it. Push. One last time--"

There was no crowning. No peek of a head. No sight of hair.

Our daughter simply emerged.

The doctor lifted the baby for Jess to see. "Meet your baby girl."

"Charlee," Jess said in an exhaustive breath. "Her name's Charlee."

The doctor handed Jess our daughter. While our mothers peered over my shoulder and admired their granddaughter, I thanked God for trusting us with the gift of a healthy child.

Jessica's eyes met mine. We didn't speak. I doubt either of us could have. We simply shared a moment as she held our newborn daughter against her chest.

While the doctor stitched Jessica's perineal tear, I cleared my throat. "Put an extra stitch in that, would ya, Doc?"

"Scott!" Jessica snapped. "Stop it."

"When is it, exactly, that he sleeps?" the doctor asked with a laugh.

When the doctor finished her work, she stepped to Jessica's left side. "I need to get her cleaned up and weighed."

"Before you take her, Doc," I said. "I need something."

The doctor looked up.

I clenched my fist and extended my arm over Jessica and the baby. The doctor looked at my hand and then at Jess.

Jess grinned.

The doctor met my gaze, smiled, and then pounded her knuckles to mine.

CHAPTER FIFTY-EIGHT

With Landon and Lily trailing close behind, I carried the pies and Jessica carried our baby. Thanksgiving was once again upon us. In the year that had passed since the dessert debacle, Jessica mastered the art of baking the pecan-laden pies.

When we walked through the door, my father straightened his posture. "Scott's got the soup, and Jess has my granddaughter."

"It's not soup this time," Jess said.

He waved his hand in my direction. "I don't give a shit about that," he said. "I need to see Charlee."

Jess took the sleeping baby from the car seat and carried her to my father. After laying her in his waiting arms, she took a step back.

He scowled at her. "Go sit down. This isn't my first rodeo, you know."

He held her in his arms, rocking back and forth in the recliner that had all but become his home. He gazed at her with admiring eyes. A smile formed on his weathered face.

"A long time ago, in San Diego, California, your daddy was born," he said. "He was half your size. He was born three months early. He only weighed three pounds and three ounces. They told us he wasn't going to live. Ended up he was a fighter, just like his daddy."

He looked at Jess and grinned. "She's beautiful."

"Thank you."

The *big kids* arrived after dinner. The two boys ate a second meal, complaining the one they had previously wasn't quite enough to satisfy their appetites. While Erin held the baby and talked with Jess, the boys and I went outside and enjoyed the late fall sunshine.

Landon and Derek wandered into the center of the large yard and began playing catch.

Alec stood at my side, seeming reluctant to join them. After a few moments, he broke the silence.

"You ready to do this all over again?"

"Fatherhood?" I asked.

With his eyes still fixed on Landon and Derek, he nodded. "Raising kids again."

"I'm pretty excited about it, really," I said.

He looked at me, but he didn't speak. He didn't seem upset, nor was his face wearing an odd look. He did, however, seem willing to listen. I saw it as an opportunity. An opportunity I needed to take advantage of.

"You know, Son, I did what I did because I had to, not because I wanted to. I did my best to teach you and your brother right from wrong. To run toward the smoke and flames instead of running away from it. To help those incapable of helping themselves. To stand up when everyone else is afraid to. That old man in the recliner taught me the same thing. His father taught him. Your great-grandfather fought his way out of the trenches in World War I in a battle that may have played a part in changing that war. Imagine if he hadn't. What's right doesn't become wrong when the risk associated with standing up for it is great. I stood up for what was right. In doing so, I took the risk of losing my family and my freedom. I lost. When I lost, I lost you. I regret losing you, but I don't regret standing up."

I paused, exhaled a breath through my teeth, and looked at him. "I hope that makes sense."

He gave a sharp nod. "I'm proud of you, Pop."

Hearing him say that made me much prouder of him than he ever could have been of me. Sadly, he day turned into night, with Charlee being the point of interest for all who were in attendance. When it came time for everyone to leave, hugs were given.

Once again, Alec somehow managed to forget Jess.

With a wave of his hand as he backed out of the door. At the last moment, he acknowledged her. "See you at Christmas, Jess."

With Charlee cradled in her arms, she waved in return. "See you at Christmas."

I could have easily either asked Alec to hug Jess or I could have demanded it, playing the *I'm your father, and you're my son, therefore you'll do as I say* card.

Alec may not have always agreed with the decisions I made as a father, but he respected me. Respect is a two-way street. In the biker world, there's belief. To get respect, it must be given.

I was respecting Alec's decision. In time, all I could do was hope that he'd see the love Jess and I had for one another. In seeing it, I further hoped he'd realize she was an asset in my life, and in turn, in his.

No differently than his sister had.

As he drove away, I gave a mental nod. With it, came respect.

CHAPTER FIFTY-NINE

We enjoyed Christmas morning that year in our new home, and then celebrated it again at my parent's home. Afterward, we drove to St. Louis, and had a late Christmas with Jess' family. A New Year's party followed, and then we came home.

I grew a year older one day but didn't celebrate the occasion. I signed a contract with Harlequin Romance to produce a three-book series and turned the first book in for publication. Lily attended a private Christian school, while Landon attended his magnet school, which focused on technology.

Then, on one February day, the phone rang.

Surprised to see my mother calling early on a Saturday from her cell phone, I answered.

"Everything okay?"

"Well, not really. There's been an accident."

"Everyone alright?"

"Your father was making breakfast, and he dropped an egg," she said.

She seemed fairly calm, but then again, she was always calm.

"Want me to come clean it up?" I asked.

"I already did. He uhhm. Your father got mad when he dropped it. He went to kick it across the floor. His foot got mixed up in the yolk, and he slipped on the tile. You know how that kitchen floor is when it's wet."

My father's temper was no different than his father's temper. I inherited it from him, and Alec inherited it from me. Attempting to kick an egg across the kitchen floor seemed par for the course.

"Is he okay?" I asked.

"He's in the hospital, and he wants you to come get him out. They won't let him leave."

"How long's he been there?"

"Since yesterday."

"Why didn't you call?"

"You know how your father is. He's stubborn. He didn't want me to."

"What, exactly, is wrong with him?"

She sighed. "He's got a broken knee cap, a broken ankle, and a broken wrist. The knee is on one leg, and the ankle is on the other. He's going to be in a wheelchair."

"Fuck," I shouted. "Which hospital?"

"Susan B. Anthony."

"I'll be there in fifteen minutes."

"Don't speed."

"Be there in fifteen."

It was a thirty-minute drive at eighty miles an hour, which was the speed that could be driven on the highways in Kansas. In the BMW M5 that replaced my Craigslist SUV, it took fifteen.

In fifteen minutes I parked at the entrance of the hospital and stomped through the doors.

"You can't park there unless you're picking up a patient," the receptionist said.

"I'm picking up David Hildreth," I said. "Where is he?"

She studied the monitor for a moment, and then looked up. "One forty-six."

I didn't need to rely on room numbers to guide me to him, I could hear the sound of his voice when I entered the corridor.

"My Son's taking me out of this son-of-a-bitch, and I'm going home."

"Mister Hildreth, you aren't capable of operating a wheelchair," a voice said. "Furthermore, your heart cannot handle the stress associated with getting in and out--"

I stepped through the doorway.

"See," he said. "I told you. He's here to get me."

The doctor looked at me. "His kneecap is in four pieces. Once the swelling goes down, we'll perform the operation to repair it. His ulna is cracked, his collarbone is broken, his wrist is broken, and his ankle is broken. He's immobile. I'm sorry."

"What do you want to do, Pop?"

"Well," he growled. "I didn't have you drive your ass over here to gawk at me in the goddamned gown. Take me home, Son."

I looked at the doctor. "Sounds like we're leaving."

He shook his head. "I can't let you take him home."

"Is it against the law?" I asked.

His pursed lips gave all the response I needed.

"You can't stop me, then," I said.

With the assistance of two nurses, I loaded my father in the front seat, and then placed his wheelchair in the trunk. After driving him home, I attempted to carry him up the stairs. At two hundred and thirty pounds – and with five broken bones – he was simply too much for me to carry alone.

I set him at the bottom of the steps.

He looked up at me. His eyes were filled with fear. It was the first time I'd seen him give an outward sign of fearing anything. To me, my father would always be the invincible Marine that raised me.

"What are we going to do?" he asked.

"Are you cold?"

He coughed a laugh. "Not right now, but I might get that way about midnight, Son. It's fucking February."

I was angry, disappointed in myself, and fearful for what the future held. His dry sense of humor extracted a laugh from me, nonetheless.

"I'm calling an ambulance," I said.

"I'm not going back to the hospital," he hissed. "Just leave me here."

"You stubborn prick," I snapped back. "I'm not leaving you. When they get here, I'll make them help me carry you in."

He grinned a fractured smile. "You're not as dumb as you look."

An hour later, he was sitting in his chair. With his Kindle clutched in his hand, he looked around the room. "I think your work's done here, Son. Go home to your wife and kids."

"What are you going to do when you have to go to the bathroom?" I asked.

"I'll figure something out."

I looked at my mother.

She shrugged. "This is where he wants to be."

"I'm sitting right here, Anita. Don't act like I can't hear you." He looked at me. "Go home, Son."

After some argument, I did just that.

Two days later, the phone rang again.

CHAPTER SIXTY

Sunday visits to see my parents now consisted of driving to an assisted living home. My father was scheduled to stay there until he could walk with a cane. The doctors explained that the severity of the trauma was such that it may be months before they could operate on his knee. They assured us until then, he was in good hands.

For the following months, my mother spent her evenings and nights with him. Despite being in her seventies, she continued to work doing what she loved – managing a safe house for battered women. Leaving him was difficult for her when the time came, and she often stayed much later than she should. Being separated from him wasn't easy. In the fifty-eight years that they'd been married, she'd spent every day with him without fail. From the day they met – when she was sixteen – he had been her *everything*.

Her only man.

Her only love.

If anyone knew how to care for my father, she did.

The phone rang late one evening, three months after my father was admitted to the home. I cringed when I realized who it was. My sister rarely called me. When she did, it was always about one of my parents. She lived in Houston, Texas, and visited quite frequently, but she had never been one to want to talk on the phone.

Reluctantly, I answered.

"Mom's in the hospital," she said.

"Exhaustion?" I asked.

"She wrecked her car."

"Fuck. Is she okay?"

"The car flipped end over end, and then slid for a hundred yards. She was on the highway between Augusta and El Dorado. It's bad. They've towed the car to Cook's Salvage. I need you to go see if you can find her purse and house keys. Oh, and don't tell dad. She's pretty insistent on that."

"Jesus, Amy. Is she okay?"

"By the grace of God. She was tossed out the window, and the car rolled over her, but somehow it missed her. They found it about a hundred yards from where they found her."

"Goddamn it. Is she at Susan B. Anthony?"

"She is. Room 724."

"Thanks, Amy."

"Keep me in the loop."

"Will do."

When I saw my mother's car, I all but collapsed. It looked like it had been hit by a speeding train. None of the windows were intact. The top was crushed. All four doors were crushed. The front, the back – everything – was crushed.

How someone could live through such an accident was incomprehensible to me.

A thirty-minute search aided by a flashlight produced the key. An hour later, my mother was at home nursing a concussion.

That weekend, her face was plastered with extra makeup to hide her bruises. Luckily, my father was more interested in Charlee than anything else, and he didn't notice.

"She's what? Eight months now?" he asked.

"She will be in a few days."

"She's going to be tall. Like Alec," he said.

"Every doctor's visit, she's off the charts," I said. "One hundred percentile on height, and fifty on weight. Tall and skinny."

He smiled. "Just like her granddad used to be."

In his younger years, my father, like my sons, was an athlete. He played basketball and ran cross country. He grew up in Leon, Kansas, and my mother lived in El Dorado. He didn't have a car at the time, and my mother wasn't old enough to drive.

It didn't diminish his desire to see her. Nor did it prevent him from doing so.

He'd lace up his Chuck Taylor's, stretch his long legs, and then he'd run the thirteen miles that separated them. After their visits, he'd run home.

I often told myself I'd write a romance novel based on their experiences as lovers. Their love for one another would act as an inspiration for anyone with a heart. Far more inspirational than the motorcycle club romance novels I'd been writing, that much I was sure of.

"What's the plan for the summer," he asked Landon.

"We're going on vacation," Landon replied.

"Where?" my father asked.

"Florida. For a whole month."

My father nodded. "I bet you'll have a good time."

"We're going to the beach."

My father's eyes closed for a moment. When he opened them, he smiled. "Your dad used to love the beach. Tough dragging him away from it, that was for sure."

Landon looked at me and grinned. "We're going to surf."

My farther pointed at his knee. "Be careful."

"I will," Landon assured him.

A week later, I stood on the beach and gazed out at the Gulf of Mexico. With my toes in the sand and my mind deep in a dream, I closed my eyes. I dreamed of my childhood, and the magic the beach caused me to believe in.

As a child, I struggled with the existence of God. Even then, my world was black and white. If I couldn't see it, taste it, or touch it, it simply didn't exist. One day, while playing along the area where the ocean met the land, I peered out at the vast blanket of water that stretched to the horizon.

I gazed up at the sky.

I tried to comprehend how it worked. What made it function. The waves. High tide. Low tide. It was unconceivable. As the Pacific Ocean's waves crashed against my feet, I decided what was before me was nothing short of proof that God did, in fact, exist.

The ocean's waves were confirmation that He was alive.

I convinced myself it was God breathing that caused them to wash ashore. As long as they continued, I was certain that He was watching over me. The closer I was to the waves that tickled my feet, the closer I was to God.

The Gulf's warm water covered my feet each time the tide pulsed.

"What are you doing?" Jess asked.

I didn't respond.

"Scott?"

I raised my index finger.

Then, I said a prayer.

We left the beach that day and drove from Marco Island, Florida to Naples, a city a few miles north. The streets were lined with palms for as far as the eye could see. The median that separated the eastern and western traffic ways was landscaped with lush tropical plants and flowers.

"This is beautiful," Jess said.

I agreed. "It's unbelievable."

In my fifty-plus years on earth, I'd driven from one end of the United States to the other. I'd visited every body of water that touched its edges. I had never, however, seen anything as beautiful as the city we were driving through. Despite having prepaid for a condo on the island for a month, we decided to spend the remaining portion of our vacation in Naples.

While Charlee slept, Jess and the kids swam in the hotel's pool. I Googled *Naples*, to find out more of the paradise-like city. A quick check of the statistics revealed the odds of being the victim of a crime were less than one-one-thousandth of one-percent.

The city was primarily occupied by seasonal visitors. The average age of the permanent residents, according to Wikipedia, was sixty-seven. I checked the school system. Federally, the schools throughout the nation are ranked on a scale of one through ten, with ten being the best.

The private schools in Wichita were the best the city had to offer. They were ranked a four. Even so, the cost of attending was fifteen thousand per student, per year.

The public schools in Naples were a ten.

When Jess returned from swimming, I put my phone away. "Do you like it here?" I asked.

"At this hotel? Yeah, it's really nice."

"No," I said. "In Naples."

"Oh my Gosh. I love it. It's like paradise."

"Would you want to live here?"

Her face lit up. "Could we?"

After Charlee's birth, I decided I didn't want Jess to work any longer. My career had advanced enough that she didn't need to. I wanted to have both of us at home, playing an active part in raising our daughter.

She soon began designing book covers for other authors. Then, she began designing graphics. Building websites. Designing and publishing coloring books. Before I knew it, she had a full-time career, and could barely keep up with what was in front of her.

Thoughts of returning to the beach shot through me. Visions of playing in the sand with the kids, seeing them develop a love and respect for one of God's greatest gifts, and watching Charlee hunt for sea shells ran through my mind.

My heart raced.

I straightened my posture and cleared my throat. "We both work from home," I blurted. "We can live anywhere."

"What about the big kids?" she asked.

They were all enrolled in college at Kansas State University. It would be Derek's freshman year in the upcoming August.

"They're all away in college. This is when parents often leave. When the last kid goes to school."

"I'd love to live here," she said. "Want to look at houses?"

We spent the next week looking at homes. Our criteria was difficult to meet. A bedroom for each of the children, a yard, an in-ground pool, and we preferred the home be in one of the city's many gated neighborhoods.

During that week, we found not one home that qualified.

Two weeks after we arrived, and two weeks before we planned to leave, the realtor called. According to him, he'd found the perfect place.

We came to a stop at the manned guard shack. Thirty-foot palms lined either side of the professionally landscaped entrance. Two fresh water lakes were within view, complete with fountains.

"Good morning," the guard said. "What can I do for you?"

"We're here to look at a home."

"I'm sorry," he said. "You'll have to be accompanied by a realtor. When he or she gets here, I'll gladly let you in."

We moved our SUV to the side and waited.

"They're not going to let us live in a place like this," Jess said. "Look. There's tennis courts and a clubhouse. This isn't for tattooed authors that write smut."

A few minutes later, when we pulled in the driveway of the home, Jessica's jaw was in her lap. Upon walking through the entrance, she gasped.

I didn't need to go any further. "Call her," I said. "Tell her we'll take it."

Jess spun around. "Can we afford to live here?"

"Tell her we'll take it," I said. "Call her right now."

"There's only one more step that you'll need to take," the realtor said.

"What's that?"

"The neighborhood association will need to do a background check. If you pass the check, they'll let you move in."

I glanced around the newly remodeled home. I was quite certain a background check wouldn't produce favorable results.

If nothing else, it was nice to dream.

CHAPTER SIXTY-ONE

After returning home from our vacation, we waited for news from the neighborhood association, fearing the worst, but hoping for the best. Every morning, Jessica would check her email before she made her coffee, only to find that no contact had been made.

Days passed. Then, a week.

Then, another week.

"They're not going to let us move in, are they?"

"If it's meant to be, it's meant to be."

"I really want to live there," she said. "I love that house. The kids can come home from school and swim. Even in the winter. It'd be so nice."

I could care less about the home. I'd live in a coastal city in a cardboard box.

"We'll just have to see what happens," I said.

I put the finishing touches on book one of my new series, yet another book about a motorcycle club. This time, it was set thirty minutes north of San Diego, in Oceanside. The men would share my love for the beach, find God in the waves that washed ashore, and be well-endowed bikers.

My readers, I told myself, would love it.

Halfway through editing the manuscript, my phone beeped. I paused, picked it up, and swept my thumb across the screen. The email we'd been waiting for stared back at me.

INBOX: *Longshore Lakes Community*

With reluctance, I pressed my finger against the screen.

Mr. Hildreth,

Welcome to the neighborhood! We at Longshore Lakes pride ourselves...

I didn't read any further. I jumped from my seat and shouted.

"Jess!"

She was ten feet away.

"Stop it, Scott. You scared the crap out of me. What?"

"Pack your bags," I said. "We're moving to Florida!"

CHAPTER SIXTY-TWO

I sat across from the foot of my father's bed. My knee was bouncing a mile-a-minute as he watched the end of a baseball game.

"Something bothering you, Son?" he asked without looking up.

"No."

"I raised you," he said, meeting my gaze as he spoke. "That knee starts doing that when you're thinking. I don't see your laptop in front of you, so my guess is something's eating at ya."

"I need to talk to you when the game's over."

He pointed the remote at the television and turned it off. "There. It's over."

I looked at Jess, drew a long breath, and then met his curious gaze. "The kids really liked it in Florida."

"When are you moving?"

I didn't know how to continue.

I stood. Jess came to my side. I looked at my mother and then my father. "We liked the city. The schools are second to none, and the crime rate is non-existent. I want to take the kids there for the same reasons you took us from San Diego. It's what's best for the family, Pop."

He pursed his lips and nodded. "I'm happy for you, Son." He looked at Jess. "Congratulations."

"Are you okay with it?" I asked.

"Would I like you to stay? Sure. I've grown kind of fond of you over the years, Son. But. I want what's best for your kids no differently than you do. Your older kids are all in school, and there's not much that ties you to this God forsaken city. Move somewhere that inspires you to write and do what you do best."

"So, it's okay with you?"

He sat up and opened his arms. After giving me a hug, he hugged Jess. When he released her, he gestured at Landon.

"Lan-dino will be hunting snakes and lizards, just like you did. Mark my words."

The thought of leaving him was difficult to digest. I fought back tears. "Probably so."

He could see my emotional struggle.

I could also see his.

With our eyes locked, he forced a smile. "It's what's best, Son. Swallow that lump in your throat and give your mother a hug, I've got a ballgame to watch."

The next weekend, we told the big kids. Alec explained that the best time of his life was when he'd spent spring break with his brother in the Gulf of Mexico, on the Texas coast. Derek agreed. Erin was excited for us and went on to explain that she wanted to move to Boston as soon as she graduated college.

It was settled.

We were moving.

We signed the paperwork, sold our home furnishings, and packed the remainder of our belongings into a U-Haul trailer.

With the trailer hooked to the back of Teddy's truck, we began our journey. Teddy and Heather drove his truck. Jess, Charlee and Lily drove her SUV, and Landon and I drove my car.

Three days later, we stepped through the threshold of our new home. I took photos, emailed them to my mother, and then called my father.

"We made it," I said.

"Kids excited?" he asked.

"You're going to like this one," I said.

"What's that?"

"There's lizards everywhere. Landon's hunting them. Already caught three."

"Chip off the ol' block, isn't he?"

The phrase, of course, meant that Landon was like his father. I wasn't Landon's biological father, but in the time that had passed since Jess and I were together, he'd forgotten about his father.

My father always said the 'sperm donor' didn't deserve to claim the children, and that I was their true father. I agreed wholeheartedly.

I gazed into the yard. Landon was chasing Lily through the grass with a lizard clutched tightly in his hand. I'd done exactly the same thing with my sister.

"He sure is," I said.

"Son?" My father asked.

"Yeah, Pop?"

"I need to tell you something."

"Okay."

"When I die, I don't want a funeral."

"Pop. That's something we can discuss one day. We don't need to do it now."

"Promise me."

"Pop..."

"Promise me, Son. I know if you do, you'll honor it. No funeral. I want to be cremated. Immediately, too. I don't want anyone looking at my dead ass."

"Pop..."

"Promise me, Son."

I sighed. "Okay. When you die, no funeral. Cremated immediately, with no one looking at ya."

"Alright. Now that we're done with that, let's see. Oh, your mother and I celebrate our fifty-ninth in two weeks. Long time to be married to one woman, isn't it?"

"Sure is Pop. Congratulations. What are you two planning? Big Scrabble game?"

"Nope. Homemade dinner for two."

"She catering it in?"

"No. I'm going home."

I jumped up. It had only been three days since I'd seen him, and I knew they hadn't fixed his knee in that time. At least I thought they hadn't.

"They get your knee fixed?"

"Fuck these dip-shits. I'm done waiting. I walked to the end of the hallway yesterday. That's what they required, so that's what I gave 'em. They're working on my paperwork right now."

"Well, good for you. I'm proud of you, Pop."

"I'm proud of you, too, Son. Give Jess my best. I've got shit to do, I can't sit here and yack all day. I'll talk to you soon."

"Talk to you soon, Pop."

"I love you, Son."

"Love you, too, Pop. Tell mom I love her."

The following Sunday, we talked. He was at home, right where he belonged. Midway through my current novel, *HARD*, he gave praise for what he'd read. The bikers in the group were vigilantes. They took the law into their own hands and administered punishment as they saw necessary.

I'd dedicated the book to a woman I didn't know. She was raped at Stanford University by a man who was then sentenced by the judge to sixty days in jail. I explained in the dedication that I couldn't correct what happened, but I could acknowledge her being raped twice.

Once by the man, and once again by the court.

It sickened my father that the judicial system could sentence him to sixty days in jail, and me to three years in a maximum security federal prison.

We ended the call with me explaining that I was going to Hollywood, and then Las Vegas for two back-to-back book signings the following weekend.

"You've come a long way, Son. I remember when you said you'd never do a book signing."

"Jess made me."

"Career took off after that, huh?"

"Kind of."

"Kind of, my ass. Give credit where credit's due, dip-shit. She's a good woman."

Charlee was crawling through the house giggling, and Jess was chasing her playfully. I glanced at them, smiled, and then agreed.

"She sure is, Pop."

"Give her and the kids my best. I've got an anniversary to plan. I'll talk to you soon, Son. Have fun in Hollywood."

"Will do, Pop."

CHAPTER SIXTY-THREE

We stayed in the historic Roosevelt Hotel on Hollywood Boulevard. The book signing was a huge success. We were scheduled to leave in a rental car the following morning. Four days of mingling with fans and readers in Vegas would follow before the book signing began at Planet Hollywood.

My father was right. I'd come a long way since I wrote my first book. I'd gone from writing good stories that were terribly written to writing great stories that were well-written. My count, at that time, was forty full-length novels. I yearned to reach a point that I wrote great stories that were greatly written.

Keeping my nose to the grindstone was the recipe for success, according to my father. Maintaining a humble attitude. Listening to those who were perceived as better than me. Learning from my mistakes. Practicing humility.

Following the Hollywood signing, Jess and I fell asleep in each other's arms.

I woke up, confused. My phone was ringing. I looked at my watch. It was four am. I leaned to the side, lifted my phone from the nightstand, and looked at the screen.

It was my sister.

With reluctance, I answered the phone.

It was silent.

"Amy?"

"Just a minute," she said.

I didn't like the emotion in her voice.

She cleared her throat. "Dad died, Scott..."

She continued, but I didn't hear a word. I didn't sit up. I didn't move. I didn't speak. I couldn't.

I simply stared at the ceiling.

"He lived long enough to celebrate their anniversary, and then he died. He came home to die. He didn't want to do it in that care home. His heart quit in the middle of the night. Mom found him on the floor beside his chair. Matt went over and picked him up and put him back in it. She didn't want the ambulance attendants to see him on the floor."

I stared.

"He said there'd be no funeral. Said he made you promise. He told mom you promised. Did you promise him, Scott?"

I managed to respond. "I did," I whispered.

"That grumpy prick," she said with a laugh. "He hated the celebration of death, just like you hate the celebration of birthdays."

Laying in the dark beside a sleeping Jess, I swallowed hard and nodded, even though I knew my sister couldn't see me.

"You've got a signing in Vegas, don't you?"

"I'll be home tomorrow," I whispered, being cautious not to wake Jess.

"You better go to that signing," Amy said. "You said you'd be there. You gave your word. If dad thought you went back on your word, he'd throw a fit."

She was right. My father was a man of his word. I, too, was a man of mine.

I sighed. "You're right."

"He told mom he wanted you to write the eulogy. Can you do that?"

"I can."

"Okay. I'll let you go. Enjoy the signing as much as you can. Call mom tomorrow once it's morning there. It's six am here, right now."

"I will."

"I'm sorry, Scott."

"Me, too."

She hung up.

I dropped my phone onto my chest. I was numb. He was my father, but he was also my best friend.

Silently, I stared at the ceiling.

"Was that your phone?" Jess asked, her voice hinting that she was half asleep and half awake.

"It was."

"Who was it?" she asked.

I didn't want to say. I knew if I did, she'd figure something was wrong. I wasn't ready to talk about it.

"Who was it?" she asked again.

"Amy," I said.

She sat up, turned on the light, and looked at me.

I stared at the ceiling. I couldn't do anything else.

"Scott?"

I stared.

"Scott?"

I looked at her.

She saw it in my face.

Her face contorted. "No." She sucked a breath. "No!"

I nodded.

"Oh my God." She gasped. "No!"

She collapsed at my side, blubbering and crying against my chest. I held her in my arms, keeping my eyes fixed on the ceiling. After a few minutes, she sat up.

"I'll need to get this stuff packed so we can fly back there."

I coughed a laugh. "We're going to the Vegas signing."

"What?" she said. "We can't. Your father just died."

"If we don't go to that signing, he'll be glaring down at us from heaven with fire in his eyes."

She laughed and cried at the same time. "That sounds like your dad."

I sat up.

The world around me collapsed.

I looked at Jess.

She opened her arms. I leaned against her. "He was a good man," I said.

"He was," she said. "And, he raised a greater man."

CHAPTER SIXTY-FOUR

In the months that followed my father's death, I couldn't write. I doubted I would ever publish another novel. I'd never suffered from writer's block, but I was suffering from something, that much I was sure of. I sat on the back deck on Sundays and stared at my phone.

The first Sunday I called home after he passed, I asked to talk to him out of habit. My mother had to remind me that he was gone.

I didn't slip into a state of depression, nor did I wad up into an emotional ball. I simply couldn't bring myself to write a story about *anything*.

One Sunday, instead of calling my mother, I called my agent. We talked for an hour. She told me many authors, following the death of a loved one, write a book about their relationship with that person.

She explained that I didn't even need to publish it. Writing it, she said, might be enough.

I decided the next book in the biker series would be about one of the members of the club losing his father.

I sat down at the computer and wrote ROUGH. The story was about a member of the club whose father fell, broke his ankle, collar bone, and arm. A move-in nurse who took care of him fell in love with the biker.

I finished the book and dedicated it to my father.

The book was well received and became a number one bestseller in a matter of days. The readers loved the banter between the Hero and his father, which was taken from what would have been a typical Sunday at my parent's home.

In the book, I included the actual eulogy I wrote for my father. It seemed writing the novel allowed me to release whatever it was that was holding me back. I was once again free. Free to live life. Free to write. Free to be the father my father would have wanted me to be.

I tucked the children into bed that night as I always did. My appreciation for them, somehow, had grown since the book was released.

The nighttime ritual was the same night after night.

"Good night. Love you. See you in the morning," I said.

"Good night. Love you. See you in the morning," Lily replied.

She extended her fist.

As I'd done every night since the day we became a family, I pounded my knuckles against hers.

Then, I turned out the light.

CHAPTER SIXTY-FIVE

When Christmas came that year, we'd lived in Florida for six months. After it passed, Erin came to visit. We spent ten days together, mostly at the beach. What time we weren't at the beach, she spent playing with her sister, Charlee.

Seeing her interact with Charlee was comforting. They chased each other, played in the yard, and swam in the pool. They played with dolls, made blanket tents on the couch, and laid in each other's arms and watched television.

In short, despite their nineteen-year age difference, they did what sisters do.

Erin and I walked along the beach one day, side by side. She, like me, enjoyed the beach in silence, allowing it to take her far away from the reality of earth. She spoke little, but when she did, it was always worth hearing.

"Do you think the boys will come soon?" I asked.

"They want to. They're just busy with school," she said.

They'd told me the same thing. Deep in my being, I wanted her to enlighten me. To tell me something of their thoughts, beliefs, or plans when it came to us being a family. I felt I'd lost so many opportunities with them, but I knew there was so much life ahead of me that I could spend with them.

I simply wanted things to be different. They had college to attend, yes. But. A phone call on Sundays, or a text message from time to time would be well received. More than anything, I wanted Alec to acknowledge Jess as being a part of the family.

Until he did, my heart would continue to break each time we were together.

I decided as we walked through the wet sand that Alec's absence was God's will. That his infrequent visits prevented Jessica's heart from being broken any more than she was capable of handling.

Erin left, but only after shedding a few tears over missing her younger brothers, sisters, and parents.

As always, she hugged everyone, thanked Jess for everything, and kissed the kids before she went to the airport.

"It sure was nice to have her visit," Jess said.

"It was. She's a good kid."

Jess chuckled. "She's a woman, Scott. She's twenty-one."

"She'll always be a kid to me."

Four months later, while leaving a book signing, I was involved in an accident at the airport in Las Vegas. With third-degree burns over forty percent of my body, I was rushed by ambulance to the trauma unit at UMC, Las Vegas.

Jessica signed a release form to allow them to amputate my left thumb. In tears, she came to my side while they were administering anesthesia.

"They're going to cut off your left thumb, Scott. You need to know that. I'm sorry," she sobbed. "They said you could die if they don't."

I was in shock, but I understood her. It was the least of my worries. I had been burned from my hip to my knee, and the burns were so severe that my muscle was exposed in places.

I gave a nod, and then everything went black.

I awoke the next day in a hospital bed. Confused, and in agony, I looked around the room. Jess was sleeping in a chair at my side.

I lifted my left hand. It was tightly wrapped in gauze. Frantic, I dug at the bandage.

"It's still there," she said. "It's really bad, but you got to keep it."

"What happened?" I asked.

"Nobody knows," she said. "The news is coming today to interview you."

For over two weeks, I was in the intensive care unit at the burn center. Several surgeries later, I was fitted with synthetic skin and a few skin grafts using my own skin. The pain was horrific. To describe it as *unbearable* would be a grotesque understatement.

At the end of the first week, I wanted to go outside. I wanted to smell the fresh air. Visions of prison promptly returned – being locked in an institution where I wasn't allowed to go outside.

"You can take him in a wheelchair," they said.

"I'll walk," I replied.

"You can't walk."

"Want to fucking bet?" I said.

I attempted to stand and collapsed. They were right. I couldn't walk. Defeated, I asked Jess to go home and be with the kids.

She laughed.

"You're my husband. We do this together," she said. "I leave when you leave."

"I might be here for months," I said. "They don't know."

"Then I guess I'll be here for months, too. I'm not leaving you Scott. Now, or ever."

On that day, she proved even further that love is much more than a word. When told by friends that she should leave me, she simply laughed and replied, *you must not be in love.*

Eventually, I used a walker. Then, one day, I used a cane. After a few weeks of walking with a cane, they performed an operation. After I recovered from it, I once again learned to walk with a cane.

When I was released, I walked out, using the aid of a cane.

My next book, *NUTS*, would be of a biker who fell in love with a burn victim. I dedicated it to the doctors and staff of UMC Las Vegas.

Erin came to visit me in the hospital, along with my niece, mother, brother, and sister-in-law. Immediately after I returned home, she came to visit again, staying for two weeks.

During those two weeks, she didn't visit the beach once. She sat and talked with us during the day and read books at night. The time we were able to spend with her during that trip was what I'd always dreamed of.

One-on-one time with my children.

Filled with a degree of satisfaction that only a child can provide to a parent, I relished in that feeling day and night for the weeks that followed.

Two months later, Erin returned.

This time, it was with her brothers.

We spent time at the beach. We barbecued. We sat and talked. They drank wine. I drank water. We went back to the beach. We had great talks. We shared laughter, told stories, and stayed up until wee hours of the night.

Derek developed a relationship with Charlee that was heartwarming to experience. They played together. He fed her. Held her. Chased her through the house. Read to her. Watched Disney shows with her.

On that trip, he became her older brother.

Upon waking in the morning, Charlee would ask. "Where's Day-Day?"

"Derek's in bed," Jess would respond.

Charlee would then run to his bedroom, push the door open, and shout at him. "Day Day!"

Derek would get up, put on a smile, and begin spending another day with his baby sister. Seeing the joy in their eyes as each day unfolded was truly a rewarding experience.

During the last Saturday of their trip, we went to the beach as a family. While Landon and Lily built sandcastles, Charlee took off in a dead run toward the ocean. Her curly hair bounced with each step she took, just as her mother's had when she entered the donut shop on the night we first met.

At that moment, Alec, Derek and I were combing the beach, looking for the perfect seashell. Alec pointed and laughed.

"Charlee's going to outrun Jess," he said.

I chuckled. "Jess has short legs."

"Not as short as Charlee's."

Jess reached Charlee when she was ankle deep in the waves. We were fifty yards away, but I could see that Jess was scolding her.

Alec paused. After bending his lanky body over, he stood erect. "There," he said, raising a perfect conch shell. "This one's perfect."

Derek found an undamaged sand dollar ten minutes later.

Proof of their trip that I hoped they'd treasure for years to come. Something tangible they could hold while I held the memories. We walked past where Jess had the sunshade secured to the sand. Erin was playing with Charlee in the sand. When she noticed us, she jumped up and joined us.

Jess, Charlee, Landon and Lily followed.

Together, as a family, we walked along the beach, looking for sea shells.

I squished my toes into the wet sand, not bothering to look back. I knew another day would come, giving another opportunity to leave more footprints along the beach. There wasn't anything – or anyone – who could drag me and my family from the place we loved.

As we walked back along the beach, the sun was lowering itself into the sea. Erin and Jess took photos with the sun at their backs. I noticed our previous footprints were gone, and I grinned.

Life couldn't get any better.

Well, it could have, but it would have required a miracle.

The two weeks passed all too quickly.

When it ended, the *big kids* packed their suitcases and dragged them to the car. As Erin and Derek passed by the kitchen, they hugged Jess.

"It sure was nice seeing you guys," Jess said. "Come back any time."

"We'll see you at Christmas," Derek promised.

"I'll look forward to it," Jess replied.

Alec loaded the car while Jess bid her farewells. When Erin and Derek reached the door, Alec met them there.

He became the man in the family when I went to prison. He may have only been eleven years old at the time, but he didn't have a choice. He maintained that fatherly position through the years, always looking out for his brother and sister.

"You guys ready?" he asked.

"Is everything loaded?" Derek asked.

Alec nodded.

"You ready?" Erin asked.

"In just a minute," he said.

He brushed past me and peered into the kitchen. "Jess?"

She turned around. Her face wore the same phony smile it wore every time Alec left.

"Yeah?" she asked.

"Come give me a hug," he said. "We gotta go."

She turned off the stove, set the skillet aside, and walked out of the kitchen with an ear to ear grin plastered on her face.

Alec opened his arms.

They embraced.

The miracle I had wished for happened. My heart swelled to the point I feared it would burst. It seemed he held her forever. Maybe it was because I wanted him to.

When he finally released her, he stepped back and smiled. "Thanks for everything, Jess. We'll see you on Christmas, okay?"

"Okay," Jess said, her face clearly expressing the emotion that was running through her. "I'll look forward to seeing you again."

"So will I," Alec said.

With that one hug, a decade of misery that had lived within me vanished.

But, that wasn't all that vanished. The cracks that once littered my wife's heart went right along with it.

EPILOGUE

Another birthday passed without celebration. Things changed significantly during that year. As always, not all the changes were welcome.

Teddy was looking for a home in Naples and intended to move as soon as his home in Kansas sold. Having him to ride with would be a far cry from the motorcycle clubs of my past, but my life had changed. Along with those changes, my priorities changed.

My family came first.

The MC had all but disbanded after continued problems with a rival club. King, Chico, and the Big O had gone on to bigger and better things. Affirmation, I decided, that there's value in riding solo. Club, or no club, my brothers would always remain my brothers.

Jessica's parents accepted me wholeheartedly, with Lisa being the driving force behind the open-mindedness. She never came to understand why I wrote the stories I did, but she recommended them to her friends, nonetheless.

An unexpected phone call one Sunday evening brought shocking news. Jessica's parents, after thirty years of marriage, were going to divorce. We struggled to find sense in the decision. We later came to the conclusion that love, regardless of its depth, requires maintenance.

We opened our home to Lisa and Jessica's eighteen-year-old brother. They lived with us for five months. She moved a few blocks away, and visits often. When I feel the need, I wrap my arms around her and give her a hug. The gesture is no longer spiteful. It's driven by love.

I stood on the scale and stared at the display.

"How many more?" Jess asked.

She'd learned over the years that I struggled with my weight on an hourly basis. It sickened her that my weight fluctuated no more than five pounds while she seemed to wear whatever it was she chose to eat on her hips.

"One point three to go," I said. "The holidays suck."

"The boys get here tonight, don't they?"

"They do."

"It'll be exciting to see them." She turned away. "But you'll gain two more pounds."

I didn't need a reminder. The boys ate like horses. In turn, I did the same when they visited. I got off the scale, got back on it, and then shook my head. "It will be nice to see them. And, you're right."

Seeing the gleam in her eyes when she mentioned them was enough to convince me that our lives were truly in order.

I'd penned fifty novels, satisfied my three-book contract with Harlequin, and had sold the rights to two of my biker series'. None of that mattered as much as the fact that Alec had accepted Jess into his life.

He never explained what happened to cause him to change, but he didn't have to. I expected he eventually saw the love that we shared and believed it to be true. It wasn't surprising, most who knew us claimed to see the same thing.

My love for Jessica wasn't manufactured, nor was it a claim I made simply to satisfy her. It was a part of my being. Driven by each beat of my heart, my love for her pumped through my veins right along with the blood that kept me alive. As long as my heart was beating, I would be able to express it.

One day, if my heart chose to stop, I knew my love for her would continue. Each wave that washed ashore along the beach would act as proof of my continued existence, and of my love for her.

The smiles our children – and our children's children – wore would act as proof of the lives I touched while spending a lifetime walking along those beaches.

Eager to see the boys, I showered, got dressed and waited for their plane to arrive. Three hours later, I picked them up at the airport.

I learned on the drive home that Alec decided to go to law school. He was going to make a career out of standing up for what was right. His brother Derek was graduating with an accounting degree and intended to be an actuary. Not surprising, as his father was a man who constantly made reference to statistics.

Erin wrote for the school newspaper and enjoyed writing as much as she enjoyed reading. Her degree, and chosen career, however, differed considerably from what I originally expected.

She intended to manage a care home for the elderly.

Her passion mirrored her grandmother's.

I couldn't have been more pleased with each of them, nor could I have been prouder.

"Jesus, Pop," Alec said as we pulled into the driveway of our new home. "It's *huge*."

Two weeks before their arrival, on the day after Christmas, we moved a few blocks away, but stayed in the same neighborhood. Contrary to our beliefs and expectations, the people in the neighborhood welcomed us with open arms.

When we went to the clubhouse, we were always the youngest family there. We were certainly the only ones covered in tattoos. The residents of the community saw us for who we were, not what we appeared to be. We couldn't imagine living anywhere else.

"We wanted enough room for you guys to have a place to sleep when you came," I said. "It's got enough bedrooms for everyone to have a bed. Pool's big enough to swim laps in."

He peered over the windshield of the Mustang and grinned. "No more sleeping on the floor for Dee, huh?"

"Nope."

Contrary to my belief that they'd spend their days at the beach or chasing college girls, they didn't. When asked if they wanted to go to the beach, the response was always the same.

No, we'll just hang here.

We spent the two weeks as a family. During that time, I got lost in the feeling of having them home, laughing while recalling their childhoods, and hearing them tell stories of their grandfather's colorful life.

As a family, we ate dinner. As a family, we watched movies. As a family, we laughed until we cried. As a family, we bonded. As a family, we grew two weeks older, and lifetimes richer in our experiences.

The boys and I rented a boat one day and took it to a remote island. It reminded me of trips to Point Loma when I was a kid. We combed the beach alone, once again searching for the perfect shells.

Derek found two sand dollars, and Alec found an entire bucket of perfect conch shells. While we walked the length of the Gulf side of the island, Alec searched for a lettered olive. Although I doubted he would find one of the rare shells, he eventually did.

Derek mentioned Alec's luck, and seemed disappointed that he hadn't found one like it.

"We'll be back here plenty of times," Alec said. "You can find one next time."

Hearing his response filled me with hope that their trips to see us would continue at the same pace.

When we returned from our day-long excursion, we sat by the pool as Jess cooked hamburgers. Her hair was curly that day, the blond locks tickling her shoulder as she flipped the burgers to the other side.

"Almost ready," she said over her shoulder.

I gazed at her with loving eyes as she tapped her foot to music only she could hear. Once again lost in admiring the woman she'd evolved into, I recalled meeting her the second time. The immediate attraction I'd felt. The grip she had on my heart. The undeniable love that still remained from the day we'd met.

"Did A-Train tell you about that girl he pissed off?" Derek asked.

I snapped out of my daze. A-Train was a nickname I'd given Alec when he was three. He moved non-stop, and at one speed. Full throttle. Just like a train.

"I guess not," I said.

"Tell him, 'Train."

Alec sighed. "Erin set me up with this chick, and she was really hot. Tall, blond, athletic. So, we started hanging out--"

Mid-sentence, Jess stepped to our side, holding the plate of burgers. "I want to hear this," she said.

We stood and walked in the house together.

Alec continued his tale as we walked. "So, we hung out for a few days, and then it had been a few weeks. She was awesome. We went to the show, got coffee together, and kicked it back at the crib. Then, after about a month, she was like, *what about that dick?*"

He looked at Derek and laughed. "So, I said, *uhhm, you're not gonna get it. I don't just give away, it takes time. You've got to earn it.* She got pissed, and texted Sis, saying I was a douche, and that I wouldn't give her the dick. She wanted to know what was wrong with me. I told Erin to tell her there wasn't a damned thing wrong with me. Some chicks are just crazy, huh, Pop?"

I'd never explained to Alec what happened with Jessica and I regarding the thirty-day rule. Hearing him tell his story, in many respects, gave affirmation that he resembled his father in many ways than met the eye. It also gave me hope that he valued love as much as his father.

I looked at Jess and smiled. "Yeah, some of them are nuts, Son. When you find that one that isn't, you better grab ahold of her."

We ate dinner, and eventually ended up back out on the deck, sitting by the pool with a cup of coffee.

Alec peered over the top of his cup. "Pop, I got a question."

"I'm like Dumbo the elephant," I said, reciting one of my father's sayings. "I'm all ears."

"Dee and I were talking. You think you'd let us come stay for the summer? We'd get jobs and work while we were here."

I tried to hide my excitement. "We'd love that," I said. "You're always welcome here. You can stay as long or as short as you'd like."

He looked at Derek. "What do you say, Dee?"

Derek nodded. "Let's do it."

"I'll start looking for jobs when we get back," Alec said. "But, plan on it."

"Look forward to it," I responded.

The two weeks came to a close. In a day, their sister was showing up to stay for a two-week stay. On the night before they left, they washed their clothes and packed their bags.

Jess got ready for bed and bid them farewell. Their plane left at six am, and we were planning a trip the airport at four, long before she would be awake.

"Gimme a hug," Alec said. "I won't get a chance to give you one tomorrow."

After hugging both the boys, she walked up the stairs wearing a prideful grin. As we laid side by side in bed, she expressed her satisfaction regarding the changes that had transpired since we moved to Florida.

"Alec's come a long way, hasn't he?"

"He has. I feel like we're a family now. A normal, cohesive family."

"So do I," she agreed.

We fell asleep that night, both satisfied about the same things.

At four am the next morning, I dropped the boys off at the airport. Before Jess took the kids to school, she joined me at the desk to check her emails. We worked side by side at the same desk, all day, every day. It was a drastic change from writing books as a hermit, but I couldn't imagine life any other way.

Spending twenty-four hours a day with Jess wasn't a burden, it was a gift.

"I need to decide what I'm writing next," I said.

"Erin will be here tomorrow."

"I know. I'm just trying to decide what's next. Between the books in this series."

My phone beeped.

I swiped my thumb across the screen. Surprised to see a text from Alec, I opened it.

When I read the message, a lump rose in my throat.

Pop. Got out before Jess and the kids woke up. Forgot to tell Jess I loved her. Tell her for me, will you? Tell the little kids, too.

I typed my response.

Will do son. Let me know when you land. Talk to you soon.

"Who was that?" Jess asked.

"Alec," I said.

That one-word response got tangled in my throat.

"What did he say?"

I couldn't respond. If I had, I would have cried. With the screen of the phone illuminated and still on the text message, I handed it to her.

She read the message, and then looked up. Her eyes welled with tears. I nodded in acknowledgement, still incapable of speaking. She read the message again, and then handed me the phone.

As she wiped her eyes, I let what happened sink in.

Jess may have been *my* missing puzzle piece, but throughout or relationship, our family was missing one piece from being complete. Alec's text message snapped the last piece of our family's puzzle firmly into place.

Our family was complete.

"I think I know what I'm going to write," I said over the top of my screen.

"What?" Jess asked.

"A memoir."

"About what?"

"Well, a memoir is like a piece of a person's life. A slice of their life's pie. I was thinking our relationship. That piece."

She scoffed. "Nobody would want to read that."

"There's one way to find out," I said.

I labeled a new folder *Lover Come Back* and grinned at the thought of writing a memoir. In an instant, the power of Alec's message hit me, and I struggled not to cry.

"Babe, are you okay?" Jess asked.

"I'm fine," I lied as I wiped something from my left eye.

Then, with a full heart, and eyes that were brimming with tears, I began to type.

A REFLECTION FROM JESSICA

It was July 4th. I usually looked forward to this holiday. Barbeques and fireworks by the lake brought back cherished memories of my childhood. Memories that I clung to as an escape of the previous 4 years of my life. I wasn't necessarily miserable with my life at that time. I had a boyfriend. I had two kids. I had a decent job doing hair at a salon my friend had opened. All in all, things could have been worse.

My phone vibrating in my purse caused me to snap out of my thoughts and remember where I was. My boyfriend's family had invited us to come to town forty-five miles north of Wichita to celebrate the holiday with them. While the kids were jumping in and out of the pool, he and I sat in lawn chairs drinking beer on the deck. I hated beer. Just the smell of it made me want to throw up the hotdog I had eaten thirty minutes prior. Not wanting to disappoint him, I finished the one I was drinking and got up to grab us both another.

I opened the red Coleman cooler and grabbed two Coronas. My phone vibrated again, reminding me I had a new message. I tucked the beers under my arm and dug in my purse until I found my phone buried at the bottom. I clicked the side button to illuminate the screen.

316-988-7363: *You.*

Confused, I typed in my unlock code and opened my messages. I knew *that* number. *That* number hadn't texted me in almost a year. I dropped the Coronas. My phone vibrated again.

316-988-7363: *I wrote a book. Broken People. You should read it. I think it would benefit you greatly.*

As if on cue, my boyfriend walked up at that moment. I felt him peering over my shoulder and instinctively shoved my phone back in my purse.

"Who was that?" he asked.

Not wanting to lie or cause an argument I simply replied, "Scott. He was just telling me he wrote a book."

He winced at the mention of Scott's name.

I met my boyfriend at the gym about a month after Scott and I had decided to go our separate ways. I had unintentionally mentioned *my friend Scott* in conversation a few times. My new boyfriend didn't like the thought of me having a male friend of any kind.

"Let me see your phone," he demanded.

Reluctantly, I handed him the phone. I'd rather let him see it than deal with the fight that would surely ensue if I didn't.

After opening my messages, he typed a response and pressed *send* before I could see what he said. He then picked the beers up from the grass and went back to his lawn chair.

I nervously fumbled with my phone before opening it to see his response.

His reply wasn't as bad as I was expecting. But a part of my heart sunk at the thought of Scott leaving me alone for good. I had waited almost a year to hear from him and now I was certain I never would again. It was silly to let a man I would never see again make me feel this anxious over one little text message, but I couldn't deny it.

I shook off my feelings, blaming them on the buzz I was feeling from the beer and went back to watching the kids splash in the pool.

Later that day we ate again, drank some more and set fireworks off in the driveway behind the house. It made me happy to see the kids enjoying themselves. I had always wanted days like this for them. Spending the summer playing outside, swimming in the pool, barbequeing in the backyard... being a carefree kid. It seemed, at least for that moment, they had that. I wasn't, however, sure that this was where *I* belonged.

I spent the next few weeks questioning my relationship with my boyfriend. My family liked him, he was pretty good with the kids, and was going to school to get his doctorate.

On paper he would be the perfect husband.

But.

He wasn't Scott.

Scott came into my life like a tornado without warning. He was kind. He was caring. He was responsible. Dependable. Honest. Confident. The list could go on and on. Every single box on my checklist of requirements, he checked off.

He was also the epitome of everything my parents hated. He was a biker. A felon. An older man. A man with children. A divorcee. None of it mattered. I knew I loved him when we met, and I still loved him now.

I had spent the past thirteen months of my life suppressing my feelings for him, even masking them while in my new relationship. The time had come to be honest. With myself, and with boyfriend.

The relationship with my boyfriend ended soon thereafter. I knew I needed to take some time to reflect on the life I wanted for myself, and for my children. I decided to do anything that I could, within reason, to better my life.

I started spending my mornings *and* evenings at the gym, sending the kids to the childcare center while I worked out. I got a new job at a salon in the downtown district of Wichita. I bought a new (to me) car. I chopped my hair off into a curly asymmetrical bob.

Nothing I did filled the Scott-sized void I felt.

One evening after putting the kids down for bed, I downloaded the Kindle App on my phone and purchased Broken People, by Scott Hildreth. After devouring the book over the next couple days, I concluded that the only thing that could fill my Scott-sized void...was *Scott*.